THE ISRAELI-EGYPTIAN PEACE PROCESS IN THE REPORTING OF WESTERN JOURNALISTS

MOHAMMED EL-NAWAWY

Civic Discourse for the Third Millennium
Michael H. Prosser, Series Editor

ABLEX
WESTPORT, CONNECTICUT • LONDON

Library of Congress Cataloging-in-Publication Data

Nawawi, Muhammad ibn'Abd al-Ghani.
   The Israeli-Egyptian peace process in the reporting of western journalists / Mohammed
El-Nawawy.
       p.   cm.—(Civic discourse for the third millennium)
   ISBN 1-56750-544-9 (alk. paper)—ISBN 1-56750-545-7 (pbk. : alk. paper)
   1. Arab-Israeli conflict—Mass media and the conflict.   2. Arab-Israeli conflict—Press
coverage.   3. Foreign correspondents—Israel.   4. Foreign correspondents—Egypt.
5. Mass media—Political aspects.   6. Government and the press—Israel.   7. Government
and the press—Egypt.   I. Title.   II. Series.
   DS119.7.N385   2002
   956—dc21   2001046315

British Library Cataloguing in Publication Data is available.

Library of Congress Catalog Card Number: 2001046315
ISBN: 1-56750-544-9
        1-56750-545-7

First published in 2002

Ablex Publishing, 88 Post Road West, Westport, CT 06881
An imprint of Greenwood Publishing Group, Inc.
www.ablexbooks.com

Printed in the United States of America

The paper used in this book complies with the
Permanent Paper Standard issued by the National
Information Standards Organization (Z39.48–1984).

10 9 8 7 6 5 4 3 2 1

TO RASHA

My Wife and the light of my Life

For a journalist, Israel is the best country in the world to work in because it is far more open than what you would find in many Third World countries. On the Palestinian side, as it is the case in the rest of the Arab World, there is always that deep divide between Islam and the West.

—Walter Rodgers, former CNN bureau
chief in Jerusalem

CONTENTS

PREFACE

There have been tens, if not hundreds, of books published on the Arab-Israeli conflict, most of which have focused on the historical perspective of the strife. Some of these books have tried to offer a critical analysis of the political dimensions of the peace process in the Middle East. However, none of these books have included an on-the-spot thorough investigation of both the official and the news sides of the conflict. This book seeks to provide a succinct overview of the main political, cultural, and religious issues in Israel and Egypt through the eyes of Western correspondents operating in the two countries.

The initial study, which was conducted in the fall of 1998, investigated how access to information about the Middle East conflict by Western correspondents in Israel and Egypt is affected by the governments' information delivery systems; the demographic and educational backgrounds of the correspondents and their professional and newsmaking roles; and the cultural environments (language and religion) in which those correspondents work.

This book conveys the opinions of 168 Western correspondents (94 correspondents in Israel and 74 in Egypt) representing more than 88 percent of the whole population of foreign correspondents in the Middle East region during the time the study was conducted. These correspondents are considered to be the best sources to give the readers some "feel" of the day-to-day interactions between government officials and news reporters. I should note here that some of the correspondents might have moved to other countries or returned to their home countries after the study was conducted.

I traveled to Israel and Egypt to interview these correspondents. Not only was I able to get a visa to enter Israel, which is in and of itself very unusual for an Egyptian citizen, but I was able to obtain intensive interviews with all of the correspondents, who are extremely busy and hard to get hold of. And to present the official side, I also include interviews with the three top public relations officials in the Israeli and the Egyptian governments during the time the study was conducted.

Egypt and Israel were chosen for this study because they lead the two sides in the Middle East peace process. Moreover, most of the Western correspondents operating in the Middle East are stationed in these two countries. Although Egypt is no longer a direct partner in the Arab-Israeli conflict, still it is the leading Arab country, and a major mediator in peace negotiations between the Israelis and the Palestinians.

The importance of this study emanates from the argument that decision makers rely on information available to them via the news media to formulate state policies. This information, reflecting the concerns, capabilities, and orientations of their adversaries, is a key factor that influences government negotiation strategies in periods of conflict.

At the heart of the Arab-Israeli conflict is a recurrent pattern of misunderstanding and failed communication between the Middle Eastern governments. Western correspondents in two major Middle Eastern countries (Israel and Egypt) can enhance the information flow between the Israeli and the Egyptian governments in a way that can reduce or cause misunderstanding on the political scene. Consequently, information exchanged between the governments and the news media in Israel and Egypt can affect the decision-making process in both countries.

My purposes for this book are to provide information on how and why news about the Middle East conflict in general and the Israeli-Egyptian relationship in particular comes to be shaped and presented not only in the U.S. news media but also in the Western news media in general. Moreover, I believe this book will offer a good idea of how Israeli and Egyptian government officials try to manipulate the news media and how the news reporters react to the official attempts at manipulating them.

A Western correspondent, as defined in this study, is a citizen of one of the democratic industrial nations of Central and Western Europe, North America, or Australia (Safire, 1993, 868). This Western correspondent is stationed in the Middle East and reports to an international audience. I focused on the Western correspondents in this study because the international news scene is still dominated by the West, and therefore, the Western correspondents play a major role in the international news flow. Many of the correspondents I interviewed for this study might have left Israel and Egypt since 1998 because of their rotating assignments.

This book is structured to examine the political and cultural issues of the Arab-Israeli conflict by initially presenting a wide-ranging historical overview of the conflict and its most recent developments and the stereotypes held by the Western news media about the Arab and the Israeli sides, followed by topical chapters. The first topical chapter highlights the Israeli and Egyptian cultures in detail. The following topical chapter considers my personal experience in Israel as an Egyptian citizen, and how my visit to Israel has affected my predetermined views about this country. The succeeding topical chapters look separately at the views of the leading Israeli and Egyptian public information officers, the newsmaking and the public relations asymmetric models for the analysis of government-media relationships in Israel and Egypt, and the role of culture in affecting the reporting of Western correspondents in both countries.

I would like to acknowledge the efforts of James D. Kelly, Associate Professor of Communications at Southern Illinois University at Carbondale, whose guidance, encouragement, and personal understanding were major factors in the completion and success of this study. I would also like to thank my mentors, Leo Gher of Southern Illinois University at Carbondale and Hussein Amin of the American University in Cairo, who have always been and will continue to be like family to me.

No words can express my thanks and gratitude to Professor Michael Prosser, the series editor of "Civic Discourse in the Third Millennium," in which this book is included. Professor Prosser has been unfailingly kind, sincere, and patient with me. I owe him a lot as my mentor before being my editor.

I will be forever grateful for the help and guidance I received from Walter Jaehnig and Gerald Stone of Southern Illinois University at Carbondale.

I would like to thank Deborah Bassett, a graduate student at the University of West Florida, for her help in the proofreading and indexing of the book.

And last but not least, I thank my family: my mother, who not only gave me life, but guided me to the right path; my father, whose continuous support and encouragement have always been the inspirations that carried me through tough times; and my brother, who has always made me laugh with his wonderful sense of humor.

INTRODUCTION

Several books and autobiographies have been written by foreign correspondents who recite their memoirs and recall certain events that they witnessed throughout their professional careers. The way that journalists present their memoirs depends on their cultural and political experiences in the countries where they were stationed, and it also depends on the degree of congruence between those correspondents' backgrounds and expectations and what they actually witness in these countries.

I think that there is no better way of starting this book than presenting some selective memoirs, anecdotes, and feature stories written by Western journalists who served in the Middle East in general, and in Egypt and Israel in particular. I believe that these memoirs are a good indication and illustration of the way Western journalists regard their coverage in the Middle East.

You will notice that most of these memoirs were written by American correspondents. The reason for this is because very few European correspondents have written their memoirs on the Middle East.

MEMOIRS FROM THE 1967 WAR

Several Western journalists were in the Middle East during the 1967 war between the Arabs and the Israelis. One of those journalists was Thomas Friedman, a former *New York Times* correspondent in Jerusalem. In his book titled *From Beirut to Jerusalem*, Friedman (1989) said:

After the 1967 war, the perception of Israel in the mind of many American Jews shifted radically, from Israel as a safe haven for other Jews to Israel as the symbol and carrier of Jewish communal identity. This radical transition, I believe, can be understood only in the context of the foreboding that preceded the Six-Day War, when many American Jews feared Israel was going to be erased: the people who came out of the death camps were going to be thrown back in. (455)

In his memoirs titled *Black September to Desert Storm: A Journalist in the Middle East*, Claude Salhani (1998), a French freelance photographer in the Middle East, referred to the 1967 war by saying:

Israel launched a preemptive strike against Egypt, Syria, and Jordan. In six grueling days, Israel doubled its territory by taking the Gaza Strip and the entire Sinai Peninsula from Egypt. The Israelis then captured the West Bank from Jordan, including Arab East Jerusalem, and in fierce hand-to-hand fighting they seized the strategic Golan Heights from Syria. (13)

MEMOIRS FROM THE 1973 WAR

Thomas Friedman (1989) wrote in his memoirs about the 1973 war: "For American Jews, discovering the 'real' Israel began in earnest in 1973, when Egyptian troops overran the Israeli army along the Suez Canal and American Jews realized that their Israeli heroes were not supermen after all" (469).

Salhani (1998) said about the 1973 war:

For the Arabs, the October war shattered decades of belief that Israel was invincible. In the Arab world, Israel was often seen as a giant impenetrable and incapable of losing a war. Israeli intelligence was thought to be infallible. The Mossad [Israeli Intelligence] was reputed to have penetrated the highest military and government circles in Syria and Egypt. It was thought that the Arabs could never launch an offensive of this magnitude without alerting the Israelis. Yet for the first time since the creation of the State of Israel, Egypt and Syria managed to plan, prepare, and implement a major attack . . . The crossing of the Suez Canal was a major victory for the Egyptian army and a fantastic morale booster for the Egyptian people . . . The mood in Israel was reversed, as the people questioned their leaders. Prime Minister Golda Meir and her minister of defense, Moshe Dayan, the hero of 1967, were harshly criticized by the public. How could the Arabs prepare and launch such an attack without Israel [and the United States] learning about it? (20)

MEMOIRS FROM THE 1978 CAMP DAVID ACCORD

Camp David witnessed a breakthrough in the bilateral relations between Israel and Egypt when both countries signed their peace treaty in 1978.

Among the Western journalists who witnessed the Camp David accords was Henry Brandon, an American freelance journalist, who authored a book in 1988 reciting his memoirs of 35 years of reporting from different countries of the world. In one section of the book, he talked about his experience in covering the Camp David accords by saying: "Base camp for the press was in the foothills to Camp David, but for almost all the thirteen days the conference lasted there was nothing much of substance to report, partly because a news blackout had been imposed, partly because the outcome remained in doubt almost to the very last day" (350).

CNN correspondent Wolf Blitzer (1985) referred to his coverage of the Camp David accords by saying:

On the morning after the dramatic announcement of the Camp David breakthrough between Israel and Egypt, Begin and Carter found themselves publicly disputing the exact nature of the Israeli commitment to freeze new settlement construction. Begin said it was for only three months; Carter insisted that it was for the duration of the negotiations leading up to the establishment of a Palestinian self-governing body. (29)

MEMOIRS FROM THE OSLO ACCORDS

Some Western journalists operating in the Middle East have been very pessimistic about the adoption and continuation of the Oslo accords between the Israelis and the Palestinians. One of those journalists, Robert Fisk, a BBC correspondent in Lebanon and one of Britain's most highly decorated foreign correspondents, was quoted in an interview with Rothschild (1998) as saying:

(Oslo Accord) is buried. I'm afraid there's going to be an explosion in the Middle East. I fear very much that there's going to be a great deal of violence in the coming months, years, and I can't see at the moment that there's any determination on the part of the people involved or the U.S. government to prevent it . . . It is said that Oslo was based on U.N. Security Council Resolution 242, but in fact it wasn't . . . What Oslo did was to allow the Israelis to renegotiate 242. It allowed them to say, "OK, instead of talking withdrawal, we'll withdraw from this bit and we'll let you keep this bit, and we'll negotiate this later." That is no way to make a peace. That is a way to make a war. (37)

MEMOIRS FROM LEBANON

Thomas Friedman (1989) commented in his memoirs on the convenience of working in Lebanon by saying:

Being a reporter in Beirut [Lebanese capital] was like being at a play in which the audience could, at any time, hop right up onto the stage and interview the actors as they were reciting their lines or acting out some dramatic scene . . . There were no ushers to hold you back, no press pools or limits on access. Because of this, I got to witness encounters and to describe scenes that would have hidden away behind an official shroud in any normal country. (52)

Friedman also said, referring to the way the Lebanese were dealing with him:

Because I have dark Mediterranean features and a mustache, Lebanese were always asking me whether I was of Arab origin. "No," I would say, "I'm American. One hundred percent." But then they would ask, "What were you before that? What kind of name is Friedman?" I would always answer "Romanian," because my paternal grandparents emigrated to America from there, and somehow that would satisfy people and there would be no further questions. They would say, "Romanian," and nod their heads as if that explained everything. (55)

Robert Fisk (1998) said about his experience in Lebanon:

You do see people die, and you realize how easy it is to be killed. You go through the risk and the danger. At the end of the day, either you get back to Beirut and file your story and go out to a French restaurant, or you end up in a fridge. (36)

MEMOIRS FROM BAGHDAD DURING THE GULF WAR

Peter Arnett (1994), the only Western correspondent who was in Iraq during the 1991 Gulf War, said in his memoirs titled *Live from the Battlefield*:

My joy at being in Baghdad went much deeper than covering the story. From my early youth I had thrilled to the exoticism of the Arabian Peninsula. Dried dates fruit arrived at my local grocery store in boxes from Basra [a city in Iraq]. I read in my schoolbooks that the hanging gardens of Babylon [a popular tourist site in Iraq] were one of the wonders of the ancient world. The songs from the broadway musical *Kismet* wove rich tapestries of longing in my imagination. I was now older and wiser, but the magic carpet of journalism had carried me from New Zealand and over thirty-five years to my destination. (352)

Another comment from Arnett reflecting the atmosphere in Iraq while being bombed by the allied troops during the Gulf War reads:

As long as there were bombers in the skies overhead, no one could feel safe. The price for the invasion of Kuwait was that everyone's lives were put at risk. At a large rally [in Iraq], several hundred angry relatives and friends marched and shouted anti-American slogans and chased off the foreign press. It was the first large, open assemblage of people we had seen since the war began. They did not seem to care that they made an easy target. (413)

These memoirs show that correspondents' access to information is affected by the nature of the news sources, the amount and quality of information they release, and the correspondents' understanding of foreign cultures.

I

HISTORICAL VIEW

In the last half century, the Arab-Israeli conflict has led the Middle East into six major wars and has cost thousands of lives. It has also left the Palestinian people stateless and dispersed, creating frustration and anger that exacerbate regional tension. Moreover, this conflict has diverted billions of dollars from productive investments to the purchase of armaments and has blocked regional cooperation for economic development that would have permitted a more rational and effective use of national resources (Granham & Tessler, 1995, xiv). The world remains concerned about the future of the Arab-Israeli conflict, with finding a solution, and with helping peace prevail in the Middle East.

WHAT IS THE ARAB-ISRAELI CONFLICT?

The Arab-Israeli conflict and the Middle East conflict are two sides of one coin used to describe the regional dispute between the Arab states and Israel. The conflict, which started with the establishment of the state of Israel, has been one of the longest and seemingly unresolvable conflicts of this century. In 1948, Walter Lippmann, the dean of American pundits, declared: "Among the really difficult problems of the world, the Arab-Israeli conflict is one of the simplest and most manageable" (Webster, 2001). Not exactly as it turned out. More than half a century later, we are witnessing a fresh eruption of diplomacy around what has become the bitterest, most intractable, and most destabilizing problem of world politics.

"To Jews and Judaism, the establishment of Israel is the pivotal event of the past 2,000 years of Jewish history. To Islam and to Muslims, the existence of a Jewish state in the midst of the Muslim world is perhaps the greatest challenge it has faced in its history" (Bickerton & Klausner, 1998, 1). Throughout their long conflict, both the Arabs and the Israelis have tried to legitimize their positions by seeking to set favorable political and cultural images and symbols of themselves, and unfavorable ones of their opponents. "The tragedy of the Arab-Israeli conflict is that it is the collision over the same land of two sets of historic and moral rights of groups who are both victims of each other's violence" (3).

A BACKGROUND OF THE ARAB-ISRAELI CONFLICT

In the Balfour Declaration of November 2, 1917, the British government informed the Zionist movement that it favored the establishment of a "national home for the Jewish people" in Palestine. "By offering to help the Zionists establish this home, Britain could place its own troops in Palestine and thereby control that strategic prize near the Suez Canal as well as preside over the holy places in Jerusalem" (Lesch & Tschirgi, 1998, 8).

During the 1920s and 1930s, Jewish and Palestinian nationalists, each seeking statehood in the same territory, struggled against each other. Arabs could not stem Jewish immigration, which became increasingly urgent once Adolph Hitler and the Nazis seized power in Germany in 1933. Arab governments became concerned about the Palestine problem, and they articulated their grievances in meetings with the British government in 1937–1939.

World War II led to a groundswell of support in the United States and Europe for a Jewish state, as a result of the shock of the near annihilation of European Jews by the Nazis. Zionists hardened their political position, insisting that the Jewish state must encompass all of Palestine. In 1946, the Anglo-American Committee of Inquiry recommended that one hundred thousand Holocaust survivors settle in Palestine. The Committee of Inquiry also proposed that Palestine become a joint Jewish-Arab state. By then, however, the Arab and Jewish communities were each determined to create their own state.

The U.N. General Assembly Resolution 181 of November 1947 endorsed a plan to establish separate Jewish and Arab states. At that time, Palestine's Jewish community totaled 30 percent of the population and owned seven percent of the land. However, the partition plan allotted 55 percent of the land to the Jewish state. Jerusalem and its environs, some five percent of Palestine's area, would form an international enclave under U.N. control. The Arab state would comprise 40 percent of Palestine's land. Palestinians and the Arab states rejected that partition plan, insisting that Palestine gain full independence as an Arab state. The Zionist leadership, however, accepted the partition plan as "the indispensable minimum."

THE FOUNDATION OF THE STATE OF ISRAEL

As the United Nations was reexamining the "Question of Palestine," Zionist planners were busy establishing their authority on the land of Palestine. As Chaim Weizmann, the president of the World Zionist Organization, reminisced, "Our only chance now . . . was to create facts, to confront the world with these facts, and to build on their foundation. . . . While the United Nations was debating trusteeship, the Jewish State was coming into being" (quoted in Nassar, 1997, 79).

The manner in which the Jewish state "was coming into being" was not peaceful, rather, it was characterized by "violence and bloodshed." The most violent incident that led to a massive exodus of the Palestinian Arab inhabitants and opened the door for the creation of the Jewish state was the massacre of Deir Yassin. On April 9, 1948, 254 men, women, and children in the village of Deir Yassin were massacred by a militant Zionist group named Irgun led by Menachem Begin, who became Israel's prime minister in 1977. Begin later justified the massacre in these terms: "The massacre was not only justified, but there would not have been a state of Israel without the victory at Deir Yassin" (quoted in Nassar, 1997, 79).

In his memoirs about the Deir Yassin incident, Edward Said (2000), a renowned Palestinian American scholar, said: "More than any single occurrence in my memory of that difficult period it was Deir Yassin that stood out in all its awful and intentional fearsomeness—the stories of rape, of children with their throats slit, mothers disemboweled, and the like. They gripped the imagination, as they were designed to do, and they impressed a young boy many miles away with the mystery of such bloodthirsty and seemingly gratuitous violence against Palestinians whose only crime seemed to be that they were there" (157).

Israel proclaimed its independence on May 15, 1948, just as the last British troops departed. By then the Jewish army had seized most of the territory allotted to the Jewish state and captured major Palestinian towns. So, Israel was created as a Jewish homeland almost three years after the end of World War II and the Nazi Holocaust that killed six million Jews in Europe. For the Jewish people, the significance of that piece of Middle Eastern land bordering the Mediterranean went back millennia, to biblical times. The founding of Israel was, for them, a return home after 2,000 years in exile (Cantor, 1998).

Prior to the establishment of Israel, volunteers and donations (aside from diplomatic moves) characterized Arab involvement. But it was not until after the declaration of Israel and the mass exodus of Palestinians to neighboring Arab countries that the Arab armies entered Palestine. On the same day that Israel was born, Egypt and other Arab countries, such as Syria and Jordan, decided to defend the Palestinians, but their forces were ill-prepared for combat. The fighting lasted from May through December 1948, after which agreements between the warring parties left Israel in control of three-quarters of Palestine. Jordan took control of the remaining part of Palestine, including the old city of Jerusalem, with the exception of the Gaza district which went to Egyptian control.

In the Palestinian Arabs' memories, "1948 stands as the year of *al-nakba* (the tragedy). Ever since, the notion of the return to the homeland became a Palestinian obsession" (Nassar, 1997, 79).

Israel used its victory to consolidate its hold territorially and politically. As Jews migrated to Israel from Europe and the Middle East, Israel's Jewish population doubled from 650,000 in 1948 to 1.3 million in 1952. The United Nations admitted Israel as a member in 1949, with the condition that it compensate Palestinian refugees and internationalize Jerusalem. Less than a year later, Israel defied those terms by proclaiming West Jerusalem its capital.

THE 1956 WAR

During the early 1950s, Palestinian intellectuals believed that the remedy for their plight rested on Arab unity. To bring about unity, many Palestinians felt that the first step would be to change the traditional leadership, whom they felt had betrayed their cause. Most Palestinians hailed the overthrow of King Farouk of Egypt in 1952 and became the strongest supporters of Egypt's revolutionary leader Gamal Abdel Nasser.

Nasser, who came to power in Egypt after a military coup that that put an end to the monarchy, championed the cause of Arab unity. It is noteworthy that Israeli Prime Minister David Ben-Gurion publicly welcomed the 1952 coup in Egypt and extended an offer of peace to Nasser. Secret negotiations did in fact ensue, but Nasser's regime in 1953 made it clear to the Israelis that Egypt preferred to maintain the status quo of "no war, no peace" (Mufti, 2000, 72).

Nasser did not believe that he had much to gain from a peace accord with Israel, and he was afraid to lose the Arab public opinion, an important element in Egypt's regional ambitions at the time. Therefore, the result was a steadily escalating level of tension between 1953 and 1956, driven by Israeli insecurity and further exacerbated by Arab border infiltrations.

A major factor that affected the situation in the Middle East during that time was the way in which both the United States and the Soviet Union were preoccupied in such a manner as to limit their freedom of action. The United States was in the throes of a presidential election, during which it was assumed that President Dwight Eisenhower would not make any vital international decision that might prejudice his chances of reelection. Similarly, the Soviet Union was busy quelling the national urge for liberalization that had begun to be expressed in Poland and Hungary.

However, the Cold War still intruded into Middle East politics when the United States tried to get Arab countries to join an anti-Soviet military alliance that included the non-Arab Moslem countries of Turkey, Iran, and Pakistan. The pro-British government of Iraq joined the alliance in April 1955, which was then named the Baghdad Pact.

Israel became concerned about American cooperation with the Arabs and was also concerned about Egypt's refusal to allow Israeli ships to pass through the Suez Canal. Although Egypt searched only three of 267 vessels that entered the canal from 1951 to 1955, Israel feared its vulnerability to a blockade and stressed that it would go to war if its access were denied.

In September 1955, President Nasser turned to the Soviet Union to negotiate an arms deal after the United States and the West European governments refused to sell him arms. The Egyptian-Soviet arms deal angered and frightened the United States because it enabled Moscow to gain influence in the heart of the Arab world. The United States also became angry when Egypt extended diplomatic recognition to the Communist Chinese government in May 1956 (Lesch & Tschirgi, 1998).

On July 26, 1956, Nasser nationalized the administration of the Suez Canal, which had opened in 1869 under international management. Nationalization helped provide revenue for Egypt to construct the Aswan High Dam, which the United States, Britain, and the World Bank had refused to fund. The United States recognized Nasser's right to nationalize the Suez Canal Company so long as Egypt compensated the stockholders. However, Britain and France, who were the major shareholders in the company, were determined to regain control of the canal. Britain denounced Nasser as "a new Hitler, who would dominate the Middle East if appeased" (Lesch & Tschirgi, 1998, 16).

Britain and France assembled naval and air forces in the eastern Mediterranean to invade Egypt. Israel shared the British and French desire to overthrow Nasser. The canal crisis provided an opportunity for Israel to seize the Gaza Strip, gain control of the Sinai coast along the Gulf of Aqaba, try to force Egypt to sign a peace treaty, and perhaps cause Nasser's fall from power. Leaders of Britain, France, and Israel secretly met in Paris on October 16, 1956, and invented an elaborate cover story to disguise their plans.

On October 30, 1956, Israel attacked Egypt with the stated purpose of stopping guerrilla raids from Gaza and opening the Gulf of Aqaba and the Suez Canal to Israeli shipping. One day after the start of the Israeli invasion, Britain and France issued an ultimatum to both Israel and Egypt to withdraw from the canal, which would have left Israeli forces in control of the Sinai. They also demanded that Nasser accept a temporary Anglo-French occupation of the canal to protect international shipping. When Nasser, as expected, rejected the ultimatum, Britain and France announced a joint expedition to seize the Suez Canal, and they attacked Egypt (Andersen, Seibert, & Wagner, 1998, 115).

Britain and France hoped that the United States would support the attack because the American public generally sympathized with Israel, and Washington was preoccupied with the Soviet crackdown on Hungary as well as its presidential election. However, President Eisenhower sternly opposed the invasion of Egypt, viewing it as "a throwback to colonial-era gunboat diplomacy" (Lesch & Tschirgi, 1998, 17).

Both the United States and the Soviet Union supported United Nations resolutions that condemned the three countries' attack on Egypt, called for an immediate cease-fire, and demanded their withdrawal. The United States encouraged the establishment of a U.N. Emergency Force (UNEF) to police the Israeli-Egyption border. UNEF was stationed in the Gaza Strip and at the southern end of the Gulf of Aqaba. UNEF prevented Palestinian raids into Israel and ensured that Israeli shipping could pass through the gulf. But Israel did not gain the use of the Suez Canal, and its political conflict with Egypt festered.

On November 1, 1956, the United Nations adopted a U.S.–sponsored resolution calling for an immediate cease-fire, a withdrawal of Israeli forces from the Suez zone, and the reopening of the Suez Canal which was closed by Egypt before the invasion. The resolution also asked Britain and France to "refrain from introducing military goods into the area" (Diller, 1994, 24).

After the 1956 war, Arabs and Israelis made no progress toward resolving their conflict, for they disagreed on how to negotiate: Arabs wanted indirect negotiations under U.N. auspices; Israel insisted on direct talks. They also disagreed on negotiating priorities. Arabs viewed the Palestinian refugee problem as key: The refugees' status must be resolved before Arabs would recognize Israel and agree on borders. On the other hand, recognition was Israel's top priority: Only after achieving diplomatic recognition would Israel discuss the refugees. Even then, Israel would not consider allowing refugees to return to their pre-1948 homes. Israelis hoped that over time, refugees would assimilate into surrounding countries. Instead, the refugee problem continued, and the armistice lines remained unstable (Lesch & Tschirgi, 1998).

Following the 1956 war, the Soviet influence increased markedly in Egypt, Syria, and Iraq. Moscow became the major arms supplier and a significant trading partner for those states. Eisenhower's support for Egypt during the Suez crisis encouraged Arab nationalists, but U.S. preoccupation with the Cold War dampened that support because Arab regimes were more concerned about Israel than about potential Communist threats. In the aftermath of the 1956 war, the Arab-Israeli conflict took a backseat to intra-Arab tensions in Middle East politics, as Nasser, whose political prestige had risen in the Arab world following the conflict, sought to extend Egyptian influence over the rest of the Arab world.

[During the decade following the 1956 war,] Arab politicians were preoccupied with their search for political identity. Under the banner of pan-Arabism, politicians in Egypt and Syria attempted to achieve political unity by forming the United Arab Republic, which lasted only from February 1958 to September 1961 because Syrians resented their junior role in the union. During those years, Arab rulers avoided confrontation with Israel, but tension along the armistice lines separating Israel, Syria, and Jordan occasionally created new crises (Lesch & Tschirgi, 1998).

THE FOUNDATION OF THE PALESTINE LIBERATION ORGANIZATION

During the 1950s, Palestinians were attracted to various forms of pan-Arabism that asserted that regaining Palestine required Arab political and military unity. But the idea of Arab unity received a blow in 1961 when Syria ended its union with Egypt. Moreover, "the sense of being discriminated against by fellow Arabs and disappointment with Arab regimes led many Palestinians to stop being passive. They sought to transform their situation through their own actions, rather than wait for Arab governments to rescue them" (Lesch & Tschirgi, 1998, 74).

Small underground guerrilla cells sprang up in the early 1960s. Fatah, the main Palestinian faction founded in Kuwait in 1959 by Yasser Arafat, launched its first raid into Israel in 1965.

The growing discontent among Palestinians worried Arab governments, who sought to channel that alienation by forming the Palestine Liberation Organization (PLO) in 1964. Egypt appointed the PLO leaders, who convened the first Palestine National Council (PNC) in East Jerusalem in May 1964. The equivalent of a parliament-in-exile, the PNC adopted an uncompromising political charter that refused to accept Israel's existence and called for the destruction of the state of Israel and a return to the situation as it was before 1948.

After the Arabs' defeat in the 1967 war (to be discussed in the next section), the PNC amended the charter to reflect the new situation. The amendments emphasized popular armed struggle, rejected Zionism and the partition of Palestine, termed Judaism "a religion . . . not an independent nationality, and called for the total liberation of Palestine" (Article 20; cited in Lesch & Tschirgi, 1998, 75). The PNC charter upheld Arab unity, but emphasized that just as the PLO would "not interfere in the internal affairs of any Arab state" (Article 27; cited in Lesch & Tschirgi, 75), "it rejected control by Arab regimes" (Article 28; cited in Lesch & Tschirgi, 75). The charter could only be amended by a two-thirds vote of the more than four hundred members of the PNC.

THE 1967 WAR

From 1948 to 1966, the Arab-Israeli conflict could be described as an interstate conflict, however, the 1967 war changed it into a regional dispute. The

Israeli occupation of the Sinai Peninsula, the Golan Heights, East Jerusalem, the West Bank, and the Gaza Strip in the 1967 war added new elements to the conflict and marked the beginning of an extensive conflict in the Middle East region (Battah & Lukacs, 1988).

In mid-August 1966, the Palestinians launched attacks against Israel from the Jordanian and Syrian borders, leading to a major clash between Israel and Syria. In the meantime, Egypt strengthened its military forces on the borders with Israel to back Syria against an expected Israeli attack. Moreover, President Nasser, weakened domestically by economic hardship and popular discontent and alarmed by the American tilt toward Israel, marched some troops into the Sinai on May 14, 1967, and he closed the Gulf of Aqaba to Israeli vessels or any vessels carrying goods to Israel.

Nasser was hoping to score a propaganda victory without actually going to war. He apparently calculated that the Americans would restrain Israel as they had in 1956 and that he would thereby emerge as a hero to the Egyptian and Arab masses once again. This interpretation was supported by Yitzhak Rabin, chief of staff of the Israeli forces at the time, who told *Le Monde* in 1968, "I do not believe that Nasser wanted war. The two divisions he sent into the Sinai on May 14 would not have been enough to unleash an offensive against Israel. He knew it, and we knew it" (quoted in Mufti, 2000, 80). It was also supported by Menachem Begin, who said in a speech in 1982, "In June 1967, we again had a choice. The Egyptian Army concentrations in the Sinai approaches do not prove that Nasser was really about to attack us. We must be honest with ourselves. We decided to attack him" (quoted in Mufti, 2000, 80).

On May 30, 1967, King Hussein of Jordan arrived in Cairo, Egypt, and signed a defense agreement that put his armed forces under Egyptian command. By early June, after the creation of a war cabinet in Israel, Nasser called on the United States to mediate, dispatching his vice president to Washington on June 4, 1967. The next day the Six-Day War broke out during which Israeli planes destroyed most of Egypt's air force on the ground. After the initial Israeli air strike, Israeli ground troops defeated the Egyptian army, seizing the Gaza Strip and the Sinai Peninsula. That day, most of Egypt's approximately four hundred aircraft were either destroyed or so severely hit that they were put out of action indefinitely. Israeli aircraft also bombed Syrian airfields in the Golan Heights, taking a toll of at least 50 Syrian aircraft. On June 7, the Israelis captured Old Jerusalem, with its fifty thousand Moslem citizens and ten thousand Jordanian troops.

During the first two days of the war, U.S. President Lyndon Johnson and Soviet Premier Aleksei Kosygin had been exchanging messages, leading to an agreement by both sides to press for the U.N. cease-fire. The U.N. Security Council convened in New York on June 5, only a few hours after the Israelis had struck the first blow, but the delegates could not agree on the terms of a cease-fire. The Soviets wanted the fighting to stop, with all sides returning to their positions before the first Israeli attack. The United States, however, called for a simple cease-fire, which was the Israeli position because it permitted the Jewish state to retain its territorial gains. Then the Soviets complicated the matter by demanding a resolution condemning Israel for starting the war, which was opposed by most of the delegates (Hohenberg, 1998).

On June 23, 1967, President Johnson and Premier Kosygin had a summit meeting at Glassboro State College in New Jersey, but there still was no way of settling the tensions in the Middle East. The Glassboro summit resulted only in an urgent plea for a treaty on arms control between the two great adversaries, the United States and the Soviet Union.

At the beginning of July 1967, the U.N. Security Council was in session on the Middle East conflict. "The Soviet Union called an emergency session of the Security Council's General Assembly under the 1950 'Uniting for Peace' resolution that allowed two thirds of the General Assembly membership to agree to become involved in a crisis which the Security Council had been unable to solve. In the 1967 War, Israel took control over the West Bank, the Gaza Strip, and the Golan Heights, all of which became known under international law as 'the occupied territories of Israel' " (Donahue & Prosser, 1997, 247). The Arabs' refusal to change their aggressive stance toward Israel, even after the damage that had been inflicted on them, served to delay for some time any agreement between the Soviets and the Americans to reduce tensions.

Even though the Arab League opposed negotiations and peace at its summit conference in Sudan's capital, Khartoum, in September 1967, it approved the use of diplomacy to achieve tangible results. The diplomatic solution to the 1967 hostilities was U.N. Resolution 242, "a masterpiece of diplomatic ambiguity that became the key document in all attempts to arrive at a peaceful solution to the conflict. . . . The Resolution proposed the idea of peace in return for territory—without specifying which should come first" (Bickerton & Klausner, 1998, 155).

The resolution, which was passed on November 22, 1967, did not demand withdrawal from all the territories; rather, it recognized that negotiated boundaries must be "secure." In return, the Arab states should end their state of belligerency with Israel and recognize Israel's right to live in peace. The resolution also called for freedom of navigation through international waterways, which meant the Gulf of Aqaba and the Suez Canal, and a "just settlement" to the refugee problem. In that context, Palestinians were merely refugees, not a nation. "The resolution did not specify the content of a 'just settlement' of the refugee problem" (Lesch & Tschirgi, 1998, 22). The regional Middle East governments continue to debate the meaning of the resolution and differ as to whether it is merely a declaration of principles or a blueprint for a peace settlement.

Israel's victory in 1967 created a new map of the Middle East, with Israel three times larger than it had been in 1949. The Arabs' swift defeat destroyed Nasser's credibility as the preeminent Arab leader and undermined the Syrian regime's claim to be the Arab world's radical savior. Egypt faced economic collapse when it lost revenue from oil wells in the Sinai and from the Suez Canal. King Hussein's credibility was also destroyed because he lost the holy sites of Jerusalem and failed to protect the Palestinians on the West Bank.

Israelis reacted with amazement, jubilation, and relief to their victory. After feeling besieged by the Arab armies, they now seemed to have won space and security. Many Israelis flooded East Jerusalem to visit the holy places. "For Israel, a new image of strength and power replaced the previous one of the threatened underdog, the gallant little country surrounded by enemies who wished to exterminate it. Israel's victory had a profound effect on Jews, engendering self-confidence, pride, and assertiveness" (Bickerton & Klausner, 1998, 153).

In an interview with a *New York Times* correspondent after the 1967 war, one of Israel's preeminent diplomats said, "Although the Six Day War was a tremendous military salvation and political gain, and enabled us to get the peace with Egypt, we went a little bit crazy intellectually as a result of it. We interpreted the war . . . as a kind of providential messianic event that changed history permanently and gave Israel the power to dictate the future. . . . The reality was quite different. The Arab world remained intact, with the power of refusal largely untouched" (Brown, 1988, 145).

Before the 1967 war between Egypt and Israel, the Arabs opposed the very existence of Israel in the Middle East. However, "the 1967 War marked the beginning of a shift in the conflict's essence: from the issue of Israel's legitimacy to the question of its boundaries. In other words, the conflict began to turn away from 'paradigmatic,' that is cultural, religious, and ideological, to a 'normal' political—and thus more manageable—dispute" (Sela, 1998, 28).

The 1967 war brought about a reawakening among the Palestinians. The Arabs, they learned, were unable to bring about their "Return." The speedy and devastating defeat of the combined forces of Egypt, Syria, and Jordan left most Palestinians in shock. "During the earlier phase, Palestinian political culture was characterized by its emphasis on the lost homeland and the dream of 'Return.' It was alienation from the homeland that gave the Palestinians their most powerful common cultural bond. Now, after the defeat of 1967, Palestinians began to combine their longing for the 'Return' with emphasis on the maintenance of their identity. Thus, Palestinian nationalism began to replace the traditional Arab nationalism which had dominated Palestinian political culture prior to 1967" (Nassar, 1997, 82).

The regional tension in the Middle East was exacerbated by the Cold War. During the fighting in 1967, Egypt and Syria broke diplomatic relations with the United States. The Soviets broke diplomatic relations with Israel. Because each superpower had its client states, Cold War polarization complicated efforts to foster diplomacy.

SECRET NEGOTIATIONS BETWEEN ISRAEL AND JORDAN

When King Hussein of Jordan lost control over the West Bank and East Jerusalem to Israel in June 1967, he initially accommodated the Palestinians by allowing the PLO to operate from Jordanian soil. He also took advantage of the cover provided by Nasser and accepted Resolution 242. Moreover, King Hussein removed a major source of tension by cracking down in September 1970 on the PLO guerrillas, who had provoked Israeli retaliatory strikes with their cross-border infiltrations during the previous two years.

Toward the end of 1970, Golda Meir, the then Israeli prime minister, seemed confident that an agreement could be reached with Jordan. The presumption among Meir's advisers was that Hussein was ready to grasp the opportunity for a peaceful settlement if granted decent terms. What the Meir government secretly offered Hussein was a plan in which Jordan would be given a narrow corridor of land leading from Amman to other Arab areas on the West Bank of Jordan, plus a few other minor considerations. However, Hussein refused, and he demanded Israel's removal from his occupied territories including the Old City of Jerusalem. He said this was the only solution that would make him agree to sign a peace treaty as the first major Arab leader to do so and thereby accept Israel as a regional partner. "So, the opportunity passed and Hussein returned . . . to the all-or-nothing Arab fold" (Hohenberg, 1998, 109).

THE 1973 WAR

The period from 1969 to 1973 witnessed a prolonged "war of attrition" between Egypt and Israel. Egypt was hoping that "a campaign of artillery bombardments and commando raids would produce a steady trickle of Israeli casualties, thereby eroding Israel's triumphalist mood and forcing it into a more accommodating stance" (Mufti, 2000, 83).

The full implications of Anwar Sadat's inauguration as president of Egypt after the death of Gamal Abdel Nasser in September 1970 were not at first fully understood. Unlike his predecessor, Sadat saw a certain amount of merit in negotiating for peace with Israel. He was determined to end the Arab-Israeli conflict, which had drained Egypt's resources for almost three decades.

In February 1971, Sadat offered partial peace in return for a partial Israeli pullback in the Sinai, which would have allowed the Suez Canal to reopen. Israel rejected that partial withdrawal, which made Sadat realize that the Jewish state would not respond so long as the Arabs lacked both military credibility and U.S. diplomatic support. Therefore, he expelled Egypt's Soviet military advisers in 1972 to enlist Washington's mediation. Sadat also sent a special envoy to Washington in February 1973 to repeat the offer of partial peace in return for partial withdrawal.

   In the early summer of 1973, having explored a half dozen other methods, Sadat determined that he had no alternative but to go to war. "Sadat's decision to wage war in 1973 was a desperate act aimed at accomplishing what his diplomatic campaign of the previous two years had failed to do—to force Israel and the United States to the negotiating table by jolting them out of their complacency. His war plan reflected this limited objective: crossing the Suez Canal and overwhelming Israel's fortifications; penetrating at most five or six miles into Sinai; then digging in and resisting counterattacks until—he hoped—the superpowers worked out a cease-fire" (Mufti, 2000, 85).

   On October 6, 1973, Egypt and Syria attacked Israel in what the Israelis call the Yom Kippur War. This is because the war started on the Jewish Day of Atonement. In this war, the Egyptian troops succeeded in crossing the Suez Canal and demolishing the Bar-Lev Line, which was established by the Israelis on the East side of the Canal. Syria initially seized most of the Golan Heights, but Israeli troops then pushed the Syrian forces east toward the Syrian capital of Damascus.

   During the 1973 war, the Egyptian troopers made use of the missiles imported from Soviet sources. On the other hand, the United States engaged in a massive effort to provide Israel with military supplies.

   The main objective of the 1973 war was not to recapture all of Egypt's lost territory, but to change the political environment. The limited purposes of the war were to restore Arab honor by erasing the humiliation of the 1967 defeat so that Egypt could negotiate with Israel from a position of dignity, and to get the superpowers more actively involved in the negotiating process. Sadat succeeded on both counts. The 1973 War resulted in an emotional and psychological shock in Israel, where there was severe public criticism of Israel's overconfidence that had prevented accurate intelligence assessments.

   Two new elements entered into the 1973 war. First, oil was used as a diplomatic weapon by the Arab states. Second, the United States and the Soviet Union, frightened by their near confrontation during the crisis, cooperated to bring the war to an end.

   The Organization of Petroleum Exporting Countries (OPEC), formed in 1960, had gained influence internationally by the 1970s. Moreover, its Arab members sought to coordinate their policies within OPEC. During the October War, Saudi Arabia and other oil-rich Arab countries instituted a 25 percent cutback in oil production and increased the posted price of oil by 50 percent. They also refused to sell oil to the United States and other countries, such as The Netherlands and Portugal, that armed Israel or allowed U.S. supply planes to refuel in their airports on the way to Israel. Those measures were instituted within hours of the U.S. dispatch of arms to Israel. "Production cutbacks, price increases, and embargoes led to long lines at gas stations in the West and increased the pressure on the United States and Europe to resolve the crisis diplomatically" (Lesch & Tschirgi, 1998, 26).

The United States and the Soviet Union reached a common understanding that resulted in U.N. Security Council Resolution 338 on October 22, 1973, which called for a cease-fire and immediate negotiations among the concerned parties to implement Resolution 242 in all its parts. Egypt, Israel, and Syria accepted the resolution (Bickerton & Klausner, 1998, 179). The 1973 war set the stage for the peace process of the late 1970s.

STEPS TOWARD PEACE

The Palestinian issue and the liberation of the West Bank and the Gaza Strip, which were occupied by Israel in 1967, are the "core issues" that have been topping the agenda of all regional and international summit conferences held to try to solve the conflict peacefully.

Currently, the conflict is crystallized in the abandonment of the diplomatic option by the Arab and Israeli sides and the refusal of some Arab states to "normalize" their relationships with Israel.

ISRAELI-EGYPTIAN PEACE TREATY

Among the Arab countries, Egypt plays a pivotal role in the negotiations for solving the Arab-Israeli conflict. Besides its political, ideological, and military weight in the Middle East region, Egypt has entered wars against Israel in 1948, 1956, 1967, and 1973. Moreover, Egypt's separate peace treaty with Israel in 1979 marked the beginning of bilateral talks between Israel and an Arab country (Sela, 1998, 29).

"Sadat's success in demonstrating the bankruptcy of the 1967–73 status quo led to Israel and American reassessments. Since it was now clear that ignoring Egypt altogether was not a cost-free policy, the Israelis—particularly after the ascension of Yitzhak Rabin to the prime ministership in April 1974—reverted to their earlier strategy of trying to reach a separate peace with it" (Mufti, 2000, 86).

The 1973 war was a turning point because it made it possible to think about negotiations and peace and created opportunities for effective diplomatic action. Much credit is due the U.S. Secretary of State of that period, Henry Kissinger, for the way he managed American power. He made it clear that the United States would give massive aid to prevent Israel's defeat, but he also managed the ending of the war, satisfying some Arab claims and bringing the Russians into the process.

As a result of Kissinger's diplomatic efforts during 1974–1975, there were three important Arab-Israeli agreements, two with Egypt and one with Syria. The Sinai I agreement of January 18, 1974, resulted in Israel's withdrawal from the west side of the Suez Canal and the establishment of a new armistice line 20 miles east of the canal. As payoffs to the United States, Egypt restored diplomatic relations with Washington, and Saudi Arabia lifted the oil embargo

in March 1974. The Golan accord of May 31, 1974, resulted in Israel's withdrawal from the land captured from Syria in the October War and from the city
of Qunaitra, which Israel had occupied in 1967. As a result, the United States
and Syria restored diplomatic relations. The Sinai II agreement of September
1, 1975, yielded further Israeli pullbacks east of the mountain passes in the Sinai and from the oil fields in the Gulf of Suez (Lesch & Tschirgi, 1998).

In a secret annex between the United States and Israel, the United States
pledged to neither recognize nor negotiate with the PLO as long as the PLO
did not recognize Israel's right to exist and did not accept U.N. Security
Council Resolutions 242 and 338.

As for the situation in Jordan, King Hussein's inability to regain territory on
the West Bank and his crackdown on the PLO in September 1970 persuaded
the Arab League to set aside Jordan's claims to represent the Palestinians. Instead, at a summit conference in October 1974, the Arab League recognized
the PLO as the sole legitimate representative of the Palestinian people.

The election of U.S. President Jimmy Carter in 1976 produced the first
U.S. administration that attempted to try for a comprehensive settlement by
incorporating the PLO into efforts to bring peace to the Middle East. Carter's
administration broke new ground when it conceded that Palestinians had "legitimate political rights" that should be upheld by a Middle East settlement
(Lesch & Tschirgi, 1998, 97).

Carter had extensive contacts with Middle East leaders. However, his administration failed to obtain the PLO's unconditional recognition of Israel's
right to exist and was therefore unable to negotiate with that body. On the
other hand, the Israelis rejected the PLO participation in a peace conference
and distrusted the Carter administration. The election of an Israeli Likud government (right-wing conservative) under Menachem Begin in May 1977
heightened Israel's hostility toward Washington's policy.

Amidst all these obstacles to peace, Sadat issued a startling declaration during a speech before the Egyptian National Assembly on November 9, 1977:
He would go anywhere to achieve peace—even to Israel. True to his word, on
November 19, 1977, he went to Israel to meet with Israeli Prime Minister Begin. "For the first time in modern history, an Arab leader on a mission of state
under the eyes of a captivated world stepped onto Israeli soil . . . Sadat came offering peace and acceptance, that 'sacred message . . . of security, safety, and
peace to every man, woman, and child in Israel' " (Saunders, 1985, 1). In his
speech to the Israeli parliament on November 20, 1977, Sadat spoke of compromise and reconciliation and initiated the "first real breakthrough in more
than thirty years of Arab-Israeli hostility" (Lesch & Tessler, 1989, 3).

Sadat believed that his visit to Israel would quell Israeli fears and transform
the negotiating climate. He also felt encouraged by Carter's personal request
that he break the diplomatic stalemate. He did not anticipate, however, the anger that his move would cause in the rest of the Arab world. Indeed, he ex-

pected that—despite momentary criticism—Arab governments would support Egypt in its move for peace with Israel.

For its part, the Soviet Union strongly criticized the Sadat visit to Israel as a legitimization of Israeli occupation of Arab lands and an effort to isolate both the PLO and the Soviet Union. Despite strong Soviet criticism of the Sadat visit, U.S. Deputy Secretary of State Warren Christopher sought to downplay Soviet negativism, claiming that the Soviets had a role to play in the outcome of the negotiations. This position was challenged, however, by former United States Secretary of State Kissinger, who attacked the Soviet Union for opposing the Sadat visit and discouraging other Arabs from endorsing it. "The maximum role that the Soviets should play, argued Kissinger, would be to participate in endorsing an agreement that the parties had reached directly" (Freedman, 1979, 68).

The Israeli-Egyptian negotiations were on the verge of collapsing when Israel attacked Lebanon in March 1978 in response to PLO commandos who hijacked a bus near Tel Aviv and killed Israeli civilians. Although the United States pressured Israel to withdraw in June 1978, Israeli forces retained a security zone in south Lebanon.

To prevent Israeli-Egyptian negotiations from collapsing, Carter invited Sadat and Begin to his retreat at Camp David to resume negotiations. On September 17, 1978, the Camp David accords were signed by Sadat, Begin, and Carter. The accords included two agreements. The first, "A Framework for Peace in the Middle East," set forth guidelines for treaties between Israel and each of its Arab neighbors, with a focus on the West Bank and the Gaza Strip, in order to reach a solution to the Palestinian problem. The second, "A Framework for the Conclusion of the Peace Treaty between Egypt and Israel," was a draft proposal for a peace agreement to be negotiated and signed within three months. This called for a phased Israeli withdrawal from the Sinai over a period of three years and a full restoration of the Sinai Peninsula to Egypt. The United Nations would oversee provisions of the accords to satisfy both sides. In this accord, the parties agreed to enter into negotiations over the establishment of a self-governing authority for the West Bank and the Gaza Strip, based on U.N. Resolution 242. The accord did not stop settlement construction or resolve Jerusalem's status (Diller, 1994).

"The Camp David agreements simultaneously lessened Arab rejectionism and Israeli suspicion. In this context, the accords could be viewed as a major step forward and, however viewed, must be regarded as a vast improvement on the methods of violence and terror so often employed by both sides" (Bickerton & Klausner, 1998, 202).

Although the Camp David accords resulted in a peace treaty between Egypt and Israel, they ignored the future of the West Bank, Gaza, the Golan Heights and East Jerusalem. These issues are still unresolved.

Most Arab governments were shocked at the terms, which they believed satisfied Egypt's interests at the expense of the Palestinians. An Arab League summit convened in the Iraqi capital of Baghdad in November 1978 to orga-nize opposition against Egypt. When the Israel-Egypt peace treaty was signed, all the Arab states—except Oman and Sudan—broke diplomatic relations with Egypt and suspended Egypt from the Arab League. They also expelled Egypt from inter-Arab banks and investment companies, banned the sale of oil to Egypt, and closed their airspace to Egyptian planes.

In his comment on the Camp David accords, Johan Galtung, author of the book *The Arab-Israeli Conflict: Two Decades of Change* (1988), said:

"The core conflict is between Jews and Arabs in this area, more particularly between Is-raelis and Palestinians, over the exercise of the type of territorial rights associated with national sovereignty. . . . There was a process associated with Camp David, but that was a 'peace process' imposed by Egypt and Israel [and the United States] on the Palestin-ians with no Palestinians present. By that process, the Palestinians were fragmented." (322)

Sadat failed to achieve gains in the West Bank negotiations that would have restored his credibility and gained him the trust he lost in the Arab world after signing the Camp David accords. The Israeli government accelerated the con-struction of Jewish settlements on the West Bank and the Gaza Strip, and de-clared unified Jerusalem the eternal capital of Israel in July 1980.

Nevertheless, President Sadat and Prime Minister Begin shared the 1979 Nobel Peace Prize while President Carter, their host at Camp David, led the applause for the risks they had taken at home and the sacrifices they had made.

During his final year in office, Carter was preoccupied with the Soviet inva-sion of Afghanistan and revolutionary Iran's seizure of U.S. hostages. When Ronald Reagan replaced Carter in the White House in 1981, Reagan dis-tanced himself from his predecessor's policies and signaled to Israel that his priority was U.S. support for a strategic partnership to curtail Soviet influence in the Middle East.

For Sadat and Begin, the price of peace became discouragingly high. "From Palestine to Iran, raging Moslem fundamentalists for some time had been try-ing to arouse the Arab world in turn against all 'foreign' influences, including Israel and the United States, with grave consequences for both. Each dispute, whether it involved Egyptian dealings with Israel, or the religious sanctity of the rights of the Palestinian or Iranian peoples, became a cause that was fought for with violence that often burst all bounds" (Hohenberg, 1998, 211).

In the summer of 1981, Sadat cracked down on his increasingly vocal critics inside Egypt, which triggered a violent reaction. Members of the Islamist-oriented Jihad group assassinated Sadat on October 6, 1981, while he was viewing a military parade celebrating the October War. Sadat was suc-ceeded by his vice president, Hosni Mubarak, also a trusted American ally. Even though President Reagan could not risk appearing in Cairo (on the ad-vice of his Secret Service guards), he sent three former presidents—Jimmy Carter, Richard Nixon, and Gerald Ford—to the funeral of the slain Egyptian leader. "Another among the eighty chiefs of state who attended, Prime Minister Begin, came from Jerusalem to pay his tribute to the Egyptian leader who had given his life to peace" (Hohenberg, 1998, 215).

ISRAELI-EGYPTIAN BILATERAL RELATIONS

With respect to bilateral relations between Israel and Egypt, the Israeli withdrawal from the Sinai was completed on schedule. Also, both countries started exchanging ambassadors early in 1980. In addition, they coordinated the development of tourist exchanges, established a joint agricultural development company, and planned to produce cooperative ventures in several other areas (Lesch & Tessler, 1989, 6).

Egypt was the first Arab country to make peace with Israel, but that peace has always been a "frosty affair" that involves little real partnership between the two countries. Despite their trade and cultural ties, both Egypt and Israel continued to distrust each others' motives, "a distrust that was enhanced considerably by their inability to make any significant headway in negotiations over the West Bank and Gaza. Israelis wondered about and debated whether Egypt was sincerely committed to peace or whether Sadat's overture was simply a tactical shift in Arab efforts to destroy the Jewish State. Egypt expressed similar doubts about Israeli sincerity, often questioning whether Israel had any intention of fulfilling its promise to accept Palestinian self-determination" (Lesch & Tessler, 1989, 7). Ten years after the Camp David accords, Begin said that "full normalization of relations with Egypt still hasn't arrived and we're watching it" (Diller, 1994, 202).

Throughout the 1990s, the Egyptian and Israeli leaderships have clashed publicly over a wide range of issues that have brought the two countries to the brink of crisis. "The verbal war [between Israel and Egypt] reveals deep insecurity, suspicion, and hostility . . . This (verbal war) raises disturbing questions not only about the future direction of Egyptian-Israeli relations but also about the long-term viability of the peace process itself" (Fawaz, 1995, 69).

The main point of contention is the character and composition of the new Middle East order and the roles of Egypt and Israel in it. Their competing visions struggle to shape the region's dynamics in their own images. Most segments of Egypt's civil society have expressed deep mistrust of Israel. Most intellectuals, trade unions, and cultural and religious figures have called on the government to refuse normalization with Israel and even to reassess its position on the peace process. For example, the former Grand Sheikh of al-Azhar, Egypt's most important center for Islamic learning, refused a request to meet the former Israeli President Ezer Weizman, during the latter's visit to Cairo in December 1994, saying that "the climate was wrong because of the continuing Israeli occupation of Arab countries and Jerusalem" (Fawaz, 1995, 75).

Although much of the verbal war between Israel and Egypt is mere rhetoric designed to test the other nation's will and commitment, the fundamental political differences between Egypt and Israel should not be minimized. These disputes revolve around Israel's and Egypt's political and economic roles in the Middle East order and the lack of progress on both the Israeli-Palestinian and Israeli-Syrian fronts. Given their political and military weights and geostrategic positions, Egypt's and Israel's interests are bound to clash in the new Middle East. The challenge for both will be to keep their competition in check and prevent their cold peace from turning into cold war.

The frightening thing is that the verbal escalation between Egypt and Israel finds deeper and more hostile echoes within the public opinion of both countries. In the absence of public opinion polls and a probing press, it is difficult to gauge accurately Egyptian public opinion about Israel.

However, a poll conducted by one of the national Egyptian newspapers in December 1994 found that for most Egyptians the "psychological barrier" with Israel is still very much in place 15 years after the signing of the Egypt-Israel peace treaty. The poll, which sampled the views of 1,505 Egyptians 18 years of age and older, showed that the public was opposed to formal ties with Israel. Asked whether they would buy Israeli goods and whether they would like to visit Israel, 71 percent of respondents said no. An even greater majority—75 percent—said no to the eventuality of industrial cooperation with Israel. Although a majority expressed little faith in the ability of the peace process to restore Palestinian rights, the poll revealed much greater dissatisfaction regarding Egypt's relations with Israel. Results of the poll showed that "the Egyptian public felt it had its own ax to grind with Israel" (Fawaz, 1995, 76). Ironically, the upper strata of the Egyptian society, who are expected to have more crystallized and enlightened views, were highly represented in the poll.

In a similar vein, Israeli public opinion polls conducted during the early 1990s revealed a hardening of views regarding concluding peace agreements with the Palestinians and Syrians. The Israeli newspapers published several articles fretting about the state of relations with Egypt and calling for retaliatory measures against the Egyptians.

DOES PEACE MEAN NORMALIZATION?

Since Israel and Egypt signed their peace treaty in 1978, the two countries have been maintaining "normal" political and diplomatic relations; however, the Israeli-Egyptian normal relations were only on the political level, not on the popular level. From my point of view as an Egyptian who was born and raised in Egypt, the average Egyptian person can neither comprehend nor accept maintaining a normal relationship with Israel.

The Israelis want to maintain "full" normal relations with Egypt because they have always felt isolated in the Middle East, and maintaining a normal relationship with a leading Arab country like Egypt would help them end their isolation in the region. The Israeli society has a deep human craving for accep-

tance. "Because Jewish experience has included rejection and traumatic persecution (during the Holocaust), the yearning for acceptance is especially strong
in Israel. The Israeli attitude reflects the weariness of war and isolation and the
view that long-term security will depend on developing some reciprocal political relationship with neighbors. The Israeli people search every Arab statement
and move for implied acceptance of the Jewish state" (Saunders, 1985, 39).

The Israeli government allows its people to visit Egypt for business, and
even for tourism. In fact, many Israeli citizens regularly visit the Sinai Peninsula, which is a very popular Egyptian tourist site on the southern borders of
Israel. However, to this day, the only Egyptians who actually visit Israel are the
official political and cultural delegations. But average Egyptians who want to
visit Israel are not free to visit. Before going to Israel, they would have to be interrogated by the Egyptian intelligence service and in most cases would be denied. I believe that even if average Egyptian citizens were allowed to visit Israel
freely without any governmental restrictions they still would not consider visiting Israel. I cannot imagine an Egyptian family, for example, taking a weekend vacation in Tel Aviv. Why? Because of the psychological barrier. It is a
barrier that has been created by years and years of antagonism with Israelis; a
barrier that was strengthened by the Egyptian and the Arab news media at
large which have enforced the Arabs' stereotypes about the Israelis as invaders
of Arab land. Many Egyptians stereotype the Israelis as heartless, aggressive,
and stingy. Many Egyptians cannot even imagine watching an Israeli soap op-
era on television, let alone visiting Israel.

In Egypt today, there are some pro-peace groups who call for proceeding
further with the normalization of the Israeli-Egyptian relations; however,
there are other groups that totally oppose this normalization and ostracize any
Egyptian who visits Israel for business. For the latter groups, maintaining normal relations with Israel is considered to be a "betrayal" of Arab nationalism.
They say they do not want to shake hands with the Israelis who are occupying
Arab land. They feel that Israel's settlements in the West Bank and the Gaza
Strip demonstrated a lack of Israeli good faith in honoring the Camp David
commitment to leave the question of sovereignty in those territories open.

The Israelis have their own complaints. Many of them are disillusioned
about the situation of the bilateral relations between Israel and Egypt. They argue that maintaining full normalization with Egypt would provide a lift to the
peace process and an opportunity for Egypt to speak openly and directly with
Israelis within Israel about the effect on normalization of a continuation of the
larger process.

FROZEN COMMUNICATION

Throughout much of the Arab-Israeli conflict, the Arab nations have expressed their reluctance to communicate directly with Israel, and several U.N.,
national, and nonofficial representatives have acted as intermediaries. Those

intermediaries have, on several occasions, distorted the messages, leading to misperceptions by both the senders and the recipients of the conveyed information. "The governmental mediator may be motivated by self-interest. . . . He/she may sincerely want to facilitate a solution but can never be wholly detached from the national interest of his or her state" (Bailey, 1990, 425).

Since the late 1970s and the early 1980s, the level of government control over the flow of information in the Middle East conflict has been dictated by the fact that this is a crisis over peace rather than over war. "While the public and journalists are willing to suspend certain freedoms during times of war, they insist upon full disclosure in times of peace" (Wolfsfeld, 1997, 95).

Egypt should continue to play its role as a major mediator and facilitator of communication between Israel and the Arab countries. Egypt has already negotiated its treaty, so the issue is not so much Egypt's judgment about Israel's readiness to negotiate. The important contribution that Egypt can bring to further negotiations is its experience in dealing with Israel. "The first step in reviving the broader peace process is to put the Egyptian-Israeli relationship back on the tracks. . . . Showing that the relationship is still alive and can grow . . . could help create a political environment in which Israelis could assess other opportunities to negotiate against the background of a positive experience" (Saunders, 1985, 102).

THE *INTIFADA*

Palestinians appeared to be divided in the 1980s. However, a drastic transformation took place at the grassroots level that reinvigorated the national movement. The *Intifada* (uprising) that swept the West Bank and the Gaza Strip during the period 1988–1990 was a mass movement rather than one run by the political elite. It was a clear manifestation of a social revolution that involved the entire Palestinian body politic. The Israeli army responded massively to the *Intifada*, but the diffuse nature of the protests was very strong. Teenagers played cat-and-mouse games with soldiers, throwing stones at them and then dashing away when the soldiers shot rubber-coated bullets and tear gas. The *Intifada* compelled Washington to turn its attention to the Middle East and to open a dialogue with the Israelis and the PLO (Lesch & Tschirgi, 1998).

The *Intifada* had the immediate effect of redrawing the border between Israel and the Occupied Territories. It forced the Israelis to rethink their position on the occupation. The PLO leaders made use of the opportunity offered to them by the uprising. In November 1988, the PNC officially called for an independent Palestinian state on the West Bank and the Gaza Strip, with its capital in East Jerusalem. For the first time, the PNC accepted U.N. resolutions that called for territorial partition and that recognized Israel. The U.S. administration responded positively and opened a dialogue with the PLO.

ARAFAT AT THE SECURITY COUNCIL

In 1988 Arafat sought to address the U.N. General Assembly. However, the Reagan administration blocked his visa access, in contravention to its agreement with the United Nations, and during a period of otherwise improved relations between the United States and the Soviet Union. The entire General Assembly met in Geneva, instead of New York, to hear Arafat speak at a cost to the United Nations of nearly a half million dollars (Donahue & Prosser, 1997).

In response to the killing of Palestinians by Israeli troops in 1990, Arafat called for an urgent Security Council meeting. The Bush administration had to consider its stated immigration policy, its past support of Israel, the ongoing *Intifada* against Israeli military forces, and the recent Israeli attacks against Palestinian civilians. The United States agreed to hold the Security Council meeting in Geneva if Arafat would not push his visa request. By this arrangement, the PLO was awarded a small victory.

In his speech before the Security Council on May 25, 1990, Arafat said:

Over the past 30 months, 1,200 Palestinian martyrs have fallen under the bullets of the occupiers. More than 80,000 citizens have been injured as a result of various kinds of repression ranging from severe beatings, the breaking of bones and the use of rubber bullets and live ammunition to the use of internationally prohibited poison gases, which have caused more than 60,000 miscarriages and permanent handicaps to thousands of children, women, and men, in addition to other kinds of terrorism and repression. . . . The heroic people's *Intifada* against the Israeli occupation of our country will continue until we wrest our right to freedom and national independence on our national soil. (quoted in Donahue & Prosser, 1997, 256–257)

CONCLUSION

This chapter shed some light on the historical background of the Arab-Israeli conflict, how it originated and developed, and how complicated it became. Also discussed was the relationship between Israel and Egypt within the context of the Arab-Israeli conflict, and how various factors, such as concern about security and public opinion, have affected the communication between the two countries.

In the next chapter, I will discuss the signing of the Oslo accords, the Camp David 2000 negotiations, the new uprising, and Egypt's position regarding these developments.

2

Oslo and After

Under President George Bush, the United States called for comprehensive negotiations between Israel and its Arab neighbors. That led to the Madrid Peace Conference, which opened on October 30, 1991. For the first time, Syrian, Lebanese, Jordanian, and Palestinian delegates sat down with Israeli representatives to address their fundamental problems. The altered climate was signaled by the Soviets' restoration of diplomatic relations with Israel in December 1991.

Following the Madrid conference, bilateral negotiations opened between Israel and each of its opponents—Lebanon, Syria, and a Jordanian-Palestinian team. The bilateral talks were initially deadlocked for two reasons. One reason was that Israel's Likud government adhered to a position that opposed giving up any land, even in the context of peace. The other was that the Palestinians' status in the talks remained vague: "Because Israel refused to deal officially with the PLO and because the Arab states supported the PLO's claim to be the official voice of the Palestinians, negotiations could not be very productive in the PLO's absence" (Lesch & Tschirgi, 1998, 34).

OSLO ACCORDS

Even when the Labor Party formed a new Israeli government in July 1992, negotiations barely moved forward. However, Israel opened secret talks directly with the Palestine Liberation Organization (PLO) under the auspices of the Norwegian foreign ministry. These talks resulted in the signing of the Oslo I agreement by the then Israeli Prime Minister Yitzhak Rabin and the Palestine Liberation Leader Yasser Arafat on September 13, 1993. This was a major turning point in the Middle East. The Israelis and the Palestinians agreed in their "Declaration of Principles" to recognize each other's legitimacy and, moreover, to establish Palestinian self-rule within the West Bank and the Gaza Strip.

A second agreement in May 1994 enabled the PLO to form a Palestinian Authority in Jericho and the Gaza Strip, followed by the establishment of a Palestinian civil administration over the entire West Bank for a five-year interim period. This agreement enabled Arafat to become president of the Palestinian Authority. Arafat and the PLO officials returned to Gaza and Jericho in July 1994—for the first time since 1967.

Many Palestinians were disappointed that executive power remained concentrated in the hands of Arafat, and polls indicated that the public overwhelmingly expected Arafat to implement laws and resolutions passed by the legislature. In practice, Arafat ignored most legislative acts and even jammed the airwaves to prevent legislative sessions from being broadcast live by radio. When a poll was taken in late 1996, nearly a quarter of the respondents had a negative view about the status of human rights under the Palestinian Authority (Lesch & Tschirgi, 1998).

The Israeli–PLO agreement led, in October 1994, to Oslo II, a second major agreement between Israel and the PLO. This agreement gave the PLO partial authority over villages on the West Bank but remained subject to stringent Israeli security controls.

The breakthrough in Israeli–PLO relations had immediate consequences for relations between Israel and the Arab world. Jordan used its bilateral negotiations with Israel to conclude a formal peace treaty on October 26, 1994. That accord delineated their territorial border, established complementary security arrangements, specified their allocations of water in the Jordan River basin, and opened up trade, communications, and tourism. King Hussein of Jordan then became an important intermediary between Israel and the PLO.

Other Arab regimes also cautiously contacted Israel. For example, Israel exchanged economic liaison offices with Tunisia and Oman in early 1996 and negotiated with Qatar to purchase its natural gas. In contrast to the accords involving Israel, the PLO, and Jordan, Israel and Syria could not reach a complete agreement with regard to the future of the Golan Heights.

Following the Oslo II agreement, Rabin shared the Nobel Peace Prize in 1994 with his foreign minister, Shimon Peres, and Arafat. However, polarization inside Israel was so severe that some Israelis viewed Rabin as a traitor for reaching an accord with Arafat and conceding the principle of land-for-peace. At the end of a peace rally in Tel Aviv on November 4, 1995, Rabin was assassinated by an Israeli Jew opposed to the peace process (Freedman, 1998).

In its meeting on April 22–24, 1996, in Gaza, the PLO revoked from its charter the articles that called for the destruction of the state of Israel and that thereby violated the 1993–1995 accords with Israel. On January 19, 1997, the PLO authorized its legal committee to begin drafting a new PLO charter.

In his comment on the Oslo accords, Edward Said (2000), in his book *The End of the Peace Process: Oslo and After* said:

Oslo brought one significantly new thing, namely, the first-time official admission by an Israeli prime minister that there was a Palestinian people [approximately 7.5 million in number] with its own representatives. Beyond that, the terms of the agreement exactly reflected the huge difference in power between the two sides. Nothing was said about Palestinian sovereignty and self-determination. No end to the presence of the settlements was mentioned. . . . East Jerusalem remained under Israeli control: Oslo passed that over. The refugees expelled in 1948 were left as they have been for the last fifty years, homeless and uncompensated, despite numerous international and UN covenants and resolutions. (313)

EGYPT'S REACTIONS TO THE OSLO ACCORDS

At the official level, Egypt's reaction to the Oslo accords was, not unexpectedly, one of sweet vindication. The agreement reinforced Egypt's own 1979 peace treaty with Israel and made its endless rounds of peace-process diplomacy over the last few years before the accord seem justified. On the popular level, the Oslo accords received a warm reception. Though some leftist and Islamist intellectuals pontificated about its loopholes and flaws, most approved in the end, saying it was the best that could be hoped for. Only the radical Islamic movement rejected it completely. "But the ink had hardly dried on the landmark document before its visions of expanding Middle East horizons and opportunities began provoking fear and loathing among Egyptian policymakers and businesspeople" (Murphy, 1994, 80).

For one, Egypt worked itself out of a job. In the past, its special relationship with Israel gave Egypt the unique role of interlocutor between Israel and the Arabs. However, after the Oslo accords, which allowed the Palestinians to talk directly to the Israelis, some Egyptian pundits started to ask the question: On what will Egypt's regional role be based? Another whispered apprehension was that once the Palestinian deal was supplemented by similar Israeli pacts with Lebanon, Syria, and Jordan, "the Levant will rise to reclaim its traditional position as the commercial leader of the Middle East" (Murphy, 1994, 81).

Many Egyptian businesspeople spoke with dread of the competition they could face from Israelis teamed up with Palestinian businessmen. To allay such fears, Egypt moved quickly to hold business seminars with Palestinian and Israeli businesspeople and announced bureaucratic "reforms" to facilitate foreign investment. And even as the Israeli-Palestinian self-rule pact was being signed, senior Egyptian and Israeli economic officials were meeting in Cairo for the first time since 1981 to discuss improving trade ties.

The Egyptian ruling elite resented and mistrusted Israel's decision to by-pass Egypt and establish direct ties with other Arab states. They felt that Egypt should continue to be the mediator between Israel and other Arab states. Egyptian Foreign Minister Amr Moussa made it clear that Egypt was opposed to the formation of a Middle East common market before a comprehensive political settlement was reached. Egyptian President Mubarak intervened to allay the fears of Egyptian intellectuals: "Any assumption that Israel is capable of swallowing up Egypt is wrong. Egypt has always been, and will continue to be, a pivotal state in the region" (Fawaz, 1995, 70).

These tensions have made a cold peace downright arctic. Today, both of the two great breakthroughs in the Middle East process—the Camp David accords and the Oslo accords—are at risk.

TERMINATION OF THE PEACE PROCESS

Rabin's successor, Shimon Peres, sought to expedite the peace process by accelerating the withdrawal of Israeli troops from major Palestinian cities on the West Bank. The peace process, however, received a major blow in February and March of 1996 when a series of suicide attacks by Palestinian Islamic militants in Jerusalem and Tel Aviv shook Israel's support for the peace accords and put an end to the dialogue between Israel and the PLO. These attacks were the primary reason behind the election of the right-wing coalition government headed by Likud leader Benjamin Netanyahu on May 29, 1996. Netanyahu was elected prime minister by 50.4 percent of the vote. He was far less interested in the Middle East peace process than his predecessor had been. The Likud Party formed a coalition government that stated its determination to resume constructing Jewish settlements on the West Bank, retain the Golan Heights, and prevent the formation of a Palestine state. Likud had benefited politically from terrorist attacks by Palestinian groups in Israel, which made Israelis fear that peace had not brought them national security. Netanyahu closed Israel to residents of the West Bank and the Gaza Strip for extended periods of time, which led to clashes between Palestinian and Israeli soldiers in several West Bank towns.

The Netanyahu government shattered the status quo on the issue of Jewish settlements. "It was Netanyahu's commitment to expand settlements as part of a broader hard-line ideological policy—a policy that rejects the principle of territorial compromise, a Palestinian state, and negotiations over Jerusalem" (Rosenblum, 1998, 64). Netanyahu used his settlement policy as an instrument of denial of another nation. He eased procedures for obtaining building permits in the West Bank and Gaza and approved a request by Jewish settlers to set up three hundred mobile homes in settlements. Moreover, he pledged $5 million of immediate aid to help compensate for past financial burdens the Jewish settlers had to bear "as a result of the Israeli-Palestinian agreements" (Rosenblum, 1998, 64). Furthermore, Netanyahu put forward approximately two hundred plans for building thousands of new houses for Jewish settlers. By the end of 1996, the Palestine Council sent Arafat a request to study the possibility of suspending the negotiations should the Israelis continue with settlement activity. Therefore, the peace process passed through a period of stagnation from mid-1996 to the end of 1998 (Freedman, 1998).

EGYPT'S REACTIONS TO NETANYAHU'S POLICIES

Most Egyptians at both the official and popular levels did not approve of Netanyahu's dealings with the Palestinians. The mood in Cairo during Netanyahu's term was angry, and the reason was simple. Egypt likes to see itself as an "elder brother" among Arabs. With the Netanyahu administration's perceived lack of interest in the peace process, Egypt felt obliged to step in, if only to shout and flex its muscles. The shouting was loud and personal. Immature was the least of the insults that Egyptian officials directed at Netanyahu. Some called him "clinically paranoid."

The Egyptian press revoltingly stuck a Hitler mustache on Netanyahu's pictures and called for assassins to "do it" to him. An editorial that appeared in the weekly edition of *Al Ahram* (one of the generally staid official newspapers in Egypt) in October 1996 stated: "Violence is all but inevitable if Mr. Netanyahu continues to reside in one world, while the rest of us on planet Earth seek to sort through the mockery he has made of the peace process."

Netanyahu accused the Egyptian government of deliberately stirring up popular feeling, especially after the Egyptian opposition parties, university students, and retired generals started calling for the punishment of Israel. Moreover, senior religious figures in Egypt joined in to denounce what they called the "Judaisation of Jerusalem." Pope Shenouda, leader of Egypt's six million Coptic Christians, raised cheers by reaffirming his church's ban on pilgrimage to the Holy City.

WYE RIVER PLANTATION AGREEMENT

On October 23, 1998, Arafat and Netanyahu agreed to a land-for-peace deal on the West Bank after a nine-day summit organized by then U.S. President Bill Clinton, at the Wye River Conference Center in Maryland.

At the time the Wye agreement was taking place, the West Bank was divided into three areas: Area A, which was entirely run by Palestinians except for security, water, and exits and entrances; Area B, jointly patrolled by Palestinian and Israeli soldiers, with security, water, building permits, exits, and entrances entirely controlled by Israel; and Area C, which is completely Israeli. Before Wye, these amounted respectively to 2.8 percent, 24 percent, and 72 percent of the land area. Wye gave the Palestinians an additional one percent from Area C, and 14.2 percent from Area B, thus putting 18.2 percent under full Palestinian

Authority control with the same exclusions and provisos. In addition, Israel would transfer 13 percent more from Area C to Area B.

In his comment on the Wye agreement, Edward Said (2000), stated:

The U.S. press as usual reported the proceedings of a flagrant disregard of the facts. No one bothered to point out, to take one example, that the 40 percent of the West Bank's surface supposedly being given to Arafat's corrupt Authority was broken down into bits and pieces that tell a very different story, all of it subject to Israel's choice of date and location of the land to be partially vacated. No settlements and no bypassing roads are to be given: on the contrary, Israel asked the United States for an additional $1.3 billion for the redeployments. (294)

In his memoirs titled *A Durable Peace: Israel and Its Place among the Nations*, Netanyahu (2000) commented on the Wye agreement:

Instead of a process in which Israel would retreat to the virtually indefensible pre-1967 line even before final settlement negotiations were concluded, I sought and achieved a different result at Wye: that most of the West Bank would remain in our hands pending the start of these negotiations. Israel would retain some 60 percent of the territory with all the West Bank's Jewish population; the Palestinian Authority would have some 40 percent of the area with virtually the entire Palestinian population. (344)

The few months after the Wye agreement witnessed the suspension by Netanyahu of further implementation of the agreement after the first phase of withdrawal, ostensibly because of the failure of the Palestinian Authority to fulfill its security-related obligations toward Israel.

BARAK REPLACES NETANYAHU

On May 17, 1999, Ehud Barak of the Labor Party was elected prime minister of Israel after defeating Netanyahu by a 56 to 46 margin in the popular vote. Netanyahu announced his decision to resign from politics within hours of his stunning personal defeat. During the election campaign, Israeli ads dramatized the fact that Barak, a former chief of staff and foreign minister, had led the successful antiterrorism campaigns and was Israel's most highly decorated soldier. The ads were effective in countering the Likud charges that a Labor victory would endanger Israel's security.

Upon his victory Barak promised that he would rapidly implement the Wye River agreement, enter into permanent status talks with the Palestinians, and vigorously pursue resumption of peace talks with Syria and Lebanon, which had been suspended in February 1996. Barak also managed to put together a broad-based coalition that gave him a comfortable initial majority of 75 in the 120–member Knesset (Gruen, 2000).

Barak's victory was welcomed by most of the Arab world, most notably by late President Hafez al-Assad of Syria and young King Abdullah of Jordan, who had succeeded King Hussein after his death in February 1999, and who pledged to continue his father's commitment to peace.

During his first few weeks in office, Barak single-handedly reenergized the peace process, and he agreed with then U.S. President Clinton on an ambitious agenda: to make peace not only with the Palestinians but also with Syria and Lebanon. However, Barak announced that he wanted "physical separation" from the Palestinians. He also vowed never to give up Israeli sovereignty over any part of Jerusalem, which Palestinians also claim as their capital. Then, in the summer of 2000, Barak withdrew his troops from southern Lebanon, hoping that this move would be part of a rapprochement with Syria, which had 35,000 troops there.

Barak continued to press for closure on final status talks with the Palestinians and a possible deal with Syria to include withdrawal from the Golan Heights. Barak said his goal was the creation of a Palestinian state in 50 percent of the West Bank. However, "he failed because in one essential way he was too similar to Rabin to break from his mentor's mold: he too is a loner, convinced that only he is smart enough to be entrusted with war and peace. He refused to involve most of his Cabinet in the peace process. . . . The leader who insisted that Israelis make peace among themselves before making peace with their neighbors couldn't even make peace with the ministers in his own government" (Halevi, 2000, 15).

In his comment on Barak's policies in the Middle East, Edward Said (2000) remarked:

For Barak, Jerusalem (remained) basically unnegotiable (except for giving Palestinians authority over a few sacred places in the old city and allowing Abu Dis to become their new Jerusalem); the settlements for the most part will stay, as will the bypass roads that now crisscross the territories; sovereignty, borders, overall security, water, and air rights will be Israel's. . . . The real problem (was) that Barak (did) not seem inclined to visions of coexistence or of equality between Palestinians and Israeli Jews. He clearly said that separation is what he (wanted), not integration." (xv)

CAMP DAVID 2000

Arafat and Barak met during a 15–day summit (July 11–25, 2000) hosted by U.S. President Bill Clinton at Camp David. The involved parties discussed a solution to the Middle East conflict and the progress in the peace process.

At the time these negotiations were conducted, nearly a decade after the "peace process," Israel was in full control (security and administrative) of 61.2 percent of the West Bank and 20 percent of Gaza, and in full security control of 26.8 percent of the West Bank. That left the Palestinians with full control of 12 percent of the West Bank. The number of Jewish settlers—now about 200,000—has doubled during the life of the "peace process."

Barak's offer at Camp David to withdraw from 90 percent of the West Bank was contingent upon Arafat accepting the settlements and Israeli rather than

Palestinian citizenship for the settlers and accepting Israel's denial of legal or moral responsibility for the Palestine refugees. Arafat refused Barak's proposal. The Camp David summit, which was intended to prepare the ground for a final push toward a comprehensive agreement, fell apart (Omestad, et al., 2000).

According to Nuechterlein (2000), in an article titled "Peace When?" published in *First Things* magazine, Clinton pushed the "peace process" beyond its capacity to respond. Reliable sources indicated that Arafat urged the U.S. not to insist on the Camp David summit in July because the Palestinians were not willing to accept Barak's concessions. According to Nuechterlein,

Prime Minister Barak was as eager to [go to] Camp David as Arafat was reluctant, and he apparently persuaded himself that he had proposals for a settlement so forthcoming that they would constitute an offer the Palestinians could not refuse. He would grant statehood, make concession on territory in the West Bank and on the right of return for refugees, and even—something no Israeli government had ever before considered—put up for negotiation the status of Jerusalem as his nation's united and undivided capital. . . . But the Palestinians—supported by the major Arab powers—would not take yes for an answer and refused the deal. (7)

THE NEW *INTIFADA*

After the failure of the Camp David negotiations between the Palestinians and the Israelis in July 2000, the situation in the Middle East remained extremely tense, unsettled, and edgy. The relations between the parties involved in the Middle East conflict were not just worse than they were before the Camp David negotiations, but they were about as bad as they could be short of war.

The region exploded on September 28, 2000, when the hawkish leader of Israel's opposition Likud, Ariel Sharon (later to be elected Israel's prime minister), visited the Temple Mount (Al Aqsa Mosque) in Jerusalem, protected by one thousand riot police. This visit sparked violence between Palestinian youths and Israeli troops. Since then, Israelis and Palestinians have seemed to be mobilizing for possible war. The youthful street fighters of the new *Intifada*—the *Tanzim*, released a communique calling for a unified front against the "Zionist enemy." It was like old times again. For four months, Arafat and the Palestinians had hoped for the sympathy of the world with the mounting civilian deaths, many of them children (Omestad, et al., 2000).

Whatever middle ground existed for Israeli and Palestinian moderates vanished. Palestinians talked of a war of independence, and the conflict took an ugly turn as the stone-throwing crowds of Palestinian youths were replaced by masked men armed with machine guns and rocket-propelled grenade launchers.

Israel complained that Arafat suddenly released 60 jailed terrorists from the fundamentalist groups the Islamic Jihad and Hamas. Anti-Israeli emotions overcame divisions between Palestinian supporters and opponents of the peace process. Palestinians were citing as their inspiration and model the Hezbollah guerrillas, who forced Israel out of southern Lebanon in June 2000, ending 18 years of occupation (Omestad, et al. 2000).

On January 4, 2001, Arafat accepted President Clinton's general outline for an end to the 52–year Palestinian-Israeli conflict, sustaining Clinton's hopes, however faint, for a Middle East breakthrough in the last days of his presidency. However, no sufficient progress was made to bring the two sides together for one last stab at a deal before Clinton left office on January 20, 2001. Today, the conflict is very complex with the persistence of the Palestinian-Israeli violence that has claimed hundreds of lives and thousands of injuries since the Palestinian uprising began in late September 2000 (Lancaster & Richburg, 2001).

EGYPT'S REACTIONS TO THE NEW *INTIFADA*

During the months of September through December 2000, Egypt continued to play a major role as an Arab mediator and a leading country in the Arab Middle East, trying to stop the violence between the Palestinians and the Israelis and to facilitate talks between the two sides. Moreover, the Egyptian government organized several summits at the Egyptian resort of Sharm el Sheikh that included Palestinian and Israeli leaders.

A former senior aide to late President Sadat said in October 2000,

We in Egypt, and the rest of the Arab world, will have to reexamine the American position and the American bias toward Israel. Egypt will try to rein in the violence, but unless Israel helps, Egypt will fail [to do that] . . . Land for peace was the whole process, so taking more Palestinian territory, that will not bring peace . . . The Israelis can defeat the Palestinians, but they cannot rule the Palestinians. (Radin, 2000, A1)

The Egyptian media are continuing to whip up popular sentiment against Israel. State-controlled newspapers and broadcast outlets are awash in images of fighters against the Jewish state, pictures of the corpses of Palestinian youths, and commentary on Israel's rocketing of Palestinian territories (Radin, 2000, A1).

On November 21, 2000, Egypt recalled its ambassador from Israel, Mohammed Bassiouny, indefinitely, condemning "aggressive acts" by Israeli forces and expressing "deep displeasure" at the Israeli administration after it pounded targets in the Gaza Strip in a reprisal raid. "This step constitutes a very important and basic message that Israel has to understand: We cannot take it any more—the aggressive acts, the excessive use of force and the use of force against Palestinian civilians in their territories . . . Everything has an end . . . The situation cannot be continued like this; however, we stand firm behind a fair and balanced peace process," said Egyptian Foreign Minister Amr Moussa. Stunned Israeli Prime Minister Barak tried to downplay the recall, saying he was unhappy with the Egyptian move and hoped that it would be temporary.

Israel said it would not recall its ambassador to Egypt. "Egypt has a role in the peace process, a positive role, and I do not think that the recall of the ambassador . . . contributes to continuation of this positive role" (Drees, 2000, 3).

Following Egypt's recall of its envoy, Israel's ambassador to Egypt, Zvi Mazel, accused Egypt's mostly state-owned media of deliberately misleading public opinion with biased news coverage. He said that many Egyptians had no idea what was really happening in Israel and the Palestinian-ruled areas and were basing their decision on incorrect information. But he said that top-level talks between Egypt and Israel would continue, and said he hoped that Egypt's envoy would return to his post quickly. "Egypt has an important role to play [in peace efforts] . . . I must say that I personally, and all of us in Israel, are very sorry (about Egypt's decision to withdraw its ambassador). We have had relations with Egypt for 20 years and relations should not reach this kind of occurrence" (Drees, 2001, 3).

On January 21, 2001, Egypt hosted what was described by political observers as "marathon peace talks" between Israeli and Palestinian negotiators at its Red Sea resort of Taba. Pessimism characterized these negotiations, which have not achieved a breakthrough (Curtius, 2001, 4).

ASSESSMENT OF THE AMERICAN ROLE IN THE MIDDLE EAST CONFLICT

Since the establishment of Israel in 1948, its well-being and security have been singled out as a major U.S. policy interest. After the late 1940s, U.S. Middle East policy was characterized by a fundamental contradiction—how to maintain close and friendly relations with Arab nations while maintaining intimate relations with Israel, America's principal ally in the region. This contradiction was compounded by the Cold War between the Soviet Union and the United States, in which Moscow used the Arab-Israeli conflict to its advantage by aligning itself with the Arabs against the Jewish state. During the Cold War era, resolution of the Arab-Israeli conflict remained a primary U.S. objective, along with containment of Soviet influence in the region and maintaining free access by the West to Middle East oil (Peretz, 1998).

Some argue that the United States, particularly since the 1967 war, has followed shortsighted policies that caused it to miss several opportunities that might have helped end the conflict years ago. Proponents of this view point to Henry Kissinger's apparently complacent certainty that the Arab world would not go to war in order to break the 1967–1973 diplomatic stalemate, and to Washington's refusal to negotiate with the PLO between 1975 and 1988. However, opponents of that view argue that the United States managed to contain, or at least limit, the frequency and intensity of outbreaks of war between Arabs and Israelis. They also argue that U.S. policy was responsible for conditions that eventually led to the Egypt-Israel, PLO-Israel, and Jordan-Israel peace agreements as well as to negotiations between Syria and Israel and the recognition of Israel's legitimacy by most of the Arab world (Lesch & Tschirgi, 1998).

Every American president from Harry Truman to Bill Clinton had his own proposal for ending the Middle East conflict. Truman urged Israel to take back thousands of Palestinian Arab refugees; Dwight Eisenhower sent Eric Johnston to the region with a scheme for developing its water resources; John F. Kennedy sent Joseph Johnson with a new refugee plan; Richard Nixon's and Gerald Ford's emissary, Henry Kissinger, spent months in shuttle diplomacy; Jimmy Carter played a major role in the Camp David accords that put an end to the conflict between Israel and Egypt; George Bush's secretary of state, James Baker, succeeded in persuading Israel, Syria, Lebanon, Jordan, and the Palestinians to join in negotiations at the Madrid Middle East Peace Conference in October 1991; and Clinton always put the Middle East conflict on top of his foreign policy agenda (Peretz, 1998).

Whether the United States attains its objectives in the Middle East will depend less on its foreign policy than on the course of internal economic, political, and social developments within the region. However, Washington can still influence the pattern of these developments through, for example, encouraging or discouraging large expenditures for weapons, support for or censure of undemocratic regimes, and extending or withholding economic assistance to creative development programs (Peretz, 1998).

ASSESSMENT OF THE SOVIET ROLE IN THE MIDDLE EAST CONFLICT

The Soviet Union has been involved in the Arab-Israeli conflict since the birth of Israel in 1948 when it gave Israel both military and diplomatic aid in its war against the Arabs. Following the 1948 war, however, Soviet-Israeli relations cooled, and by 1954 the Soviet Union had switched to the Arab side. The Soviet Union backed the Arabs in the 1956, 1967, and 1973 wars, and in the aftermath of the 1973 war, it became increasingly opposed to U.S. Secretary of State, Henry Kissinger's efforts to work out a settlement of the Arab-Israeli conflict, which the Soviets saw as detrimental to their interests (Freedman, 1979).

The decision by Egyptian President Sadat to visit Jerusalem in 1977 was strongly opposed by the Soviets. They were afraid that if Sadat and Begin successfully negotiated a deal there was a good chance that Jordan, Syria, and moderate Palestinian elements might follow suit, thus leaving the Soviet Union isolated in the Middle East with only radical Libya and Iraq, whom virtually all the other Arab states distrusted, as backers of Soviet policy.

Soon after Sadat's return from Israel, a parade of Arab leaders visited Moscow. The Soviets' invitation to the Arab leaders was aimed at reinforcing Soviet ties with each Arab opponent of Sadat. Then, the Soviets supported the Tripoli Conference, which was held in Libya in December 1977. The conference, which called for opposing Sadat's negotiations with Israel, was attended by five Arab states: Syria, Iraq, South Yemen, Libya, and Algeria.

When Mikhail Gorbachev took power in the Soviet Union in March 1985, the Middle East was clearly an area of superpower competition. Moscow backed the Arab rejectionists, such as Syria, the PLO, Iraq, Algeria, and Libya, in their confrontation with Israel. Moscow viewed Egypt, an ally of the United States, as an enemy. The U.S.S.R. had no diplomatic relations with Israel, had reduced Jewish emigration from the U.S.S.R. to less than one thousand per year (as opposed to a high of 51,000 in 1979), and continued to champion the anti-Israeli "Zionism is Racism" resolution of the U.N. General Assembly.

Before Gorbachev was ousted from power during the collapse of the Soviet Union, there had been a massive transformation in most Soviet policies toward the Middle East. He had restored full diplomatic relations with Israel in October 1991 and had joined the United States in cosponsoring a U.N. resolution reversing the "Zionism is Racism" resolution. He allowed hundreds of thousands of Soviet Jews to emigrate to Israel, and he joined the United States in cosponsoring the Madrid Arab-Israeli peace conference. Gorbachev also cultivated Egypt, making it the centerpiece of Soviet policy in the Arab world. At the same time, Syrian-Russian relations deteriorated when Gorbachev refused to give Syria the weapons it needed for military parity with Israel (Freedman, 1998).

When the Soviet Union collapsed in August 1991, Boris Yeltin came to power following a coup. In its policies toward the Middle East during Yeltsin's years, Russia had moved from active cooperation with the United States on virtually all Middle East issues to assertions of its independence of U.S. policy in the region. By the summer of 1996, Moscow clearly was pursuing an independent policy in the region, as indicated by its call for a lifting of the sanctions against Iraq (set after the Gulf War in 1991), its mediation attempts in the conflict in southern Lebanon, and its sale of increasingly sophisticated arms to Iran (Freedman, 1998).

Today, with a weakened economy and with the newly independent states to its south, Russia is far less a power in the Middle East than the Soviet Union was. Whether a revived economy and more adept diplomacy will enable Moscow to play a more significant role in the region is a question for the future.

SHARON BECOMES PRIME MINISTER OF ISRAEL

On February 6, 2001, Ariel Sharon, the Likud right-wing leader won the election race against Ehud Barak and became prime minister of Israel. "Sharon, 72, once considered unelectable because of his role as the architect of Israel's unpopular war in Lebanon, won by an unprecedented margin in Israeli electoral history" (Morris & Demick, 2001, 1). With 99 percent of the vote counted, Sharon had 62.5 percent of the vote; Barak, had 37.4 percent. Voter turnout was a record-low 62 percent.

Many political experts believe that Sharon being in power is a blow to the whole peace process, as he is known for his extremist views. He even announced that he is against all of the terms that were included in the Oslo accords. Moreover, he is a "hated" figure in the Arab world, and therefore no real progress in the Palestinian-Israeli negotiations is expected during his term.

Sharon embodies the old expansionist Israel of settlements and the Lebanon war. For Palestinians, he is a symbol of the slaughter that befell them at the hands of Israel's Lebanese Christian militia allies in the Palestinian refugee camps of Sabra and Shatila near Beirut. It was Sharon's alliance with the Maronite militia forces that enabled them to enter the camps in September 1982, where they killed hundreds of civilians. The official government report found that Sharon as defense minister had "indirect responsibility" for the massacres; and that event remains an essential part of the Arab vision of him. A member of the Palestinian Legislative Council from Gaza said in November 2000: "He (Sharon) could never be anything except a murderer and a criminal" (Rees, 2000, 67).

The rest of the Arab world reacted to Sharon's election with a mixture of caution and outright hostility. Many Arabs have not forgotten that it was Sharon's visit to Al Aqsa Mosque in late September 2000 that sparked the new uprising *Intifada* in the Palestinian territories. Hosni Mubarak, the Egyptian president, said after Sharon's election: "We will wait and see what Sharon will do. Will it be a policy of peace or that of suppression?" (Drummond, 2001, 14).

Jordanian Prime Minister Ali Abu Ragheb, said: "The election of Sharon is an internal affair and we will not issue early judgments about his performance and his government" (Drummond, 2001, 14).

In Syria, a frontline state that failed to reach an agreement with Barak's government on an Israeli withdrawal from the Golan Heights, the reaction in official newspapers was much tougher, saying the election of Sharon amounted to a declaration of war.

Even in Saudi Arabia, normally the most discreet of Arab states when it comes to relations with Israel and the outside world in general, one of its newspapers, *al-Medina*, was outspoken. One of its editorials said following Sharon's election: "The rivers of blood are coming, and the Palestinians and Arabs must be prepared to confront this new attack" (Drummond, 2001, 14).

Less than 48 hours after Sharon was elected, a car bomb exploded in Jerusalem in an attack that "had the hallmarks of an attempt by his Arab opponents to signal that they will not be deterred by their arch enemy's return to power" (Reeves, 2001, 13). No one was killed by the bomb, which was claimed by the extremist Palestinian group "The Palestinian Popular Resistance Forces." A faxed statement from that group said: "It was a first message directed to the criminal and fascist Sharon" (13).

A few days after his election, Sharon succeeded in forming a coalition government with the Labor Party in an attempt to strengthen his power and form a stabilizing force that could have some influence on his future policies. Sharon continued his predecessors' policy of expanding the building of Jewish settlements in the West Bank by approving three thousand new Jewish units to be built at a controversial Jewish settlement on occupied land, a move that angered the Palestinians.

Throughout the early months of 2001, relations between Israelis and Palestinians continued the downward spiral dictated by the ongoing violence between the two sides and the insular logic of the New *Intifada*. The Israeli army launched several helicopter strikes in Ramallah and Gaza City in response to a series of attacks by Palestinian extremists that killed three Jewish children. The new Israeli coalition government threatened "a stepped-up campaign, including hit squads to assassinate alleged terrorists" (Whitelaw, 2001, 38).

The U.S. administration of George W. Bush, who started his presidency in January 2001, has been on the sidelines with regard to the Middle East conflict, urging restraint by both sides. Pointedly, President Bush called on Arafat to openly condemn terrorism. During Sharon's two-day official visit to the United States on March 20, 2001, he was assured by President Bush that the United States would not impose a peace agreement on the Middle East, giving Sharon the latitude to pursue his skeptical approach toward negotiations with the Palestinians.

EGYPT CONTINUES ITS PEACE EFFORTS

During his official visit to the United States on April 1, 2001, the Egyptian President Hosni Mubarak announced that Egypt is going to facilitate the situation so that the Palestinians and the Israelis can sit together and negotiate.

Mubarak came to the United States bearing Arab concerns that the United States was stepping back from its role as a peace broker and urged the Bush administration to stay involved in the Middle East and use its influence to save the peace process. Bush assured Mubarak that the United States would remain active in the Middle East peace process. However, he stopped short of pledging the kind of personal mediation effort his predecessor had undertaken. Bush told reporters during the conference with Mubarak: "We will work together to try to convince all parties involved to lay down their arms. We can't force a peace. We will use our prestige and influence as best we can to facilitate a peace" (Hutcheson, 2001, A-5). Mubarak told reporters that he had great hopes that President Bush "will do the maximum effort for peace so as to lessen the tensions and resume negotiations" (A-5).

CONCLUSION

This chapter gave an overview of the Arab-Israeli conflict since the Oslo accords. As I highlighted in this chapter, the Arab-Israeli conflict has been placed on a new footing since most Arab states started recognizing Israel's legitimacy.

Today, Egypt, Jordan, the PLO, and Israel explicitly recognize each others' legitimacy and right to peace. Syria and Lebanon, by attending the Madrid conference in 1991 and entering into direct negotiations with Israel, implicitly extend recognition to Israel.

However, today, the situation in the Middle East is very tense, especially after the continuous clashes between the Israelis and the Palestinians and the election of Sharon as prime minister of Israel. Egypt continues to play its role as a mediator, but the future of the peace process is yet to be witnessed.

In the following chapter, I will discuss the images and stereotypes held by the Western news media about the Arabs and the Israelis.

3

ARABS AND ISRAELIS IN THE WESTERN NEWS MEDIA: IMAGES AND STEREOTYPES

The Middle East is perhaps one of the most misunderstood, misperceived, and stereotyped regions of the world. Many Western journalists operating in the Middle East lack a comprehensive understanding of the cultures that characterize that region. They also lack an awareness of the deep cultural differences between the Middle Eastern countries. This has led to the prevalence of stereotypical images about the Middle East in the Western news media.

WHAT IS AN IMAGE?

An image can be defined as "a combinatorial construct whose subject is itself a collection of images in the individual memory of various aspects of reality. It is the totality of attributes that a person recognizes or imagines. Images are to varying degrees interdependent on one another. The structure of one is inferred or predicted from that of another; and change in one produces imbalance and, therefore, change in others" (Mowlana, 1997, 3).

It is widely recognized and accepted by social scientists that people create psychological images of the "other" or the "unknown" in order to secure their identity. People have conceived opinions, both genuine and erroneous, of people with different characteristics, whether they be racially, culturally, or gender based, without any true attempt at comprehension. As a result, misinterpretation of other cultures has revealed a common thread that runs throughout history, fostering stereotypes, discrimination, and often fear or persecution of such groups.

Images consist of affective, cognitive, and operational (action) components. The affective component reflects the individual's like or dislike of the image's focal object and is usually associated with approval or disapproval of its perceived, or cognitive, aspects. The cognitive component is the individual's view of the "inherent" characteristics of the object that he regards as existing independently of his own perception. An image's operational component reflects the behavioral effects of aggregate images, varying with the individual and the type of image involved (Mowlana, 1997).

In terms of international images, the affective reaction usually depends on the individual's or culture's overall disposition to like or to dislike foreign countries in general. The cognitive components are dependent on perceived power as being either threatening or benign.

There are two main effects of social norms on images of international focal objects. First, increased homogeneity of images held by members of groups is fostered by the relatively simplified and undifferentiated quality of social norms. Second, these group norms encourage maintenance of simple cognitive structures in which such images are embedded while at the same time either reinforcing or distorting the effects of direct contact (Scott, 1965).

Formulating an image depends, to a great extent, on the individual's perception of that image. Prosser (1978), in his book *The Cultural Dialogue: An Introduction to Intercultural Communication*, said: "Perception is the most individual process of subjective culture [; it] is formed by the memory of past structured, stable, and meaningful experiences" (198). He also believes that perception, as a cultural universal, can be seen as an inherent capability of all human beings whose cognitive abilities are functioning in a normal fashion. Each culture helps to shape this capability according to the experiences that are common in that particular culture. As individuals, both are acted upon by our culture and act upon it, so too do we perceive through our cultural experiences.

An individual's perceptions of the external world are the experiential elements that help him or her to see the world as stable, structured, and meaningful. Like images, many perceptions are consciously coded and decoded, while many others are not. According to Prosser (1978), "it is precisely such shared, often unarticulated, and sometimes unarticulable patterns of perceptions, communication, and behavior that can be referred to as a culture" (212).

Individual perceptions differ from group perceptions in that the latter do not necessarily recognize national or cultural boundaries. Groups that share the same perceptions to one degree or another develop, and they are intercultural or cross-cultural in nature. "The fewer group identities that a person shares, and the less intensely held the identities which exist with individuals with whom he or she must communicate, the more crossculturally he or she is operating on the basis of a perceptual continuum" (Prosser, 1978, 213).

STEREOTYPICAL IMAGES OF THE ARAB-ISRAELI CONFLICT IN THE COVERAGE OF THE WESTERN NEWS MEDIA

The mass media cannot be underestimated in terms of their power in perpetuating ethnic and racial bias; they are part of a cultural mechanism that promotes and exploits commercial stereotypes. "Such images become dangerous when they materialize in the complex social narratives and foreign policies enacted simultaneously on the world stage and in the human mind and heart" (Palmer, 1997, 139).

News media images of the Middle East to a great extent have their roots in the media's images of the religions and cultures of Middle East people. Indeed, the religious and cultural identities in Middle East and the media's understanding of the cultural and social structures of the Middle Eastern societies often determine the procedure through which the events, policies, and actions are portrayed. Central to this analysis is the thesis that the Western news media always misrepresent the identities and images of the Middle Easterners. This misrepresentation has resulted from two factors: Western reporters do not understand the political culture and structure of Middle Eastern politics, and the Western media cover the Middle East within the worldview of a (primarily Western) audience. By striving to make the Middle Eastern region familiar to their Western audience, the media often end up distorting the region's complex realities (Kamalipour, 1997).

In this context, Schleifer (1987) stated:

American news organizations could cover the Middle Eastern conflict more accurately if we, the foreign correspondents, were more committed on a day-to-day basis to seek out and secure an understanding of the less visible but complex patterns of social, cultural, and political life than is now the practice; and to do this not only out of a personal intellectual curiosity, by virtue of a broad liberal education, but also as a response that stems directly from professional training. (338)

According to Schleifer, the ongoing reporting of Arab-Israeli conflict by Western correspondents includes all forms of bias, such as technical, technological, social, political, and ethnic. This has distorted the popular perceptions of the region for the past 30 years (347).

Bias charges have been leveled by supporters of both the Arab and the Israeli sides with regard to Western news media coverage of the Arab-Israeli conflict. Palestinian-Americans and other pro-Palestinian groups have accused the Western news media of ignoring or downplaying alleged Israeli human rights violations. Some Arab-American families reportedly have purchased satellite dishes to watch Arab television because of their distrust for the American media (Trigoboff, 2000, 12).

The everyday stories of many Western journalists who cover the Arab-Israeli conflict, and the framing of this conflict in their reporting, tend to favor the Israeli side over the Arab side. For those journalists, "Israel is a gleaming pool and a patch of green in a baking desert inhabited by hostile elements. . . . An Israeli is a sturdy, tenacious pioneer, as well as a victim of oppression and atrocity, rightly entitled to a homeland of his own." "If American news media are any test, Israelis are also bronzed, industrious, and strong. They smile, and ride off to war singing songs with a pretty girl in fetching a uniform" (Emery, 1995, 224).

According to Steve Bell, a former anchor for ABC-TV's *Good Morning America,* many American journalists have an automatic sympathy toward the Jews of Israel because of the Holocaust. According to Bell, "one could even say Americans share guilt feelings on the subject. The human interest and potential for conflict are abundant, and the history of Israel is widely seen as the story of an 'underdog' surviving by hard work and heroism" (Bell, 1980, 56).

As defined in the 1947 edition of *Webster's New International Dictionary,* "The Arabs are one of the oldest and purest peoples, and with the Jews, constitute the best modern representatives of the Semitic race." However, the Arab Middle East has always been misperceived by the Western news media. According to Shaheen (1984),

the present-day Arab stereotype parallels the image of Jews in pre-Nazi Germany, where Jews were painted as dark, shifty-eyed, venal and threateningly different people. After the holocaust, the characterization of Jews as murderous anarchists or greedy financiers was no longer tolerable. Many [Western] cartoonists, however, reincarnated this caricature and transferred it to another group of Semites, the Arabs. Only now it wears a robe and a headdress instead of a yarmulke and a Star of David." (12)

Along the same line, Block (2000) mentioned that the world media are distorting the Palestinian-Israeli conflict by focusing on Palestinian anger, but rarely on Palestinians as victims. "When there are [television] programs on what happens, it's on Palestinian reactions, not on what they are reacting to. . . . When there is a problem of violence, Israelis are shown as humans who suffer. Palestinians are shown as aggressors . . . throwing stones" (B13).

It can be argued that the distorted media coverage of the Arab-Israeli conflict might affect the way the Arab and Israeli sides are perceived by the Western public. In this regard, CNN announced that it conducted a survey (the number of respondents was not reported) in November 2000 of American public opinion toward the Palestinians and the Israelis. The findings: 43 percent of Americans expressed greater sympathy with Israel: 11 percent with the Palestinians (Foxman, 2000, 8).

DIVERSITY OF MIDDLE EASTERN CULTURES

In our discussion of as broad a topic as Middle Eastern culture, one might ask questions such as, Is there one culture that we may call Middle Eastern culture? Are the cultural components in the Middle East universally applicable?

The Middle East consists of a large number of countries; and territorially, culturally, religiously, and linguistically, the region is diverse, encompassing nations and people who have distinctive history and heritage. The readers of this book must recognize the great variety and differences that exist among nations of the Middle East. For example, countries in North Africa are not the same as Saudi Arabia or the Arabian Gulf states, despite their Arabness. The Arabian Gulf states have Bedouin origins and traditions that might not be as prevalent in the North African countries. Countries such as Iran and Pakistan are Moslem countries, but they have Persian heritage, which is totally different from the history, language, and ethnic heritage of Arab countries in the region. A country like Egypt, which is overwhelmingly dominated by a Moslem population, has a minority of Copts (Egyptian Christians) whose religious traditions are totally different from those of Egyptian Moslems.

Even the practice of religious norms and traditions is different among Arab countries. For example, in a country like Saudi Arabia, women have to cover their hair and are not allowed to drive. However, this is not the case in other Arab countries where women can walk in the streets without the veil, and they are allowed to drive. In Lebanon and Bahrain, alcohol is served in restaurants and public places. This is not the case in more conservative Arab countries like the rest of the Arabian Gulf states. The practice of Islam is different in a country like Afghanistan where there is religious fanaticism, than it is in countries like Tunisia, Morocco, or Egypt where there is more moderation in the practice of Islam. For example, shop owners in Egypt are not forced to close their shops during prayer times, but in Saudi Arabia they do.

Although Arabic is the most commonly used language in the Arab Middle East, still some terms and phrases have different meanings and connotations in different countries; for example, the same phrase might be offensive in one country and courteous in another. The Egyptian Arabic dialect is the most popular dialect in the Arab Middle East. This is due to the prevalence of Egyptian movies and soap operas shown in the other Arab countries.

It is unfortunate that many Europeans and Americans are not familiar with the Arab and the Islamic cultures. This leads to misunderstandings and the creation of stereotypes. In this context, Edward Said (2000) commented:

A deep gulf separates Arab-Islamic culture and civilization from the United States; in the absence of any collective Arab information and cultural policy, the notion of an Arab people with traditions, cultures, and identities of their own is simply inadmissible in the United States. Arabs are dehumanized; they are seen as violent irrational terrorists always on the outlook for murder and bombing outrages. (212)

ISLAM: A RELIGION AND A WAY OF LIFE

Ever since the appearance of Islam in the seventh century, the history of Arab-Islamic interaction with the West has often been marred by misconception, stereotyping, and prejudice. Understanding the Arab-Islamic culture requires attaining a thoughtful insight of Islam as a religion and a way of life.

Most Arabs are Moslems. Even though there are non-Moslem Arabs, it has been observed that "to be Arab and Moslem is truly to belong" (Haque, 1997, 18). Followers of any religion tend to believe that theirs is the only true religion enjoying the blessings of God, and Arabs are no exception.

Islam rests on five basic pillars: creed, which is the fundamental profession of a Moslem's faith acknowledging that God is One and that Prophet Mohammed is His messenger (*Shahadah*); praying five times a day (*Salat*); paying money to the poor and needy in the amount of one-fortieth of one's income (*Zakat*); fasting by complete abstinence from food, drink, and sex during the hours of daylight during the Holy month of Ramadan, which is the ninth month of the lunar year (*Sawm*); and pilgrimage (*Hajj*) to the holy Islamic shrine *Kaaba* in Mecca, Saudi Arabia. The *Hajj* must be made at least once in one's lifetime, if health and financial resources permit.

One of the major principles of Islam is surrender to God and submission to His will. A Middle Eastern Moslem child is raised in an environment that emphasizes the notion that whatever happens in life is an expression of God's will. "In the Middle Eastern culture, human choices and attempts, successes and failures are regarded as manifestations of God's plan and will" (Haque, 1997, 22).

To the Middle Easterner, the degree of an individual's religiosity is an indicator of character forthrightness and ethicality. In most Middle Eastern countries, the civil laws are extensions of religious and theological rulings. Even in daily social, business, and official activities, religion is constantly invoked. For example, Arab Moslems often start their work by saying "*Bismillahir-Rahman ir-Rahim*" (In the name of God, the Compassionate, the Merciful).

Moslems accept in faith the religion divinely revealed in the Koran (the Moslems' holy book) and seek help of the *Sunna* (Prophet Mohammed's teachings and deeds) in order to understand it. In doing that, Moslems are always guided by rationality in interpreting a sacred text and reconciling—without forcibleness—any apparent disagreement in it with reason, and are always assured that the *Sunna* is free from fabrication and corruption so long as its content is in agreement with the Koran. Though Islamic law, the *Shari'a* is immutable as prescribed in the Koran and the Prophet's teachings, its interpretation by human beings through the instrumentality of *fiqh* (jurisprudence) is flexible and responsive to modern needs and problems (Boullata, 1990).

In politics and other matters relating to this world not dealt with in the Koran by a text and in detail, Moslems adjudicate personal opinion, their criterion being the public interest of the community and the avoidance of any possible harm to it. In doing that, they are always mindful of the general ethical ideals and universal principles laid down in the Koran.

According to Mohammed Amara, an Egyptian Islamic thinker, giving a religious character to politics and the system of government is an attempt totally alien to the spirit of Islam. For Islam, in his view, distinguishes between the community of religion and the community of politics, the former being made up of Moslem believers, the latter of citizens of various faiths. This was clear from the example of the Islamic Constitution set by Prophet Mohammed, in which the Moslem believers were referred to as one *umma* (faithful community), and the Christians and Jews (known in Islam as people of the book) were included in the *umma* along with the believers (cited in Boullata, 1990).

Islam, as correctly understood from the Koran and the Prophet's teachings, is tolerant of Jews, Christians, and other non-Moslem believers. Boullata (1990) stressed that religious pluralism, which is accepted in the Koran, "is a fact that will remain with mankind challenging Moslems and other believers to compete for righteousness and good deeds and to cooperate with one another in brotherhood within the framework of national unity" (79).

Islam affirms the lay character of political authority and emphasizes its human quality insofar as assuming it depends on consultation with other humans, on selection and public acceptance by humans, and on the fact that the ruler is responsible to a community of humans. In Islam, the political authority rests with the people. Islam has not laid down a specific political order for Moslems because the logic of its being good for all times and places requires that this be left for the people to formulate and to change in accordance with the evolution of the human mind and the interest of the community, within the framework of the general commendations and universal principles of Islam, and in light of the experience of other civilizations.

MISREPRESENTATION OF THE ARAB AND ISLAMIC CULTURES

Because nations that are not part of the Western world have cultures that are so different from Western culture, foreign cultures find themselves perceived as "the other," which opens the way for misinterpretation and possible hostility and antagonism. Presently, one of the major non-Western cultures analyzed and judged in this manner is the Islamic culture, which includes over one billion people throughout the world. Islamic culture presents concepts that might seem to be totally foreign to Western modes of thinking, such as the Moslem women having to wear the veil to cover their hair.

Arab and Islamic cultures have always been misinterpreted by the West. This misinterpretation has led to bias, misunderstanding, stereotyping, and sometimes hostility toward Islamic culture (Wiegand & Malek, 1997, 204). Most perceptions of Arabs today come not from real knowledge but from faulty and simplistic assumptions. Many Western journalists view the Arab World as "downright savage" trying to destroy the dynamic, democratic modern nation of Israel (Emery, 1995, 224).

The image of Islam in the West tends to be "totally foreign, almost sinister" (Diller, 1994, 170). This negative image of Islam has resulted from ignorance about that religion, which is considered by many Westerners to be "exotic" and "strange." Western hostility to Islam has historical roots. The Islamic people conquered and ruled parts of Europe and threatened the West for several centuries in the beginning of the second millennium. "The legacy of alienation germinated by the Islamic conquests and counter-conquests by the West was perpetuated in folk culture. . . . Later, during the nineteenth and twentieth centuries, Western industrialization and military strength spearheaded Western hegemony in much of the Islamic Middle East" (171). The revival of Islamic sentiment, represented in events such as the Iranian revolution of 1979 and the U.S. embassy hostage crisis of 1979–1981 contributed to the historically rooted Western fears of Islam (171).

The West does not seem to have done a very good job of understanding the religion and basic belief system of the Arabs. "The dread generated by the image of a virile, aggressive religion that spread its messages to the distant lands to create an empire, including vast areas of the globe, has been a part of the West's psyche for over a thousand years. Western response often has been to demonize the Arabs and their religion" (Haque, 1997, 18). Edward Said (1981) pointed out that "for most of the Middle Ages and during the early part of the Renaissance in Europe, Islam was believed to be a demonic religion of apostasy, blasphemy, and obscurity" (4–5).

In the Western news media, Moslems have often been labeled as militants, terrorists or fundamentalists. "With abundant negative reporting and opinion in the Western media about Moslem fundamentalism, it is no wonder that Western society has come to believe that Islamic revivalism—and in a more general sense, Islamic culture—is a genuine threat to the survival of democracy" (Wiegand & Malek, 1997, 204).

Jack Shaheen (1984) identified four characteristics that dominate the Western media when it comes to the depiction of Arabs: the wealthy, oil-rich sheiks; the uncultured barbarians; the sex-maniac harem owners; and the ruthless Arab terrorists. These categories emerged from Shaheen's research on more than 200 episodes of 100 television shows that featured Arab characters.

As described by Edward Said in his book *Orientalism* (1978), Orientalists have perceived the Islamic world as illogical and irrational. These impressions are rooted in the power relationship that the West has maintained through domination of the Islamic world, leading to the popular notion that the Orient, which primarily encompasses the Islamic world, is inferior to the West.

The fear of Islam and Moslems is a major factor in the negative Arab image in the West, most specifically in the United States. This is the case since, in much of the writing about Arabs, there is confusion concerning Arabs and Moslems. Consequently, to many if not most Americans the terms "Arabs" and "Moslems" are interchangeable. Ignorance about, and negative images of, Islam are, therefore, readily transferable to Arabs (Wiegand & Malek, 1997).

At a fund-raiser for the city of Jerusalem in June 1992, CBS news anchorman Dan Rather was quoted as saying that "the most dangerous ideology is fundamental Muhammadism." This biased comment made publicly by a prominent member of the news media strengthened the stereotypes held by Western societies about Islam (Wiegand & Malek, 1997, 205). In general, Western societies often have very little knowledge of the Middle East; hence, the constant barrage of disasters, coups, uprisings, conflicts, and terrorist activities, reported routinely by the Western news media, fosters a gross misimpression of Middle Eastern people and cultures. The Arab countries in the Middle East "are often lumped together as if they were a single entity devoid of any separate national identity, cultural heritage, religious ideology, political philosophy, or global sensitivity" (Kamalipour, 1997, xx).

The misrepresentation of Arab and Islamic culture in the Western news media has resulted directly from correspondents' failure to become familiar with Arab and Islamic societies. Most of those correspondents who disseminate information about the Islamic world lack an in-depth understanding of the indigenous cultures of Arab and Islamic societies. It is impossible for a Western correspondent to grasp the various language patterns, customs, and traditions of a country like Egypt by being on location in Cairo for just a few days or weeks (Wiegand & Malek, 1997).

Because it is the elite classes, and not necessarily the ordinary people in Arab countries who speak English, Western journalists are limited in where they can obtain information. For example, Egypt's political elites are products of Western education and high urbanization (Cohen, 1990, 20). Moreover, "the Western journalist is often afraid of the common man and woman who symbolizes a lifestyle that is the polar opposite of the Western ideal's sanctity for individual life" (Wiegand & Malek, 1997, 210). Thus, it is the highly secular, Western-influenced ruling classes of Arab and Islamic nations who most often relate information about the people of their countries to the Western news media. "Perception of Islamic culture through the restricted spectacles of Western cultural values hinders amiable relations between the West and the Islamic world, leaving the potential that bipolar cultural warfare will escalate" (Wiegand & Malek, 1997, 211).

The essential problem of misrepresenting Arabs in the Western news media has less to do with the shifting images in the Western media than for the Arabs' inability to project their own image. As Boullata (1990) affirms, "the Arab crisis is more internal than external. Most—if not all—Arab thinkers are unhappy with the present conditions of the Arab World" (139). The challenge of the Western media and cultural bias are only part of the demand by Arabs for change, for legitimation.

Of course, Arabs' lack of awareness of Western sensitivities and lack of understanding of the modern public relations techniques needed to work with the Western news media have always presented a problem. But the inability or sometimes the unwillingness of the Western media to admit that they were often dealing in stereotypes of the worst kind have made effective cross-cultural communication between the Moslem and the Western worlds nearly impossible.

STILL, SOME BALANCE IN THE WESTERN MEDIA COVERAGE

Not all Western journalists have presented the Arab side of the Arab-Israeli conflict in a negative way. Some programs and television documentaries produced by American journalists were successful in presenting a more balanced picture of the conflict. One of these documentaries was aired on PBS in 1975. The seven-part documentary series *Arabs and Israelis* examined the prospects for peace in the Middle East. Those interviewed spoke not of war, but of a possible peace. One Israeli interviewee said he hoped that the Israelis would recognize the PLO and the national rights of the Palestinian people. The issue at hand, he said, has been and remains "the struggle between two rights." The executive producer of this series said, "We have not tried to cover all aspects of the conflict or review the history of the Middle East, to suggest who is right or wrong . . . We listen instead for softer voices, those that may be easily drowned out but are no less important to hear" (Shaheen, 1984, 93).

Another documentary that presented a balanced point of view of the Arab-Israeli conflict was *Israel and the Palestinians: Will Reason Prevail?* The documentary, which aired on PBS in January 1981, interviewed spokesmen from the two sides of the conflict. The documentary's producer showed viewers some harsh measures that the Israelis had taken against West Bank Palestinians; and the producer discussed Israeli press censorship with editors of a Palestinian newspaper. The documentary concluded with an appeal for a mutual recognition of rights. The program's announcer said that Israel must "recognize that Palestinians are not simply 'terrorists,' that they are doctors, lawyers, and engineers who, like their neighboring Jews, believe they have an historical right to a homeland." Likewise, he said, "Palestinians must recognize that Israel has a right to exist as a nation. . . . Only then, when both Israelis and Palestinians begin addressing each other's legitimate concerns will progress be made towards a settlement."

Shaheen (1984) said of the two documentaries that they are "a kind of candle sputtering bravely in the darkness . . . The candle reveals a humanity that television all too often denies viewers . . . The series makes us feel. It makes the ordinary tears of others become our own" (94).

There are other Western-produced documentaries that were a fair presentation of the Middle East conflict. Some of these documentaries were broadcast on special news shows such as CBS's *60 Minutes* and CBS *Reports*, PBS's *World*, and ABC's *20/20*.

A MORE POSITIVE IMAGE OF THE PALESTINIANS
AFTER THE OSLO ACCORD

In 1993, Yasser Arafat, the PLO leader, and Yitzhak Rabin, the late Israeli prime minister, were selected as *Time* magazine's "Men of the Year." Their recognition followed the historic signing of the Israeli–PLO accord on September 13, 1993. The Palestinian leader, like others before him, has not always enjoyed such favorable coverage. His image has often been associated in the Western media with terrorism, violence, and ruthless behavior. For example, a political cartoon that appeared in the *Chicago Tribune* in 1990 under the theme "brotherhood of terrorists" depicted Arafat standing alongside Iraqi President Saddam Hussein and Libyan President Moammar Qaddafi with the comment: "The Three Stooges of the Apocalypse."

In the course of reporting the Middle East conflict, the Palestinian image has undergone radical transformation, moving from invisibility to high visibility. Western reporting of the Palestinians has transformed then from faceless victims to faces of violence to, now, faces of peace (Zaharna, 1997).

In the early days of their conflict with the Israelis, the Palestinians were often presented by the Western news media as unskilled and leaderless. The image of the masses of Palestinian refugees and their unresolved plight reinforced this impotent image. In contrast to this victim image, the 1970s witnessed the rise of an entirely opposite image—the Palestinian "terrorist" equipped with nothing more complex than guns, dynamite, and airline schedules. The term *fedayeen* was often used but rarely translated. This added to the mysteriousness and deviousness of the Palestinian groups. *Fedayeen* means "freedom fighters" (Zaharna, 1997).

While the main goal of the Palestinians according to Zaharna (1997) was to gain international awareness of their plight for independence, they were viewed as "dedicated, vicious political fanatics and unpredictable terrorists" (45). However, the September 1993 signing of the Israeli–PLO peace agreement was not only a diplomatic breakthrough but a breakthrough for the Palestinian image in the American media. "In terms of media images, the PLO became its people's representative not in 1974 when it received international recognition, but when it was able to align itself with the Israeli leaders in 1993. Hence, the merging of the Palestinian leadership with the [Western] people came not through the PLO identifying with its own people but through being identified with its enemy, the Israelis" (46).

The Oslo accords helped replace the "conflict" theme with the "togetherness" theme between the principal parties. According to an article in the September 20, 1993, issue of *Time* magazine cited by Zaharna, "Israelis and Palestinians . . . Arafat and Rabin . . . side by side . . . can share the land they both call home . . . these two can live . . . the two are emerging from the clutches of history . . . creating their own choices . . . the two could build their promised lands . . . they are now free to live with each other" (32–33). This theme was visually reinforced on the cover of this issue which showed the Is-

raeli and the Palestinian leaders, and had an opening picture of an Israeli soldier and a Palestinian woman sitting on a wall. As the theme continued after
the signing of the Oslo accords, a sense of mutuality emerged that had been
mostly missing from past reporting. The September 20, 1993, issue reported
that "Israelis and Palestinians embrace . . . enemies who could not live together
. . . neither Israel nor the PLO can destroy each other . . . Israelis and Palestinians now . . . attempt to live side by side . . . both have what it takes" (34–39).

WHY CAN REALITY ABOUT THE ARAB-ISRAELI CONFLICT BE DISTORTED BY THE U.S. MEDIA?

Too much emphasis is placed on the question of a pro-Israel or pro-Arab
bias in the American news media coverage of the Arab-Israeli conflict. A more
balanced analysis should consider the inherent difficulties in the media's coverage of the complex Middle East conflict. These difficulties can be catego-
rized into four groups: operational media realities, the "translation" of Middle
Eastern issues into American terms, the unique regional dimension of the conflict, in which a democracy is pitted against nondemocratic states, and personal
biases of reporters.

The Media Reality

Professional and financial constraints of the media are enormously significant. Of these, the time factor is most important. Hours and days of research
are condensed into one and a half minutes. In this process, much of the accuracy and most of the complexity of the Middle East conflict can be lost.

The competitive nature of American newsmaking must also be considered. While Middle East analysts may prefer to discuss current regional developments, broadcast executives are almost solely concerned with ratings
and the type of coverage that will best serve the ratings. Media coverage of
the Middle East today is a profit-making venture, governed by the rules of
such undertakings.

Another significant aspect of the media reality is the nature of foreign journalism in Israel. Israel hosts approximately 250 foreign correspondents—the
third largest press contingent in the world. Given the rotative nature of newspaper work, many of these correspondents know little of the Middle East region, lack any skills in Hebrew (the official language of Israel), and may have
acquired other expertise in different capacities in the past. Nevertheless, in the
eyes of editors, viewers, and readers back home, that correspondent is an automatic expert on Israel (Savir, 1985, 32).

The American Reality

An inherent dilemma lies at the root of Middle East reporting. For American television and newspaper editors, the Middle East, and Israel in particular,

are popular issues that "sell" well. At the same time, however, the conflict is complex and deep-rooted, almost to the point of being inexplicable to viewers and readers.

In attempting to resolve this dilemma, editors translate these difficult issues into terms that are comprehensible to the 17 million viewers of an evening news broadcast or the one million readers of a morning newspaper. In the process, a new pattern of coverage is created. For example, in dealing with Israeli-Arab relations, American journalists often resort to terminology from the lexicon of American Black-White relations. Here, the differences outweigh any similarities.

A second typical approach is the search for a human interest angle. When an American reporter reduces the Arab-Israeli conflict to the story of one Israeli (often a soldier) and one Arab (often a refugee), the underlying premise is that the human interest story represents the real story. However, at best, it is only a real story. This reductive process leads to serious confusion between hard and soft news.

A third discernible pattern in American reporting is the constant search for a simple solution to the conflict. Americans take the approach that everything is solvable because in America, fortunately, most problems are. In the Middle East, however, most problems are not. It is therefore futile and, indeed, misleading for the major newspapers to continuously endeavor to "solve" the Middle East conflict on their Op-Ed pages.

The Middle East Reality

The unique nature of the Middle East conflict (being a regional conflict between a democracy and nondemocratic states that is covered so extensively) governs the results in terms of coverage. The discrepancy of accessibility results in asymmetrical coverage. Thus, Israel is overexposed. The prime minister and foreign minister of Israel are household names, but the prime ministers or presidents of Jordan, Syria, and even Egypt are largely unknown.

The Arab world's political reality is rarely exposed. It is portrayed as a homogeneous entity, while it is, in fact, a heterogeneous group of 21 states with competing interests. Inter-Arab conflicts are key factors in Middle East stability—or instability. However, most Western viewers and readers remain ignorant of these salient elements because they are covered so little.

Personal Biases

The emotional underpinnings of the Middle East conflict render objectivity in reporting difficult. Many journalists who cover the Middle East for any length of time invariably develop a predilection for one side or the other. The result is a relatively "mixed bag" of pro-Israel or pro-Arab leanings.

Generalizations are facile when it comes to journalistic bias. The only safe observation is that, when the objective, aforementioned patterns of coverage create a slant, some journalists will express their personal bias more freely. A fair-minded analysis of the American media's treatment of the Middle East will seek to address seriously the inherent problems. Admittedly, though, the fundamental aspects of the problems will remain unchanged (Savir, 1985, 32).

PREJUDICES BY THE ARABS AND THE ISRAELIS

Throughout the course of their conflict, both the Arabs and the Israelis have themselves brought their own prejudices and negative stereotypes to bear on each other. For the Israelis, the most prevalent stereotype of Arabs is "the fearsome violent figure of immense strength and duplicity . . . Capable of great cruelty, given to fanatical disregard for human life, he murders easily, either out of a crazed lust for blood or as an emotional animal easily incited and manipulated by murderous leaders" (Bickerton & Klausner, 1998, 5).

Arabs also hold negative stereotypes of Jews. "Arabs regard Jews as violent aliens, as outsiders, as interlopers who do not belong" (Bickerton & Klausner, 1998, 6). These prejudices and stereotypes contribute to the intensity of antagonistic passions of the participants in the Middle East conflict. Many Arabs also do not distinguish between Jews and Israelis. For them, any Jewish person is an Israeli. In this context, Block (2000) said,

There is a discourse you could qualify as racist against the Jews. This occurs because when the Israeli army comes to the occupied territories and says, we are doing this in the name of Judaism, it is very difficult for the victim to make the distinction (between Jews and Israelis). (B13)

REMEDIES TO THE DISTORTED MEDIA COVERAGE OF THE ARAB-ISRAELI CONFLICT

A major reason for the misperception of the Arab-Israeli conflict in the Western news media and the distorted coverage of that conflict by Western reporters is the lack of a comprehensive understanding of Middle Eastern cultures and values. It is important to understand cultural values in cross-cultural communication because they serve as multifaceted standards that guide human conduct in a variety of ways.

Values

Values can be defined as "the most deep-seated aspects of culture and often cause the greatest cultural conflict when they impede upon cultural communication. They lead to behavior which seems irrational to those who do not share the same values" (Prosser, 1978, 303).

Individuals use values to determine what is aesthetically pleasing, morally or ethically acceptable, fair, or just. The values that an individual's life is governed by are those that are embedded in a culture. He or she internalizes them in the process of acculturation. "Beyond the individual, cultural values originate with laws, moral and ethical principles of the society that provide the basic criteria for evaluation of the preferred mode of conduct or existence" (Haque, 1997, 21).

Value orientations are the deepest but most visible aspects of a culture. They are the dominant ways in which members of a culture operate toward certain basic human problems, such as the role of humans in nature, their place in it, their relations to other humans, their use and relations to time and space, and their orientation toward activity. "Some values and normative systems are shared broadly throughout the world, as suggested by the Universal Declaration of Human Rights. Others are culturally specific and provide an opportunity to apply the standard of differences in the principle of similarities and differences. Still others are peculiar expressions or deviations of individuals within cultures. These are called aspects of subjective culture" (Prosser, 1978, 175).

Values are central to a comparative understanding of people and cross-cultural communication. Values are needed to rationalize actions taken by both individuals and nations. Very often, aggressive actions taken by a nation are rationalized in terms of values. Moreover, values are basic to a culture because they provide a framework for evaluating what is desirable or undesirable, admirable or despicable, in life and in society. It is through cultural communication that values are passed on within the culture and are shared with others in other cultural settings.

Ethnocentrism

One of the greatest problems of communication across cultures and of studying values and religions is ethnocentrism. According to Prosser (1978), "Ethnocentrism is the tendency of members of a culture to believe that for one reason or another their culture is better or superior to other cultures" (297). Ethnocentric individuals seek to hold on to their most deep-seated cultural patterns.

Americans historically have often been very ethnocentric in judging Middle Easterners and consequently have failed to understand the dynamics of Middle Eastern culture. Many Americans think that their national cultural characteristics are so extraordinary that all foreigners wish to become Americans or to adopt American customs. The remedy to this way of thinking perhaps lies in what might be called cultural relativism, a concept that emphasizes the need to study values of other people within the framework of their culture, not one's own (Haque, 1997).

Balance between Arab and Israeli Viewpoints

Another reason for the misperception of the conflict in the Western media is the imbalance in the coverage of Israeli and Arab viewpoints. A possible remedy to that problem is that news producers should insist that when interviews are done, there be a true balance between Arab and Israeli viewpoints. We have to recognize that even with these remedies, there will always be some of the coverage that is not liked by either the Arab side or the Israeli side. This is because "one man's context is another man's distortion" (Savir, 1985, 32).

CONCLUSION

As was discussed in this chapter, the prevalent stereotypes that distort the political, cultural, and social realities of the Middle East will continue to color the perceptions of Western journalists about this region unless those journalists try to understand more about this complex part of the world.

A comprehensive understanding of the religions and cultures of that region by providing a shared communication and other social interaction would enable Western journalists to have an insightful perception of Middle Eastern cultures. Understanding might not overcome opposing interests, but the differences at least will be clearer and more subject to discourse, negotiation, and compromise where possible.

In the next chapter, I present a detailed discussion of the Israeli and Egyptian cultures, including languages, religions, and social norms and values in the two countries.

4

THE ISRAELI AND EGYPTIAN CULTURES: AN IN-DEPTH ANALYSIS

Virtually any definition of culture, in the commonly used sense, would include such things as academic institutions, literature, the arts, theater, music, and so forth. A society is said to have a cultural life when it has such institutions, or amenities, and they are lively and in constant, popular use.

Culture is more fundamental than that, however. "It is not necessarily expressed in concrete institutions. It includes the deep-rooted and basic mores, beliefs, social customs, and notions about the home and the world" (Yael, 1998, 71).

In the shrinking world of the information age, with a variety of means of communication growing at an explosive rate, people are increasingly communicating cross-culturally at various levels. Unless people, communicating across cultures, find a way to enter into each other's assumptive worlds that are governed by the basic norms of human relations in a culture, contacts may only enhance misunderstanding and aggravate existing prejudices. It has been suggested that books on a culture may offer profound discourses on its history, religion, politics, music, sculpture, industry, and so forth; yet they may not give us the basic insight into what makes a person growing up in a culture behave in a certain way.

Despite differences, cultures and subcultures share characteristics that have been called "cultural universals." There are some who emphasize the universality of cultural patterns and supposedly assume "a psychic unity of humankind, a unity rooted in the basic similarity of the psychic structure of human beings, regardless of the differences in response to environmental stimuli reflected in different modes of behavior" (Haque, 1997, 18).

CULTURAL UNIVERSALS (DIALOGUE) VERSUS CULTURAL RELATIVISM (CRITICISM)

Two major trends have contributed to our understanding of different cultures in the realm of intercultural communication. They are cultural dialogists and cultural critics.

Cultural Universals (Dialogists)

Cultural dialogists believe that in order to understand different cultures, scholars should focus on sets of components that they select as cultural universals. According to Prosser (1978), "cultural universals are those characteristics which are shared from culture to culture, past and present, such as customs relating to cycles of life: birth, adolescence, courtship, marriage, maturation, and death; bodily care; relations with others; and customs relating to the supernatural" (296). One may assume that the more comprehensive a list of components one uses, the more thorough and deep one's examination of culture is and, consequently, the more reliable one's understanding is likely to be.

Cultural universals link humanity more by their similarities than by their differences. Such an assumption requires us to reexamine all cultural systems as actually or potentially open rather than closed systems, in which there is a constant interchange of customs and values.

Anthropologists in the early post–World War II era began developing the concept of cultural universals, or cultural traits, common to all cultures, past and present, whether or not contact with other cultures was involved. Such traits were seen as categories relating to doing and thinking that could be applied in all locations and time periods for all people (Prosser, 1978).

Cultural dialogists have focused on the possibilities of research into human culture and the differences it makes in how humans communicate with one another. They have sought to illuminate the realm of self-presentation and enlarge the human perspective to understand the culturally different. Argument, belief, values, structures, and poetics were considered basic branches of dialogue. The dialogists' work "emerged not from concentrated study of the phenomenon of humans interacting across cultures, but rather from the application of rhetorical or symbolic categories to intercultural behavior" (Asante, Newmark, & Blake, 1979, 18).

Cultural Relativism (Critics)

Unlike cultural dialogists who focus on cultural universals and similarities, cultural critics are more likely to see distinctions between cultures on a comparative basis. Instead of seeking to broaden the work of cultural dialogists, the cultural critics have left off process to argue for understanding the barriers that separate men.

Cultural critics operate on three distinct levels: classificatory, analytic, and applicative. At the classificatory level, the researcher attempts to identify the "barriers" to communication across cultures; at the analytic level, he or she explores the barriers in terms of priority, intensity, or difficulty. When the cultural critic has made the classification and analysis, application to specific settings becomes possible; this level is called applicative.

Cultural critics are seeking ways to perfect the communication process across cultures by isolating the barriers. They suggest "sensitizing persons to the kinds of things that need to be taken into account instead of developing behavior and attitude stereotypes, mainly because of the individual differences in each encounter and the rapid changes that occur in a culture pattern" (Asante, Newmark, & Blake, 1979, 20).

Integrating Cultural Universals and Cultural Relativism

I believe that analyzing the Israeli and Egyptian cultures requires using both cultural universals and cultural relativism approaches in the sense that I am comparing the two cultures in terms of their similarities and their differences. In this context, Prosser (1978) said: "It is useful for us to understand how social discourse interculturally and crossculturally can be made more workable by understanding in the principle of similarities and differences those things that help to unite us and bring us together" (166). Despite the importance of an understanding of cultural universals, we should have a critical approach to such universals.

In this chapter, I recognize the infinitely complex nature of the Israeli and the Egyptian cultures and attempt to examine only a few components of cultural universals in both cultures that are needed to have an insight into their dynamics and the distinctions between them.

Understanding the cultural dynamics of the Israeli and the Egyptian societies is essential for understanding how the two countries shape their policies with regard to the Arab-Israeli conflict. This is because politics, including the formulation and implementation of foreign policy, is very much a cultural activity. Political culture defines the value parameters for both the policy makers and the bureaucrats who are responsible for the implementation of the policy. Therefore, the external behavior of international actors cannot be gainfully examined without a comprehensive understanding of their domestic cultural values.

CULTURAL DIFFERENCES BETWEEN ISRAEL AND EGYPT

The conflict between Israel and the Arab countries is not limited to the political and military areas; it also includes the cultural differences between the

Arabs and Israel. In fact, it might be assumed that these cultural differences have contributed to the further complication of the political conflict in the Middle East. These cultural differences are very clear between the two key countries in this conflict: Egypt and Israel.

To the outsider, Egypt and Israel might seem to have more cultural features in common than in opposition. "They are ancient 'semitic' peoples worshipping in sister religions, Judaism and Islam. Their faiths share many common features: the one God reveals his word to his prophet as recounted in a sacred text— in the one case the Koran, in the other the five books of Moses" (Cohen, 1990, 19). "Early Judaic and Islamic communities were politically organized as nations of believers invoking special divine protection and in pursuit of earthly as well as spiritual salvation" (Kerr, 1973, 29).

Despite these points of similarity, profound differences exist between the Egyptian and Israeli cultures. On the one hand, Egypt, one of the world's oldest nation-states with a history of seven thousand years, is a relatively homogeneous society with a long history, self-sufficient culture, and large mass of people deeply rooted in the village life flourishing along the banks of the Nile. On the other hand, Israel is a modern nation-state with a heterogeneous population of immigrants from many lands who live in largely Western settings.

Religion and language in the two countries perform opposing national functions. Whereas Judaism and Hebrew (Israel's official lanuage) have perpetuated Jewish separateness and its sense of nationhood, Islam and Arabic (Egypt's official language) direct Egypt outward first to the wider Arab nation and then to the vast community of faithful, "the *umma*."

Egypt and Israel suffer from a very high degree of cultural incompatibility. Each culture is virtually a closed book to the other. "Imprisoned in mutually exclusive conceptual worlds and complex ecologies of assumption and habit, neither society is able to bridge the gap dividing it from the way of life of its neighbor" (Cohen, 1990, 161).

In many respects, the Egyptian-Israeli conflict is a paradigm of a relationship that "became hopelessly entangled in the snares of cross-cultural dissonance" (9). At the heart of this conflict is a recurrent pattern of cultural misunderstanding and failed communication.

A BRIEF OVERVIEW OF THE EGYPTIAN CULTURE

Egypt has always been described as "an age-old hydraulic society," with a highly centralized government and an army ready to resolve conflicts among political, economic, and ideological forces (Wilber, 1969, 1).

The core of Egypt's cultural scene is the village community. "The ineradicable natural heritage of the Egyptian people is a joint struggle for subsistence" (Cohen, 1990, 21). Most of Egypt consists of desert, and most of its settlements appear along the banks of the Nile River. In this agricultural society, the sense of group solidarity has always been very strong. Therefore, "the development of personal initiative and autonomy, characteristic of child-rearing and education in the Western world, is neglected by Egyptian culture, as it is indeed throughout the Arab world" (22).

"The cradle of Egypt's collectivist culture is the village community" (Cohen, 1990, 19). For over four thousand years of uninterrupted settlement, the vast majority of the Egyptian people have lived in the thousands of villages of the Nile Valley and Delta. Today, much has changed. Millions of Egyptians are still tied to the soil, but up to 40 percent of the population now lives in cities, and migration from countryside to town continues. Since the 1870s, Egyptian society has undergone a transformation with the emergence of working and middle classes. For many, modern education has eroded the traditional village characteristics (20). In recent years, Egyptian society has started to witness a wave of urbanization, where many villagers have moved to major cosmopolitan cities, especially Cairo. Villagers are naturally attracted to the cities by prospects of employment and prosperity (whether illusory or realistic). Rapid population growth, diminishing resources, lack of development in rural areas, the absence of new cultivable land, and the great disparities in land distribution have also served to draw people out of the villages.

Although the majority of Egyptians lived in villages as recently as the late 1980s, cities, which have been important in Egypt for more than two thousand years, continued to be important. Traditional urban society was more heterogeneous than in most other areas of the Middle East. Quarters, segregated along religious and occupational lines, were self-governing in their internal affairs (Metz, 1991, 114). "Although the physical hold of the village may have weakened, Egyptian culture still retains the indelible mark of its origins." Anwar Sadat, like his successor Hosni Mubarak, was village born and bred; Gamal Abdel Nasser also came from a village background. Thus, "there is no unbridgeable cultural gap between ruler and ruled; both draw on a common fund of symbols and experiences" (20).

Although Egypt is commonly identified by its own people and others as an "Arab" country, its unique village culture distinguishes it from other Arab nations. "There is a specific quality about Egyptian life, a distinctiveness which has its roots in a pattern of existence in the Nile Valley long antedating the rise of Arab Islam. While Egypt shares much with its Middle Eastern neighbors, it remains uniquely Egyptian" (Wilber, 1969, 2). "Islam, with its 'capacity for accepting Nature,' had no radical impact on a culture which promoted the continuity of village life and fused successive and heterogeneous systems in a syncretic whole, where the group was both agent and beneficiary" (Cohen, 1990, 21).

Despite Egypt's unique character in the Arab world, the majority of Egyptian citizens view themselves, and are viewed by outsiders, as Arabs. Their sense of Arab nationhood and belonging is based on what they have in common with the rest of the Arab countries' citizens—namely, language, culture, sociopolitical experiences, economic interests, and a collective memory of their place and role in history. "This sense of nationhood is constantly being formed and reformed, reflecting changing conditions and self-conceptions" (Barakat, 1993, 33).

The "law of assimilation" decrees that many invaders throughout the course of history who have come out of either the desert or the sea—Persians, Greeks, Romans, Arabs, and Turks who settled along the banks of the Nile—have been entirely absorbed into the Egyptian indigenous population and its long culture. Foreign conquest and occupation has had some effect on the Egyptian culture and society. However, many of the failings of the Egyptian government are blamed on previous colonial oppression. "Egyptians have also been left with an acute sensitivity to any real or apparent encroachment on their sovereignty. Proud of the antiquity and grandeur of their civilization and its centrality in the Arab World, they regard Egypt as a great power by right and bitterly resent any insinuation of subordinate status" (Barakat, 1993, 21).

The need for irrigation and unified water control along the Nile has led to group solidarity in Egyptian villages. "The villages are basically self-contained and self-reliant units, inhabited for centuries by the same kin groups, made up of people who are somewhat suspicious of outsiders. The dreary round of drudgery, lived out in hovels at a subsistence level, has been relieved primarily by group participation in marriages and funerals and in religious ceremonies" (Wilber, 1969, 4). The notion of group solidarity was initiated by late President Nasser, who called for family, village, and ethnic unity and idealized the role of the Egyptian peasant (*fellah*) as an "embodiment of the new Egypt" (7).

The Egyptian village contains several extended families (*ahl* or *dar*), each of which has a lineage or clan (*hamula*) relationship. In addition, there are secondary divisions of these families into social groups that are usually descendants of a common male ancestor. "The basic kinship unit among peasants in villages is the extended family rather than the tribe. The family structure is based on a web of relations centered on land cultivation. As such, it constitutes the basic socioeconomic unit in the villages" (Barakat, 1993, 56).

The necessities of village life have created a culture in which the individual is bound to the group by strong ties of rights and obligations ingrained from early childhood. "Complete mutual interdependence is the rule. One must help one's kinsmen, not only with mundane tasks in the home and fields, but in time of deeper need, such as illness, debt or strife with outsiders" (Cohen, 1990, 23).

One important value in the Egyptian village culture is a sense of belonging to the home, which, like the land, is a symbol of identity that must be maintained and never sold or rented. Another important value in village culture is motherhood, which, like the land, symbolizes fertility and unlimited generosity. Other village values include brotherhood, marriage, children, obedience, patience, spontaneity, simplicity, cooperation, and neighborliness. Peasants may engage in intensive rivalries and feuds when land or family values are threatened. Yet peasant culture is also distinguished by its emphasis on neighborliness as a significant value. This emphasis is reflected in often repeated proverbs such as "*Al-jar qabl ad-darr*" (The neighbor before the homefolk).

Community affiliation is given priority over individual achievement and power in Egyptian society. Indeed, *najda* (mutual support) is a critical concept in the Egyptian villagers' value system. This emphasis on helping the group—held together by informal ties—also explains the dominance of informal over contractual commitments, and the use of mediation and reconciliation to resolve conflicts in lieu of reliance on formal legal action. Disputes in Egyptian rural communities are often resolved informally and outside the official courts, according to customary law.

Village life in Egypt accords a significant role to clerics but is structured primarily around popular or folk religion. "Many of the religious values of peasants derive from their immediate environment rather than from texts and religious institutions or establishments, and from concrete expressions of faith rather than from abstract philosophical notions" (Barakat, 1993, 59). Their deep religiousness centers on saints, shrines, and rituals. It serves as a mechanism for relating to (even controlling) their environment, and for overcoming daily problems. Villagers still follow the *shari'a* (Islamic law), but they tend to develop among themselves a pattern of religious life that interprets religious texts symbolically. They use concrete experience to support abstract religious teachings. They listen to *ulama* (religious clerics), but they use their *awlia* (saints) to help them understand and interpret what the *ulama* are saying. Among the most dominant folk religious values in the Egyptian villages is *baraka* (blessedness), which emanates from dependence on seasonal harvests and direct exposure to environmental forces. Closely connected to this orientation are devotion, patience, reverence, and contentment.

Like other collectivist or communitarian cultures, Egyptian society is preoccupied with questions of shame. In the context where group power is paramount, group opinion is decisive and inescapable. The weapon of shaming is one of the group's major means of social control. "Loss of face, to be shamed before one's peers, is an excruciating penalty which one seeks to avoid at all costs . . . Punishment is administered in public and intensified by deliberate belittlement or ridicule. The humiliation is worse than the pain of the admonition itself" (Barakat, 1993, 23). In this context, Wilber (1969) said: "It is shameful [for Egyptians] to acknowledge failure, but almost as much to rejoice over success" (10).

The effect of punishment is not simply to discourage misbehavior as such but to disgrace the person in front of the group. The child is taught that the penalty for wrongdoing is public disgrace rather than a sense of personal remorse. Therefore, he or she tries to avoid humiliation as much as sin. The corollary of shame is face or honor, that is, one's reputation in the eyes of others. A pivotal concept throughout the Arab world, honor embraces various forms and may be associated with personal dignity, hospitality, the fathering of sons and the sexual virtue of one's women.

The Egyptian culture, in common with other Arab cultures, has developed an exquisite code of good manners, including the virtues of sociability, hospitality, and politeness. Social distinctions based on age, rank, or family position and other etiquette requirements are highly and strictly observed. In the Egyptian culture, "rudeness, not 'insincerity' is condemned. There is no conceivable virtue in bad manners. To protect everyone's feelings, differences must on no account be openly expressed; bluntness and undignified behavior are anathema" (Cohen, 1990, 27).

Every social situation has its own set of social conventions and etiquette. Hospitality in receiving a visitor is highly regulated. Egyptians possess a very strong sense of propriety. "Within the family circle, reserve, not effusiveness, is the rule" (Cohen, 1990, 26). A husband and wife will not openly display affection in public. A guest must always be received with a smiling face, regardless of one's mood, because any sign of unease will be taken personally by the visitor. "To spare others' feelings, to avoid embarrassment at all costs, requires the rigorous censorship of gratuitous emotions" (26).

As mentioned previously, family is the basic unit of social organization in traditional and contemporary Egyptian society. At the center of social and economic activities, it is a relatively cohesive social institution, particularly among the rural peasants. The success or failure of an individual member becomes that of the family as a whole. Every member of the family may be held responsible for the acts of every other member.

One's commitment to the family may involve considerable self-denial. Parents, and particularly the mother, deny themselves for the sake of their children. The source of the mother's happiness is the happiness and prosperity of her children. Ideally, both children and parents are totally committed to the family itself.

The centrality of the family as a basic socioeconomic unit in the Egyptian society is being increasingly challenged by the state and other social institutions. Young men and women are seeking education and careers away from their parents in urban centers within and outside Egypt. These structural changes have already begun to undermine traditional relationships, roles, and value orientations within the Arab family. Different sets of relationships are developing between family and society. However, "young men and women show less alienation from the family than from any other social institution, be it religious, political, or social" (Barakat, 1993, 100).

Islam plays a vital role in formulating Egypt's cultural values. The overwhelming majority of Egyptians are Moslems of the Sunnite rite, the largest of the Islamic groups. Egyptian Moslems follow the teachings of the Islamic *Shari'a*, which stresses the values of justice, fairness, equality, human dignity, and inviolability of person and property. The visitor to Egypt is immediately struck by the profusion of mosques and the large numbers of people visiting them at all hours of the day. Islam is also being taught as a mandatory subject at Egyptian national schools from grade school to high school.

One force working to strengthen the religious tradition in Egypt is al-Azhar University. The "Grand Sheikh" of the university hands down rulings on interpretations of the faith and is now virtually a government appointee. He is, therefore, not likely to be a man who would embarrass the secular authorities, who, respecting the strength of the Islamic tradition, are not disposed to interfere in the religious decisions made by the "Grand Sheikh" and his colleagues at al-Azhar.

The Moslem Brotherhood, which was founded in 1928 to promote religious piety, is one of the main Islamic groups in Egypt. The Moslem Brotherhood claims that Egypt's legislation, the judiciary, and economic and social systems are founded on non-Islamic bases. The group's main objective is "to institute Islamic *Shari'a* as the controlling basis of state and society in Egypt" (El-Hodaiby, 2000, 88).

The 1980s and 1990s witnessed the growth of popular interest in various forms of Islamic revival, accompanied by a local resistance to Western fashions, lifestyles, and modes of thought. "The label Western 'imported ideas' became a common expression of disapproval, and rationalist interpretations of Islam were often stigmatized as irreligious innovations" (Andersen, Siebert & Wagner, 1998, 27). The failure of modernizing secular policies to deal with internal social and economic problems and the "humiliating" defeat by Israel in the 1967 war were interpreted by some Moslems as a "divine punishment" (157). Today, the *Gamaa Islamiya* (Islamic group), an offshoot of the Moslem Brotherhood, continues to initiate widespread popular discontent against the West and to call for a return to the Islamic roots (Diller, 1994, 208).

Egypt has a Christian minority named "Copts," who represent a small portion of the Egyptian population. In my view, the Copts, who claim to be descendants of the ancient Egyptians, are well-assimilated in the Egyptian community. They hold top positions in the Egyptian government, and they represent Egypt in international arenas as consuls and ambassadors. However, many Egyptian Copts do not believe that they enjoy the same rights as the Egyptian Moslems. In fact, many of them think they are being treated as outsiders in Egyptian society.

Interaction with other cultures is an important factor of change in the Egyptian culture. Currently, Egypt is witnessing two reactions to their political and cultural encounters with the Western world. First, there is a total rejection of this world, accompanied in general with an absolute acceptance of and adherence to the Egyptian culture, which in this case becomes hegemonic and totalitarian for its own people. The group supporting that reaction represents a major portion of the Egyptian society. And, at the same time, there is total acceptance of Western culture and partial rejection of some aspects of Egyptian culture. The group representing that reaction are generally the younger generations who have been exposed to Western values through satellite dishes and other Western media, such as music, movies, books, and so on.

I cannot discuss the Egyptian culture without referring to what many scholars call "the conspiracy theory." In Egypt, as is the case in other Arab and Islamic countries, there is a general thinking among "average" individuals that the West is conspiring against the Arab and Islamic world, and that there is a major "Zionist" plot planned by the United States and Israel to stop any kind of development in Arab and Islamic countries. For those individuals, almost anything negative that happens on the political scene, or even the social and cultural scenes, would be a conspiracy plotted by the United States and Israel, which is described by those individuals as "America's pampered child" in the Middle East. These misguided understandings under the unfounded theory of international conspiracy have the potential to deepen antagonism between the Arab world and Israel.

This cultural overview of Egyptian society shows that Egypt is a collective society that rests on group solidarity, and that the Egyptian people adhere to a set of social norms and cultural values that govern their personal and social relationships. The basic value orientations in Egyptian peasant culture pertain directly to land, family, the local community, and religion. Egyptian values, most of which come from Islam, might make it harder for an outsider, especially one coming from the West, to have an in-depth understanding of Egyptian society and its people.

Based on what has been presented in this section and considering the conservative nature of Egyptian society and religious resistance to Western influence, it can be hypothesized that Western correspondents operating in Egypt might not be able to cope with Egyptian culture or mingle easily with its people.

A BRIEF OVERVIEW OF THE ISRAELI CULTURE

Israeli society is "a human improvisation patched together from amidst the debris of the shattered empires of the twentieth century with immigrants from as many countries as had Jewish communities" (Cohen, 1990, 28). Like the United States, Israel was founded by immigrants from many ethnic and cultural backgrounds. Israel has encouraged this "ingathering" of Jews to help develop the Israeli society. "This drawing-together is the essence of Zionism, which might be called 'the founding religion' of Israel" (Diller, 1994, 20).

The secular Israeli society is an "artificial creation," and the establishment of Hebrew as the spoken and written language dates back only to the first decades of the twentieth century. The parents of most native-born Israeli adults did not themselves speak Hebrew as their first language. This puts Israel in the category of immigrant countries. Israeli society as a whole "remains a hotch-potch, a strange kaleidoscope, consisting of many pieces which move against one another in various combinations, but do not mesh into a recognizable entity. The recent massive Russian immigration and the influx of foreign workers are shaking up the pieces some more" (Yael, 1998, 71).

Powerful mechanisms of socialization were established to absorb the new immigrants into Israeli society and help them adjust to prevailing cultural patterns. First among these mechanisms was an educational system that aimed at socializing new immigrants to the dominant values by helping them learn the language, norms, and appropriate social roles. There is popular agreement in Israel that schools should instill in youth sufficient knowledge of Jewish people and commitment to Jewish traditions. Among the major educational goals set by the government are "deepening one's civil responsibilities toward the state, preparing young generations for pioneering tasks, implanting a love for the national tradition and enhancing the recognition of the mutual and ultimate interdependence of the State of Israel and the Jewish people of the Diaspora" (Liebman & Don-Yehiya, 1983, 172).

The Israeli army has also contributed to the socialization of new immigrants. The army devotes much time to strengthening future officers' emotional and national commitment to the Israeli state (Liebman & Don-Yehiya, 1983, 179). Reserve duty until the age of 55 maintains the link between the armed forces and the citizens throughout the latter's working life.

The absorption and integration of Jewish immigrants in Israeli society was related to the process of modernization. The dominant framework was that of the modernization of traditional immigrants within an essentially modern society. Israel was in an almost unique situation. Unlike most cases of modern migration, in which the forces of modern economic and political processes were brought by immigrants to the traditional native groups, in Israel it was traditional immigrants who came to a relatively modern society.

The differences between the immigrants and the absorbing society meant that the immigrants had a number of adjustment problems, such as learning new social and cultural skills, becoming more future-oriented, and participating in democracy. Some factors in the absorbing structure impeded the process of absorption. These included allocation of services without consideration of immigrants' productivity, which limited incentive to work, and the dependence of immigrants on bureaucratic agencies, which resulted in passivity and apathy.

Emphasis on the relationship between absorption of Jewish immigrants and modernization of Israeli society was often accompanied by the argument that there is a pluralistic tendency among the Jewish population in Israel. There is ethnic diversity among Jewish immigrants to Israel in the sense of different cultural systems and orientations. Therefore, those immigrants found it hard to be fully absorbed in one society with a common cultural orientation.

The most important factor in the consolidation of the Israeli society has been the history of the state. Throughout their short history of less than 50 years, Israeli citizens have shared more collective experiences and challenges than other states face in generations. "As a small country, in which any event of note will impinge directly on either one's own life or that of someone of one's acquaintance, every war, border incident, or reprisal raid has strengthened that sense of joint purpose and destiny which underpins any viable national community" (Cohen, 1990, 30).

The solidarity of the Jewish community is different from that of the Egyptian village. The Jewish community is not divided along clan lines. "Jews were not, therefore, pitted against each other in the defense of tribal interests and honor— that source of so much discord in the Arab World—but were united as a minority against an alien and often hostile majority" (Cohen, 1990, 31).

The status of the individual Jew within the community is very different from that of the Egyptian *fellah*. Most of the collectivist oriental cultures, including that of Egypt, achieve group cohesion at the expense of individual rights. Israeli society, however, has a deep respect for the uniqueness of the individual and the promotion of personal autonomy. Individualism is encouraged from an early age. Israeli children are taught to express their moral responses independent of their parents and friends. "Individual discrimination and responsibility—conscience, not shame—is the guide to moral conduct" (Cohen, 1990, 32). The spirit of self-assertion in the face of pressure to conform is a popular pattern of Israeli behavior.

So, unlike the solidarity that characterizes the village community in Egypt, individuality and personal independence are the dominant cultural traits of Israeli society. "If the village is the seedbed of the Egyptian culture, that of Israeli culture is the small, often urban community of the diaspora" (Cohen, 1990, 30). Jews in Europe lived in self-contained communities where they possessed a substantial measure of autonomy. Their immigration to Israel led to a strong sense of individuality in modern Israel (31).

So, while Egypt has witnessed migration from traditional villages to big cities, Israel has witnessed the immigration of many Jews coming from the urban subcultures of Europe to the promised land of Israel. The Jews who settled in Israel came, overwhelmingly, from countries of two civilizations, from Christendom and the lands of Islam. Inevitably, they brought with them much of the civilization of the countries from which they came, including their perceptions and definitions of identity. Anyone who has visited Israel will recognize the difference between, for example, Jews from Berlin and Jews from Baghdad, not in their Jewishness, but in the German culture of one, and the Iraqi Arab culture of the other. But this contrast goes beyond city or country; it arises from the difference between the two civilizations, Christian and Moslem, that meet in this small Jewish state.

The much-discussed distinction between Ashkenazic Jews (Jews from northeastern Europe who are descendants of those who fled Germany during the Crusade) and Sephardic Jews (Jews who are descendants of those who were exiled from Spain during the Inquisition), in purely Jewish terms, is only about minor differences of ritual, each recognizing the other as valid. This distinction has no theological or legal significance. Nor does the difference arise from the conflict between Euro-American and Afro-Asian Jews. "The really profound dividing line is between the Ashkenazic and the Sephardic Jews. The Jewish immigrants to Israel brought with them, from their countries of origin, much of their cultures of origin, and it was therefore inevitable that there should have been disagreements and even clashes between them" (Lewis, 1999, 37).

The state of Israel thus brought together, with a common citizenship and a common religion, immigrant groups of two major religiously defined civilizations, in both of which the Ashkenazic and Sephardic Jews had played a minor but significant role. These groups brought with them very different cultural traditions on such matters as the relations between politics and religion, between power and wealth, and more generally, on the manner in which power is attained, exercised, and transferred.

One of the basic concepts governing the Israeli culture is the redemption of the "Zionist" land or the "Land of Israel." This concept has governed most of the Israeli government's policies and plans. For example, the land-use and land-rights policies had the effect of "stripping land away from the Arab population," especially in those areas that were placed under strict Israeli control (Andersen, Seibert, & Wagner, 1998, 113). "Zionism was a messianic movement that clothed the traditional religious goal of a restoration of the Jewish people to their historic homeland in the garb of secular nationalism" (Cohen, 1990, 34).

At a practical level, the Zionist movement was, to a large extent, successful in establishing all the constituents of an autonomous national community. It built factories, reclaimed the soil, organized representative institutions, mobilized for self-defense, introduced the Hebrew language, and developed a national literature. However, most of these social changes were negative. Religious beliefs and the *halakha*—the code of behavior that used to govern the life of the traditional Jew—were rejected and socially neglected. Traditional morality was abandoned and replaced by Western social forms. So, Israeli society started witnessing a period of informality accompanied by a neglect of traditional Jewish values. When new immigrants arrived in the country, they were encouraged to turn their backs on their traditional beliefs and ways.

This situation raised the issue of religiosity versus secularization in Israeli society. Secularization, "the process by which religious institutions, actions, and consciousness lose their social significance," has commonly been viewed either as a dimension or a consequence of modernization (Ben-Rafael & Sharot, 1991, 87). Industrialization, urbanization, the growth of science and technology, the spread of education, and the development of the mass media have been seen as contributing factors in the decline of religion.

Whatever its limitations in other contexts, the modernization-secularization perspective appears to work well in the case of Western Jews. "The precipitating factor in the decline of religiosity among Jews in Central and Western Europe was their movement out of what had been semi-autonomous and highly boundaried communities" (Ben-Rafael & Sharot, 1991, 88). The transition of imigrants into the wider societies involved concentration in large urban centers; diffusion into the modern sectors of education, commerce, and industry; and participation in the political institutions of their respective nations. Increased social interaction with non-Jews and participation in modernizing societies were accompanied or followed by a sharp decline in Jewish religious practice.

Some Jewish immigrants in Israel resolutely discarded their Jewish civilization along with their Jewish dialects and orthodox practices. In their place, they invented the "New Hebrew Man." The tenuous Jewish tradition they retained—mainly as a net for drawing and holding together the disparate immigrant Jewish communities—"consists today of rather irritating constraints on foods, marriage laws, and the like, as well as a calendar of Jewish holidays. This is probably the one vestige of the genuine civilization, but being isolated from the rest of the organic structure, it does not signify very much. Indeed, it suffers the fate of all religions in the secular, westernized worlds" (Yael, 1998, 72).

It is worth mentioning here that most Jewish immigrants from North Africa and Asia underwent comparatively little secularization, and they conceived of their immigration to Israel as a fulfillment of messianic prophecies or as a means of expressing and continuing their sacred culture. They did not distinguish Judaism from their "parochial" cultural legacy, and were not, therefore, ready to abandon those cultural attributes that they had adhered to in the diaspora. "Their contact with secularized Jews in Israel came as a shock to many, and their consciousness of the need to defend their primordial attributes led many to strengthen their traditional ways during their first years in the new society" (Ben-Rafael & Sharot, 1991, 46).

The continuing decline in the number of pupils enrolled in religious elementary schools suggests that the number of Israelis who define themselves as religious is declining. "The importance of the Jewish tradition is somewhat mitigated by the fact that the new civil religion, unlike Zionist-socialism, lacks a coherent ideological formulation. It lacks, as it were, a theory" (Liebman & Don-Yehiya, 1983, 135).

Some scholars argue that what is missing in Israel is an underlying civilization. The only Jewish society in Israel that may be said to have a civilization is the orthodox community. "The attraction of orthodoxy for certain individuals in secular Israeli society lies in the awareness of its deep-rooted civilization, with the added charm that it is 'our own' meaning that the road leading to it is wide open and free of the difficulties of assimilating into an alien civilization, however attractive. Modern Israelis who join the orthodox community feel that they are reattaching themselves to their 'roots,' i.e., their grandparents and forefathers, thus gaining a sense of solidity and security-in-continuity which is lacking in secular Hebrew society" (Yael, 1998, 75).

One of the early signs that the Zionist civilization was crumbling was the abandonment of the soil. Cultivating the soil was one of the strongest tenets of Zionism, yet the Jewish civilization for untold generations has been entirely urban. "In reality, the majority of the Jews in Palestine lived in urban communities, rather than in the agricultural ones that dominated the literature and arts and all Zionist propaganda, domestic and external . . . But in a matter of decades, and despite considerable incentives to the contrary, the percentage of Jews living on the land went down" (Yael, 1978, 75).

There is no doubt that many Israelis are uneasily aware of the situation, even if they have not formulated it in quite this way. Reactions have been varied, but the response that has dominated the cultural life of the country for a long time has been a determined effort to make it an extension of Europe. "Conscious of the thinness and artificiality of the would-be Hebrew civilization, many people strive to fill the gaps, so to speak, with cultural imports. And while the center of gravity has been shifting from Europe to the United States, the overall tendency remains the same. There is a rather desperate air about it, and the manifestations are too numerous to mention" (Yael, 1978, 78).

Based on the material presented in this chapter, it is clear that Israeli culture is more Westernized than Egyptian culture. In this context, Hess (1996) referred to Israel as an example of a culture with which the Western correspondents are familiar. Hess quoted Thomas L. Friedman, the former *New York Times* correspondent to Israel saying, "Put simply, news from modern Israel is more appealing and digestible for people in the West than news from elsewhere, because the characters, the geography, and the themes involved are so familiar, so much a part of our cultural lenses" (43). In the same vein, Schleifer (1987) argued that "Israel is one of the easiest, most convenient places in the entire world [much less an otherwise highly reserved or restrictive Middle East] for a foreign correspondent to work" (348). According to Schleifer, Israel is an outstandingly secular society as opposed to the religious atmosphere in the Arab world. On this subject, he said:

In contrast to the conservative, family-oriented, and religiously colored social life in the Arab Islamic world, Israel is "fun"; its prevailing lifestyle is comfortable and familiar to the typical young foreign correspondent. (1987, 350)

CONCLUSION

This chapter presented a brief overview of the cultural values, religious traditions, norms, and rituals practiced in both Israeli and Egyptian societies. It can be assumed from this chapter that unlike Egyptian society, whose values and traditions are different from the Western world, Israeli society is more Westernized in nature. This is because most of the Jews who immigrated to Israel from Europe have brought with them European values and styles of life.

Based on this assumption, it can be hypothesized that Western correspondents would be more familiar with Israeli society than they would be with Egyptian society.

In the next chapter, I discuss my life in Egypt and my personal experience in Israel to give the readers a sense of what it was like for someone of Egyptian origin to be exposed to Israeli culture.

5

AN "INSIDER" IN EGYPT; AN "OUTSIDER" IN ISRAEL

This chapter is a cross-cultural study. In it I present my experiece in coping with the cultural differences between Egypt and Israel, and relate how these differences could affect Western correspondents' access to information about the Arab-Israeli conflict.

Edelstein, Ito, and Kepplinger (1989) lamented that too many studies have been done on a country-by-country basis in single cultural contexts. Edelstein held that it is necessary to adopt a multicultural, comparative perspective to cope with the complicated events on international agendas. "We have taken a straightforward view of 'comparative.' It is a study that compares two or more nations (or other entities) with respect to some common activity. In international studies, region A is compared to region B with respect to the flow of news into and out of those and other regions" (4).

In these terms, I am an observer looking at nations and regions and comparing their behavior directly with respect to a certain framework or meaning that is common to both at the same (or equivalent) moment in time and space. In this context, such terms as "comparative," "cross-national," "cross-cultural," and "intercultural" can be used interchangeably.

While conducting this research in Egypt, I was a participant observer because I am part of that society and I am familiar with the various cultural situations and contexts within its realm. So, I was wearing two hats: one as an objective researcher and the other as someone who was born and raised in Egypt. However, I tried to make myself aware of my participation and my involvement in Egyptian society, and I tried to avoid becoming unthinkingly and impulsively immersed in it throughout my research. In Israel, however, I was a cross-cultural observer, and during my stay there, I encountered different cultural situations without getting intensely involved in them.

MY LIFE IN EGYPT

I would like to give the readers an insight into my years of growing up as an Egyptian, as I believe this would help them understand my approach to this study in a broader context. It is always hard to write about one's culture and one's native country because many things are taken for granted or overseen, but I will try to draw a personal portrait of my life in Egypt as I see it.

I come from an upper-middle class urban background. My father is a retired police general and a personnel manager at an investment company, and my mother is a manager of one of Egypt's national banks. I have one brother, a lieutenant in the police. I was born in Alexandria, Egypt, which is a nice Mediterranean city. I wish I could have spent more years there because Alexandria has a certain magic to it that is hard to explain. However, I moved to Cairo with my parents when I was six years old.

I was raised in a comfortable, spacious apartment in one of Cairo's nice neighborhoods. Most members of my extended family used to live very close to us, and so we visited them on a weekly basis. It is worth mentioning here that family solidarity is one of the major features of Egyptians' daily lives, whether they are living in a village or in a city. I remember, for example, that we used to go to my grandmother's house every weekend, where I would meet my uncles, my aunts, and my cousins, and we would socialize past midnight. This closeness and sense of belonging to my extended family have cultivated in me a feeling of being part of a group and a big extended family whose members would be of help to me whenever I needed it. The impact of my family on my life has always been so great that it exceeded other agencies of socialization, such as schools, peers, and the mass media. My parents have always encouraged me to have a goal in life and to be persistent and perseverant in trying to achieve it. That helped me a lot throughout my educational years and in my endeavors after that.

Having been born and raised an Egyptian Moslem, I have always tried to practice and maintain the religious rituals of Islam: praying five times a day, fasting during the holy Islamic month of Ramadan (the ninth month of the Moslem calendar), and paying money (*Zakat*) to help the poor and needy. As a child, I would accompanied my father to mosque for the Friday prayers, during which we used to listen to the Friday religious speeches. Then, after the prayers, we would socialize with family members and friends outside the mosque. Religion in Egypt was a mandatory subject at schools, and this helped strengthen and instill religious values in me.

My parents sent me to a private English school for my elementary, prepara-
tory, and secondary years. I always felt that the educational system in Egypt
was very centralized, and it was under the direct supervision of the Egyptian
Ministry of Education, which prescribed the curriculum, appointed teachers,
and set general examinations. The educational system in Egypt was also patri-
archal and paternalistic in the sense that the teachers were imposing ideas on
their students. There was hardly any discussion or interaction allowed on the
students' part. The nature of that relationship helped reinforce certain ideologies among the students and did not allow those students to express their opinions freely about those ideologies.

One of the ideologies I learned as a student and I grew up with was that Israel was Egypt's foe and that all the Israelis were "bad" people. Nobody dared
to challenge, or even discuss, that ideology, which has always been reinforced
by the Egyptian mass media. We used to buy at least two national newspapers
every day (my father has always been an avid reader of newspapers). I remember reading in Egyptian papers that Egypt was "the nucleus of Arab unity," and
that the Egyptians shared the responsibility of solving Arab problems, among
which was regaining Palestine for the Arabs. The Egyptian educational system
and mass media cultivated in me patriotism to the homeland and nationalism
to the larger Arab nation.

Many of the ideologies that we learned at school were brought up and discussed in informal settings and outings with friends and peers. Like many other
Egyptians, I used to socialize with my friends at coffee shops. However, a coffee shop was more than just a place for socializing for Egyptians; it was used
also for the dissemination of news and the discussion of political and social affairs. I remember that almost all my friends from high school had negative
opinions about Israel, but I also remember that most of them knew very little
about Israel.

During my teenage years (mid- to late 1980s), Egyptian society started witnessing an ongoing conflict between the old and the new, the traditional
norms and values of the society and the modern values imported from the
West. For example, many teenagers were listening to hard rock music and
wearing torn jeans. Those teenagers were revolting against some of society's
old values and traditions. Most of the Western values were opposed by the
older Egyptian generations who thought that Western values would contami-
nate the original cultural norms of Egyptian society.

During that time, Western influence and the general process of modern
technological and social change were affecting the family as well as other aspects of Egyptian life, particularly in the cities. One main venue for Western influence was the satellite dish. Under some pressure from me and my brother,
my parents agreed to get us a satellite dish through which we could watch
more than 140 different channels, among which were five Israeli channels. I
still remember how my curiosity to watch these Israeli channels made me
spend hours every day following their programs. This was my first direct expo-

sure to the Israeli media, and I realized after watching these programs that some of them were similar to the ones broadcast by Egyptian television. We were lucky to have the satellite dish. However, many other Egyptian families refused to get satellite dishes for fear of exposing their children to some of what they believed were obscene programs broadcast through the satellite dishes.

After finishing high school, I decided to go to the American University in Cairo (AUC), a liberal private school, which was independent from the Egyptian Ministry of Higher Education. At AUC, all the syllabi were American and so were many of the faculty members. I majored in mass communications and minored in English and comparative literature. Studying at AUC altered my way of thinking, expanded my horizons, and made me question some of the older ideologies that were imposed on me and that I used to take for granted. The liberal education I received at AUC gave me the opportunity to think creatively and to express my opinions freely without any pressures or fears of being ostracized. It liberated me from narrow interests and prejudices and helped me learn to observe reality with precision, judge events and opinions critically, think logically, and communicate effectively. It was during that time that I started to develop an interest in studying international and intercultural communication. I started to realize the importance of international dialogue and communicative interaction across cultural and political lines of demarcation.

A few years after my graduation, I decided to pursue a doctorate degree in journalism and communication in the United States. I was determined to work on a topic that would help international communication scholars understand the difficult processes of interpersonal and group interactions across cultures. That is how I thought about the idea of that study.

AN "ARAB MIND-SET"

The process of observing and exploring the political and cultural differences between Egypt and Israel through Western correspondents' eyes was not an easy task for me. Having been born and raised in Egypt, I have always been exposed to messages disseminated by the Egyptian news media, which often described Israel as the "enemy," the "aggressor," and the "intruder" on Arab land. This undoubtedly affected the way I regarded the Arab-Israeli conflict within the context of the "Arab mind-set." Before undertaking this research project, I was aware of all the personal biases and preconceptions I might have had about Israel, and I tried not to carry any of them into this study.

INVOLVEMENT IN EGYPT; DETACHMENT FROM ISRAEL

Undertaking this study made me realize that analyzing any culture in a thorough manner requires being totally detached from that culture and observing it from a distance. I was faced with the challenge of trying not to take the comments made by Western correspondents in Egypt for granted and placing their answers in the proper context. I tried hard not to let my immersion in Egyptian culture and my personal involvement and familiarity with Egyptian society affect the freshness of my perspective, speculation, and thinking about what the correspondents in Egypt said.

Analyzing the Israeli culture, however, and thinking about what the correspondents in Israel said was a much easier task. I knew very little about Israeli society. In fact, throughout my educational years in Egypt, the mere mention of any aspect of life in Israel was taboo. I had not visited Israel before undertaking this project, and therefore my knowledge of Israeli society was limited to what was written in the few books I have cited dealing with Israeli culture and society.

Initially, I thought that my minimal knowledge of Israeli society would lead to a cross-cultural misunderstanding on my part, which would hinder my comprehension and assessment of what the correspondents told me. However, this turned out not to be the case. In fact, my sense of "otherness" or detachment—much stronger in Israel than it was in Egypt—made it easier for me to speculate about what the correspondents in Israel said and to analyze their remarks in a critical manner. I realized that the less profound a cultural influence, the less likely it is to be taken for granted.

IMPORTANT REMARKS

Before discussing my personal experience in Israel in detail, I would like to highlight two significant remarks. First, although the main objective behind my visit to Israel in the fall of 1998 was to conduct scientific research and in-depth interviews among the Western correspondents stationed there, my experience in Israel went beyond doing research for a study. In fact, the month that I spent in Israel left a long-lasting impact on my life in general and on the way I view Israelis.

Second, my personal opinions that are mentioned in this chapter with regard to the Israelis and the Palestinians whom I met while in Israel are merely personal opinions about particular persons and particular circumstances. This means that they should not by any means be considered generalizations about the Israelis or the Palestinians.

PREPARING FOR THE VISIT

Throughout my planning for my visit to Israel, I was a doctorate candidate in the School of Journalism at Southern Illinois University at Carbondale. I was so anxious about the whole experience; it was something beyond my imagination to meet and talk to Israeli citizens, not to mention visiting their country and living with them. I heard from many people that it is very hard for an

Arab to get a visa for Israel, and so, I expected lots of obstacles while trying to get the visa. I applied for the visa at the Israeli Consulate in Chicago (the closest Israeli Consulate to Carbondale, Illinois), and, to my surprise, I got it very easily within a couple of weeks. I think the fact that the university supported my application made a big difference. My anxiety reached its peak during the last few days before my departure to Israel. I remember calling my parents in Egypt and telling them about my intended trip to Israel, and I remember their extreme worries about this trip, and how they strongly discouraged me from taking such a trip. They even tried to convince me to choose any country other than Israel for my research.

UPON ARRIVAL

After a nine-hour trip from the United States to Israel, I was glad to arrive in Tel Aviv. It was a Sunday afternoon, and the airport was very busy. Once I set foot in the airport, my heart was beating very fast. I felt I was going to faint. The lady at the gate checked my passport thoroughly, and then decided to keep it for a while, telling me that they had to make a quick security check on the information on my passport.

Although I had prepared myself for the worst, I started to panic, and I asked her how long it would take them to conduct this check. She told me that she did not know and asked me to have a seat until they called my name. I had no choice. I waited for almost a half hour. It was the longest half hour in my life. Finally, they called my name, gave me back my passport, and told me "Welcome to Israel."

I then took my two pieces of luggage and went out of the airport. I took the bus to downtown Tel Aviv.

IN TEL AVIV

The bus ride from the airport to downtown Tel Aviv took about 45 minutes. I was very exhausted, so I started to look for a youth hostel I knew of from the Internet. The bus stop was very far from the hostel, and I could not walk because my luggage was heavy. I started looking for a taxi, but, unfortunately, that night marked Rosh Hashana (the Jewish new year), and the streets were practically empty. It took me almost two hours to find a cab driver who agreed to take me to the hostel. The driver was Palestinian, and, obviously, he was not celebrating that event.

GOOD TIMING

The timing of my visit to Israel was very fortunate. Certainly the Arab-Israeli conflict was much more complicated then it is now, but during the period of my visit, there was a certain relative calm. I arrived in September

1998, just one month before the Israeli and Palestinian leaders agreed to a land-for-peace deal on the West Bank, at the Wye River Conference Center in Maryland.

There was nothing much going on in Jerusalem or the West Bank at the time, which gave me the opportunity to engage in lengthy conversations with the foreign correspondents in Tel Aviv and Jerusalem, something that they would not have done had there been violence going on between the Israelis and the Palestinians.

ISRAELIS ARE "HUMANS"

Before my visit to Israel, I had never had any encounters with Israeli citizens. However, I did have some Jewish friends in the United States. Those friends were not Israeli citizens. The mass media and the books I read about Israel were my only frames of reference to form a mental picture about the Israelis. Needless to say, throughout the years that I spent in Egypt, I always thought of the Israelis as harsh soldiers with weapons and heartless politicians. This mental picture started to change throughout my stay in Israel. I started to meet "average" Israeli citizens on the street; I started to mingle with Israelis at coffee shops; I started to realize that Israelis have emotions—they laugh, they cry, they play, they socialize; they are, after all, humans.

Many Israelis were very surprised to meet an Egyptian citizen. In fact, some Israelis told me that it was the first time in their lives they had met and talked with an Egyptian. I could tell they were very happy and excited. They were curious to know why I was visiting their country. They also wanted to know what I thought about them as Israelis.

I noticed that most Israelis, even those with low educational levels, were very interested in politics. I was amazed to see how knowledgeable many Israelis were about what was going on in the Middle East. I believe that the Israeli news media have contributed to the Israelis' knowledgeability about the political situation in the Middle East. This is because most of the Israeli media broadcast several political programs that analyze Middle East politics.

I still remember some encounters with Israeli citizens that reflected their human nature. Once I was waiting at a bus station, and I wanted to go to one of the newspaper offices in town; however, I did not know which bus would get me there. So, I approached one of the people standing at the station. That individual expressed a great willingness to help me, and he even volunteered to explain to me in great detail where the address was. During our conversation, several buses passed by, and he missed his bus to give me directions.

On another occasion, the driver of a bus I was riding in started a conversation with me. He told me he was a Jew from Morocco, and he had migrated to Israel. And when he learned I was an Egyptian, he shook hands with me and said: "Our grandparents have fought against each other for years, but the fact that you and me are having this conversation shows that there is some hope for a full peace in the region."

LIVING WITH AN ISRAELI FAMILY

Before leaving the United States for Israel, some American friends gave me contact information for an Israeli family who lived in Haifa in northern Israel. I called this family a few days after my arrival, and introduced myself to them. They were very welcoming, and insisted on inviting me to visit them and spend a couple of days at their home.

I spent a very nice and relaxing weekend there. They had two boys, seven and four years old. The boys could not speak English, but they seemed very excited about my visit. In fact, the elder son went to his school the next day and told his classmates proudly that he had an Egyptian visitor at his house; however, they did not believe him.

This Israeli family was very hospitable. They went out of their way to make me feel at home. They took a vacation from their work to show me around and gave me their sons' room to sleep in.

SECURITY PARANOIA

It does not take long for any visitor to Israel to realize how paranoid the Israelis are when it comes to security. I think they are, to some extent, justified in their concerns. This is because they have always been in a state of war, and they have always felt that they were being targeted by their neighbors. This security paranoia is something that I did not sense when I was in Egypt.

The streets of Israel were full of soldiers and security officers. One day, I was getting off a bus in West Jerusalem, and a security guard came running after me asking to see my ID. I was very surprised, and I refused to do that. However, he insisted, telling me that he had the right to check the IDs of people he suspected at any place and at any time. I reluctantly showed him my passport, which I carried with me all the time. He looked at the photo in the passport and then looked at me and let me go.

On another occasion, I was looking for someone to ask about a television station's address in downtown Jerusalem. I approached an individual and asked him for directions. Before I finished my sentence, he started running away from me in complete horror. On a third occasion, I was on a bus when the bus driver noticed an unclaimed bag near the front seat. He stopped the bus to inquire about who owned the bag. He did not restart the bus until he found the bag's owner.

The most striking experience that reflects the Israelis' obsession with security was at the checkpoints that I had to pass through during my daily trips back and forth between Bethany (a Palestinian West Bank city on the outskirts of Jerusalem where I was staying) and Jerusalem. Palestinians who live in the West

Bank but work in Jerusalem have to pass through these checkpoints on a daily basis. They usually ride in a van (driven by a Palestinian) with West Bank plates, which are quite different from Jerusalem plates. Whenever Israeli soldiers see such a van approaching the checkpoint, they stop it and insist that every passenger leave the van to be checked thoroughly.

Many Palestinians work in Jerusalem illegally, and they do not have a permit that allows them to be in Jerusalem. In this situation they ask the driver to take them to Jerusalem using back roads in order to avoid the checkpoints. Sometimes, the Israelis set new checkpoints on these back roads, and they take any Palestinian who does not have a Jerusalem permit to jail. Because I had a valid tourist visa stamped on my passport, I did not have problems passing through these checkpoints. However, on a couple of occasions, the soldiers held me for more than a half hour and interrogated me about the reasons for my visit to Israel.

GHOST CITY

Israel celebrates the Sabbath holiday (a Jewish religious tradition), which starts at sunset on Friday and ends at sunset on Saturday of every week. During that time, the streets are always empty; there are no pedestrians, no cars, no open restaurants or shops, no lights; everything becomes dead. In observance of the Sabbath, the orthodox Jews pray at the synagogues and abstain from traveling and doing any kind of work. In contrast, as I mentioned earlier, Moslems celebrate Friday as their holy day, during which time they go to the mosque and pray.

I was once walking in West Jerusalem on a late Friday afternoon when I heard a loud siren. Initially, I thought it was an alarm announcing the beginning of a war; however, I realized that this siren marked the beginning of Sabbath when I saw shop owners closing their stores.

EAST JERUSALEM VERSUS WEST JERUSALEM

Jerusalem is a great historical city. It is the land of three mainstream religions—Judaism, Christianity, and Islam. However, the city seemed about to explode from the high levels of tension that exist among its inhabitants. From the moment I arrived in Jerusalem, I felt that the walls of the old city were about to talk about the tension.

East Jerusalem, which is inhabited mainly by Palestinians, and West Jerusalem, which is inhabited by Israelis, are separated by one street. Yet, crossing that street is like crossing the borders from one country to a totally different country. On the one hand, East Jerusalem is very lively with narrow streets and lots of Arab *bazaars* (little markets). The shop owners call out loudly for their products, and there are several merchants who sit in the streets selling fresh fruits and vegetables. The Palestinians in East Jerusalem were very friendly to me. On several occasions, they invited me to come in to their shops for coffee and tea. When they found out I was Egyptian, they greeted me warmly and asked me about my experience dealing with Israelis.

On the other hand, West Jerusalem is quieter with wider streets. It has several European-style coffee shops, where many Israelis sit and sip Nescafe (a very popular drink among the Israelis). The shops and the restaurants in West Jerusalem close much earlier than in East Jerusalem. Also, there tends to be less traffic in West Jerusalem. Moreover, West Jerusalem has huge malls and shopping centers that do not exist in East Jerusalem.

PRAYING AT AL AQSA MOSQUE

My trip to Al Aqsa Mosque (Dome of the Rock) in East Jerusalem was one of the greatest spiritual events of my life. Because of the situation in Israel, which makes it hard for many Arabs to visit Jerusalem, not many Arabs get the opportunity to pray at that mosque, which is considered to be the second holiest place in Islam after Mecca.

I went to Al Aqsa Mosque with a Palestinian friend, who did not have a permit to be in Jerusalem. However, he graciously offered to take the risk of accompanying me, even though he knew that there would be Israeli guards at all its gates. It was a Friday noon, and we decided to have the Islamic Friday prayers there. We entered through one of the back gates, and, fortunately, the Israeli soldiers did not ask my Palestinian friend about his permit. Upon my entrance to the open court of the mosque, I was taken by the view of the Dome of the Rock, which was glowing in the sun. The scene really took my breath. I took several photos before entering the mosque.

As soon as I entered the mosque, I saw the rock which we Moslems believe that Prophet Mohammed rose from to heaven. It was such an amazing and incredible moment, that I cannot describe in words. We spent a few moments looking at the rock before we sat in one of the mosque's corners to listen to the Friday prayers' speech. After we finished our prayers, we left the mosque in as spiritual an atmosphere as we had entered.

EASY ACCESS TO GOVERNMENT OFFICIALS

Israel might be one of the easiest countries where one can meet government officials. During my interview with one of the Dutch correspondents stationed in Tel Aviv, she mentioned to me the name of the director of the Israeli Government Press Office (GPO) in Tel Aviv. The next day I showed up at the GPO without an appointment, and, to my surprise, I was able to meet with the director, who gave me all the documents that are usually given to foreign correspondents. She even called the general director of the GPO in Jerusalem and scheduled an appointment for me with him.

When I met with the GPO general director in Jerusalem, I was able to interview him for almost an hour. He was very cooperative, and he gave me his business card and advised me to show it at the airport upon my departure from Israel.

DEPARTURE FROM ISRAEL

On the day of my departure from Israel, I went to Ben Gurion Airport in Tel Aviv at 10 A.M. to catch my 2 P.M. flight. I was advised by some Israeli and Palestinian friends that I needed to get to the airport four hours before my flight to allow time for security checks. Upon my arrival at the terminal building, a security officer approached me and inquired about my passport, even before I had entered the airport. He asked me a couple of questions about my final destination (which was Egypt).

When I checked in at the departure gate, the immigration officer (a young lady in her early twenties) asked me several questions about what I did in Israel, the people I met, the places I visited, and the length of my stay at each place. I showed her the business card that was given to me by the GPO director and explained to her the purpose of my visit. After thirty minutes of asking questions, she gave me my passport back and wished me a pleasant trip. My bags were not even inspected.

CONCLUSION

Before my visit to Israel, Israeli society had always been a closed book for me. I always wondered about what life would be like in that society; how the regular Israeli citizens go about their day-to-day routines; how they communicate with each other; and how they interact with outsiders on a personal as well as a professional level. All these questions were going on in my mind, and I could not imagine that one day I would actually witness firsthand the daily interactions on the streets of Israel.

I do not deny the fact that I had several stereotypes and predetermined opinions about the Israeli culture, as do many Egyptians and Arabs. These stereotypes were instilled in me by my cultural background and upbringing. However, when I went to Israel and got involved in several social situations with Israelis, most of these stereotypes were proved wrong. This is an illustration of how situations may create their own values, transforming the meaning of culture. In this context, Edelstein said, "Perhaps the best way to distinguish culture from situation is to see the former as representing defined, related, and predictable circumstances. Situations, in contrast, interrupt the flow of culture to call attention to problems" (Edelstein, Ito, & Kepplinger, 1989, 35).

In the next chapter, I discuss the culture of foreign correspondents, and how their functioning, organizational policies, and reporting assignments affect the way they operate.

6

THE CULTURE OF FOREIGN CORRESPONDENTS

As important gatekeepers to the flow and formation of international news, foreign correspondents contribute to the way people perceive other cultures and societies. The foreign correspondent plays a vital role in the process of cultures communicating with and across other cultures and may be an important factor in the sensitivity and understanding of people of other cultures. As the desire for peace among peoples grows, the role of the foreign correspondent becomes increasingly important and requires a closer examination.

WHO IS A FOREIGN CORRESPONDENT?

The term "foreign correspondents" was defined by Starck and Villaneuva (1992) as "media personnel who report and interpret the actions and events of different societies for a selected audience of readers not native to the country" (2). For the purposes of my study, I have defined the core group of foreign correspondents as consisting of those individuals who are stationed in countries other than that of their origin for the purpose of reporting on events and characteristics of the area of their stationing through news media based elsewhere (in large part in their countries of origin). The term "foreign correspondents" in this study includes not only staff reporters but also editors, writers, producers, and news photographers working for print and broadcast media as well as for wire services.

FOREIGN CORRESPONDENTS AND INTERCULTURAL JOURNALISM

The cultural context in which correspondents operate affects the way they report the news. Several factors, such as preparation for entering a new culture, familiarity with the cultural values, and language ability, affect the correspondents in their understanding of different cultures.

The foreign correspondent is a key player in shaping people's ideas of other cultures and societies. The foreign correspondent's main task is to understand an event rooted in the complexity of one culture and report about it in the context of another culture. In undertaking their roles, foreign correspondents are involved in "intercultural journalism," which means "news and information crossing over from one nation to another" (Starck & Villaneuva, 1992, 4). Foreign correspondents must carry out intercultural journalism in a particularly sensitive way to avoid such cultural barriers as ethnocentrism, stereotypes, and preconceived frames of reference. They should translate the "foreign" into the "familiar" by placing events in cultural frameworks of understanding for the general public. This requires that they translate these events into terms that readers can assimilate and, in a sense, make their own.

Hohenberg (1964) said "it will be the role of the foreign correspondent to create understanding between peoples by bringing to them more meaningful news of each other. As such, he may very well be a decisive element. For it may fall to him in the future, as it has in the past, to represent the difference between war and peace" (452).

FOREIGN CORRESPONDENTS AND PERSONAL BIASES

Foreign correspondents are human beings, and so they might have their own biases and personal leanings and prejudices that might affect the way they report on a specific event or view a particular country. "Foreign correspondents carry with them a good deal of baggage other than their resumes and backgrounds that ultimately influences where they want to go and what they want to explore" (Hess, 1996, 58).

Rosenblum (1981) discussed the impact of bias on the process of interpreting news about other cultures. In writing about other societies, foreign correspondents, he argued, must be aware of the difficulties of overcoming cultural biases. In this context, he wrote: "the question of bias is particularly important, since readers and serious viewers add their own distortions. Logically, a person's attitude towards Jews, Arabs, black Africans or Cubans will affect how he interprets wars involving them. From far away, it is difficult to understand causes of hostilities and details of conflicts, even when they are reported with pristine objectivity. If elements of bias are added, serious misunderstanding is inevitable" (173).

Foreign correspondents might be subject to a dilemma between their personal biases and their professional duties as journalists. For example, Jewish correspondents stationed in Israel might have this dilemma: "Am I a Jew first, or a journalist first?"—this question is asked by many American Jewish correspondents in Israel. Linda Sherzer, a Jew who covered the Gulf War from Jerusalem for CNN, said she would not have reported the locations of SCUD missile strikes because to do so might have improved Iraqi accuracy (the situation was hypothetical; she was not allowed to report this type of information).

For a while the *New York Times* tried to finesse the potential clash of personal and professional loyalty by not assigning Jewish reporters to the Jewish state. The policy finally ended when Thomas L. Friedman was sent to Jerusalem in 1984. So, "journalists can be journalists first, that is, they can represent an elite fraternity, but transcending one's own history can be wearing work" (cited in Hess, 1996, 57).

THE CULTURAL FUNCTIONING OF FOREIGN CORRESPONDENTS

Several studies have been conducted among foreign correspondents to investigate how they view their profession and the way they function. One of those studies was carried out by Starck and Villaneuva (1992) who conducted in-depth interviews with six American correspondents, in which they focused on the means of functioning in a foreign culture. According to the respondents, cultural experience involves subtle aspects of communication, such as mannerisms. One correspondent said, "You have to get used to what the unwritten rules are. . . . If you use the wrong culture, you get the wrong answers" (18).

Lack of cultural preparation was a common theme agreed upon among the correspondents interviewed in Starck and Villaneuva's 1992 study as one of the main reasons behind insufficient reporting. They all argued that background reading is a key factor for the success of foreign correspondents. They also mentioned personal involvement and listening to people attentively as elements for foreign correspondents' understanding of foreign cultures. The correspondents also referred to cultural sensitivity, which they defined as "familiarity with the historical and cultural context of another society and an empathy for other ways of life" (18). According to those correspondents, the longer the stay in a country, the higher the sensitivity to that country's culture.

Pedelty (1995) noted that one of the means by which correspondents can increase their cultural sensitivity is to increase their informal relationships by cultivating friendships in the countries at which they are operating and conversing with common people. In this context, Pedelty said that informal storytelling provides reporters with information that they might not have access to through formal or government sources.

One quality that the best foreign correspondents bring to their work is a sense of the nature of the countries and regions to which they are assigned. When Jack Foisie retired in 1985 after 20 years overseas for the *Los Angeles Times*, he wrote, "I have come to join the consensus that a firm grounding in a language and a culture is essential to a foreign correspondent" (1985, 15).

But how well can a foreign correspondent communicate with his or her audience? Some believe that the news business performs its mission best if its workers are broadly representative of society, if reporters collectively resemble their audiences. However, when reporters go abroad, they are often criticized for not resembling those of whom they are reporting. Journalists debate whether—and if so, how—backgrounds that are different from those of their audiences or subjects produce different results.

FOREIGN CORRESPONDENTS AND ORGANIZATIONAL POLICIES

In the culture of foreign correspondence, news organizations have various schemes for arranging their workforces. For example, the system at the *Los Angeles Times* resembles the management of a diplomatic corps: foreign correspondents are members of a select cadre who rotate every three or four years, usually without becoming geographic specialists, and stay on the "merry-go-round" as long as they perform their duties adequately and wish to remain in the service. The rationale apparently is that foreign correspondence is essentially different from domestic journalism, or "perhaps simply that international correspondents have learned such valuable tickets of the trade that replacing them would be deleterious to the organization" (Hess, 1996, 53).

The *New York Times* seems to link a reporter's having been a foreign correspondent with promotion to the top editorships. The existence of this fast track explains why some reporters are sent abroad briefly and later return home.

The *Washington Post* has been phasing out its permanent cadre, preferring instead to send reporters abroad for one, or at the most two, tours of three or four years each. This is a personnel policy that reflects a large number of reporters who are qualified for foreign postings and a large number of challenging assignments in Washington for which returning reporters compete. The *Post* is also more likely than other papers to use former foreign correspondents as editors on the foreign desk.

The system chosen in each case has as much to do with organizational maintenance (how large enterprises try to keep their employees functioning as productively as possible), as with perceptions of how best to gather information abroad. Differences in personnel policies and other practices reflect newspapers' distinct cultures.

In television, too, there are varying corporate cultures and management practices. Because CNN was designed to be an international broadcaster, its creator Ted Turner claims he imposes fines on correspondents to encourage them to "eliminate the use of the word *foreign* when talking about other nations and other individuals on this planet" (Hess, 1996, 55). CNN also encourages a diversity of accents; correspondents in bureaus in New Delhi or Bangkok deliberately do not sound as if they were from South Dakota.

ARE FOREIGN CORRESPONDENTS BETTER THAN DOMESTIC REPORTERS?

A former Associated Press bureau chief in Madrid, Spain, once said, "There really isn't much difference between a good cop reporter and a big-time foreign correspondent" (Hess, 1996, 57). That opinion is right to the extent that many qualities desirable in foreign correspondence—tenacity, integrity, intellectual honesty, and precise and graceful writing—are also important to good domestic reporting. And, of course, seasoned reporters of whatever background can eventually learn to deal with censorship, disinformation, corrupt officials, thuggery, dysentery, and other overseas hazards.

FOREIGN CORRESPONDENTS AND LANGUAGES

An important professional tool for the foreign correspondent is the ability to converse in and read the language of the country in which that correspondent is stationed. The necessity of knowing foreign languages is a debatable issue among American correspondents. Those who underestimate its importance argue that English is the language of diplomacy, and that international conferences and official interviews are conducted through interpreters as part of routine foreign office procedures. However, correspondents who believe in the necessity of knowing at least one foreign language argue that "a good correspondent must be able to read the papers of the country not merely for general comprehension but with an eye toward the undertones of articles—which may cast more light on a situation than the article itself" (Kruglak, 1955, 64). While a correspondent may get by well with English, that correspondent cannot get involved in normal communication with the average citizen of a country if that person does not communicate in English.

A survey conducted by Maxwell in the mid-1950s on 209 American correspondents showed that a third of the respondents could speak one foreign language, a tenth could speak two, and about one-twelfth could speak three or more. One-fourth of the respondents spoke no language other than English. Hess (1996) conducted a survey on 404 American correspondents which showed that younger correspondents are less likely than their older colleagues to have a knowledge of many languages. A third of those who began their careers before 1979 claimed some ability in four or more languages; this proportion drops to one-fifth for the next generation. Hess believes that learning language on the job can be a challenge for correspondents. As Caryle Murphy, the *Washington Post* correspondent in Egypt said: "This is a 12–to–16–hour-a-day job. There is no time to learn Arabic now." On the other hand, according to Hess, in a country such as Israel, "the small number of Hebrew-speaking foreign correspondents reflects, in part, the large number of Israelis who speak English" (83).

Not many correspondents in Israel speak both Hebrew (the Israelis' official language) and Arabic (the Palestinians' official language). Some correspondents speak neither, but if they speak one, it is almost invariably Hebrew. This is hardly balanced by the fact that among those Middle East correspondents reporting on Israel and Palestine but based elsewhere (e.g., Cairo), some may speak Arabic but not Hebrew. Apart from this, most correspondents in the Middle East have to work through intermediaries and depend on translation services as they form their understandings of Middle Eastern cultures (Ulf, 1998).

FOREIGN CORRESPONDENTS AND DANGER

Foreign correspondents often talk of dealing with danger, of being scared, sometimes of exhilaration. In this context, one of the former correspondents in the Middle East said, "You get hooked on your own adrenaline." Peter Arnett, the former CNN correspondent in Iraq, wrote in his memoirs *Live From the Battlefield: From Vietnam to Baghdad, 35 Years in the World's War Zones*, "What I had learned to love [was] the thrill of covering wars, for which there was no substitute" (1994, 323).

When the Committee to Protect Journalists sought to codify safety information for reporters on their way to the former Yugoslavia in 1993, its executive director noted, "We were surprised to learn how little dialogue existed on a formal basis about safety measures, both among journalists and between journalists and their news organizations. There's a kind of hubris among reporters; they think they are bulletproof" (Hess, 1996, 58).

HOW LONG SHOULD A FOREIGN CORRESPONDENT STAY IN A PLACE?

Most foreign correspondents are likely to be stationed in one place for three to five years, although some remain longer. The question here is: what are the advantages and disadvantages of long and short stays?

It is especially the larger U.S. media organizations that show a clear preference for a rather quick rotation among foreign correspondents. The assumption here is that "going stale" is a significant occupational hazard among foreign correspondents who spend a long time in one place. One stops seeing the potential stories in what one begins to take for granted. Some stories begin to feel repetitious and boring; and one loses that sure grasp of what readers "at home" already know and what has to be explained. However, local knowledge is also useful. "The first year you are learning, the second year you are on your feet and can give more texture to stories, the third year you are getting tired," said one veteran American correspondent with experiences from postings on three continents.

The correspondents who remain for longer periods could thus possibly lose some of their freshness of perspective. They, for their part, instead tend to emphasize the intensity and breadth of their knowledge, particularly their personal involvement in the society where they are stationed. Having been around for a long time, they can place new events in the context of old ones, and they know where to turn for informed comments. In addition, there is the language factor. In most instances, correspondents who spend more than three or four years in one country will probably learn the language of that country.

CAN FOREIGN CORRESPONDENTS REACH THE BURNOUT STAGE?

There comes a time when foreign correspondents want to seek another kind of assignment or line of work. In addition to continued interest, reasonable levels of energy and stamina are also necessary to avoid burnout. In this context, one of the former *Washington Post* correspondents said, "Extraordinary demands of finding oneself on a major world story are more wearying each year."

Burnout can also be associated with particular country and regional assignments. A former Tokyo correspondent for the *Los Angeles Times* talked of "Japan burnout syndrome." He returned to take the Asia-Pacific beat on the paper's business desk in Los Angeles.

One of CNN's former correspondents defined overseas burnout as that point when the ratio of hassle to what gets broadcast or published becomes too high. One of the biggest hassles are with hostile governments. Many correspondents suffer from the way countries, especially in the Middle East, withhold visas as a means of controlling press coverage. Others suffer from official lying and surveillance. A former *Time* correspondent said in this regard, "Most of my assignments have involved dealing with repressive police states, most of which simply wear you down with delays and bureaucratic hassles" (Hess, 1996, 109).

Despite the difficulties facing foreign correspondents, many of them find coming home to be more difficult. The correspondent who has returned usually talks of lost independence: after having one's own office, a desk in a crowded newsroom becomes a symbol of a place in a crowded hierarchy. In this context, a former *New York Times* correspondent said, "It is never easy for a foreign correspondent to return to the home office, no matter how severe his life might have seemed abroad. There are compensations with those hardships.

One is not surrounded by so many editors, so much interoffice pettiness when one is thousands of miles away" (Hess, 1996, 111).

Many foreign correspondents are very content with their jobs, to the extent that they ask for nothing more. A foreign reporter was quoted as saying: "You know, being a foreign correspondent is like being a maitre d' in a fine restaurant. You meet so many distinguished people under such humiliating circumstances."

CONCLUSION

This chapter shed some light on the culture of foreign correspondents, the way they operate, the obstacles they face, and how they prepare for their assignments. It is obvious from the information presented in this chapter that being a foreign correspondent is not an easy job; in fact, it can be very challenging and difficult, but at the same time, it can be very rewarding and exciting.

In the next chapter, I discuss the correspondents' professional roles and their demographics (e.g., geographic origins, age, educational levels, and formal and informal networks).

7

Correspondents' Demographics and Their Professional Roles

The reporting by foreign correspondents of conflicts among nations is affected by their demographic and professional backgrounds. Our knowledge of foreign correspondents' demographics is limited by the lack of academic studies conducted in this area. One of the very few studies that investigated the effects of foreign correspondents' demographic backgrounds on their professional roles was conducted by Kruglak in 1955. This dated, but classic, study focused on the demographic backgrounds of 200 foreign correspondents from the United States. It showed that the early environment and background of an individual correspondent could play an important role in shaping his professional career.

Another study that surveyed foreign correspondents about their demographic backgrounds was conducted by Hess in 1992. His study, which included 370 former foreign correspondents, investigated foreign correspondents' demographic characteristics from 1960 to 1992.

CORRESPONDENTS' GEOGRAPHIC ORIGINS

The first step in examining the early environment of the correspondents is to look at their geographic origins. A foreign correspondent who was born and raised on a small isolated farm, where he did not have the chance to be exposed to other cultures, might lack the broader outlook on world affairs that his

counterpart from a cosmopolitan city might have. The ability of this correspondent coming from an isolated background to see the international scene
might be hampered by his early environmental isolation (Kruglak, 1955).

Kruglak's and Hess' studies showed that geographical origins of the older
correspondents were not important in evaluating their performance. By the
time a correspondent had served ten or twenty years abroad, his youthful pro-
vincial background was likely to have little influence on his present views. The
problem laid with the younger correspondents whose isolated backgrounds
might have affected their performance.

CORRESPONDENTS AND EDUCATION

Education is another factor that affects the correspondents' performance.
Educational background and academic training equip correspondents with
the basic disciplines needed for understanding the intricate and involved problems that will face them in later years abroad. However, an academic degree in
journalism was not the sole criterion for a successful foreign correspondent
during the 1950s. "Too many great American correspondents have come from
the ranks of copy-boys, without college training, to warrant sole use of this
gauge of a correspondent's qualification" (Kruglak, 1955, 47). A foreign correspondent could conceivably be fully prepared for the job without attending
college. But the correspondent needed to have the will to learn and the time to
study all the problems related to the job before being able to perform its duties. However, this trend changed over the years. Hess' study showed that
there is an increasing number of foreign correspondents who not only finish
their undergraduate degrees but also obtain graduate degrees.

The kind of courses selected by a correspondent during his or her university
or college years is an indication of academic and professional interests. The
foundations for understanding the world may be found in the curriculum pur-
sued by foreign correspondents in college or university. Many foreign correspondents concentrate their college studies in fields of political science,
economics, history, or international relations. This educational concentration
on the social sciences on the correspondents' part is even more pronounced in
advanced degrees and graduate studies.

CORRESPONDENTS AND AGE

Age is another factor that tends to have an effect on the correspondents'
performance. While the age of a foreign correspondent by itself is no indication of ability, it is important when correlated with other factors of experience,
education, and professional judgment. No generalization is valid about the
age of foreign correspondents. The ages differ not only according to medium
but also within each medium in which there are striking variations. The general
characteristics of a current young correspondent who has just joined a news

agency are that he is inexperienced, has been in his present post for less than a year, has little knowledge of the country in which he works, and is underpaid by American standards.

CORRESPONDENTS' FORMAL AND INFORMAL NETWORKS

The correspondents usually operate through networks of formal and informal groups with which they establish professional and social ties. Although their study was not related directly to foreign correspondents, Johnstone, Slawski, and Bowman (1976) conducted a survey on 1,313 journalists in which they studied the amount of formal and informal social contacts and nonwork activities that newspeople share with other people in the field. Results showed that one-third of all journalists concentrated their informal social relationships within the professional community. The results also showed that informal professional contacts were more characteristic of younger than older journalists. Journalists who are established in the field with prominent names have more of a tendency to be involved in formal rather than informal professional networks. "An informal network of colleague relationships . . . provides a mechanism for integrating younger journalists who are still moving up in the field, into the profession" (170).

Results from their study also indicated that a news organization's size and prominence have a positive effect on journalists' informal participation. Journalists who worked for large, nationally prestigious news media were more integrated within informal colleague networks than they were within the formal organizational structure of the profession. "This explains in part why the political and social predispositions of those in the 'elite' stratum differ so markedly from those of journalists in the rest of the industry" (108).

DEMOGRAPHIC DESCRIPTION OF CORRESPONDENTS IN ISRAEL AND EGYPT

Results of the analysis of the data obtained from the Western correspondents I interviewed in Israel and Egypt showed that the majority of those correspondents (almost two-thirds) are males (see demographics table in Appendix A). Of the total Western correspondents in the two countries, almost half fall in the median age category (between 35 and 44 years old).

Approximately half of the correspondents interviewed in Israel were bureau chiefs, and the majority of the ones interviewed in Egypt were news correspondents. There were more Jewish correspondents in Israel than there were Moslem correspondents in Egypt. However, the majority of correspondents interviewed in both countries said they practiced no religion.

Results also showed that almost one-third of the total correspondents in both countries were U.S. citizens, and two-thirds were from Western Europe, North America, and Australia.

Results showed that Arabic was more widely spoken by Western correspondents in both countries than Hebrew. Almost half of the correspondents in Israel and Egypt said they spoke Arabic, compared to only one-third who reported speaking Hebrew. Almost half of the correspondents interviewed in Israel and Egypt reported that they have been working as correspondents for more than ten years.

Finally, results showed that the overwhelming majority of Western correspondents in both countries have either a bachelor's or a master's degree.

CORRESPONDENTS' PROFESSIONAL ROLES

A significant indicator of journalists' professional roles is detachment versus advocacy, observer versus watchdog, or neutral versus participant. A neutral reporter is merely a mediator between news sources and the public, and that reporter's job is to report the news without investigation or interpretation. On the other hand, a participant reporter plays a more active role that includes investigating and interpreting the information before transmitting it to the public. In this case, the news sources provide leads but "the reporter must sift through them for the real story" (Johnstone, Slawski, & Bowman, 1976, 115).

A survey conducted by Lambert (1956) in which 250 foreign correspondents were studied showed that 74.4 percent of the respondents preferred interpretive reporting compared to 20.5 percent favoring straight factual news.

More than three-quarters (76.3 percent) of the sample in Johnstone, Slawski, and Bowman's, 1976 study strongly supported the reporter's watchdog role in investigating governmental activities. Moreover, six in 10 (61.3 percent) of the respondents thought it was essential for the news media to provide analysis and interpretation of complex problems (124). Results of this study also showed that age was strongly correlated with the reporter's stand on neutral versus participant journalism. Older reporters were more neutral than younger ones. Results also showed that reporters who entered the news media later in their careers endorsed neutral press functions most strongly. No more recent study has been conducted to show the relationship between a reporter's age and professional journalistic roles (125).

Among the other results of Johnstone and his colleagues' 1976 study was that journalists' professional values were shaped by their educational experiences. The results indicated that reporters' conceptions of participant press functions were associated with higher levels of formal schooling while neutral orientations were associated with lower educational levels. "The most highly educated and possibly the best trained journalistic practitioners thus tend to embrace participant ideologies of the press and to eschew neutral conceptions" (125).

Weaver and Wilhoit replicated Johnstone and his colleagues' study in 1986 and 1996 to investigate journalists' views on press roles. In their 1996 study, their analysis suggested that four belief systems dominate journalists' attitudes about press roles: interpretive, disseminator, adversarial, and populist mobilizer. The majority (62.9 percent) of respondents in the study, which included 1,410 journalists, supported interpretive and investigative reporting. But only a minority (17.6 percent) thought being a "skeptical adversary" of government officials was essential for the press. About 51 percent of the respondents expressed their support for the disseminator role; only 6.2 percent supported the populist mobilizer role. These results show that journalists were multi-role rather than single-role oriented. Some journalists in this study endorsed more than one role. For example, 85.5 percent of those journalists who considered the adversarial role very important also considered the interpretive role very important.

Weaver and Wilhoit's 1996 study found that having fewer years of schooling suggested that journalists were likely to hold strongly to the disseminator rather than the interpretive or adversary role. Most of the supporters of the interpretive role were "star" journalists with high salaries. Supporters of the investigative role were mainly print journalists; broadcast journalists tended to see this role as less important than their print colleagues did. The study also showed that journalists with supervisory, editorial authority tended to support the disseminator (neutral) role and to avoid either adversarial or interpreter positions. Reporters, on the other hand, were more likely to be interpretive and adversarial than their editors. Thus, "the greater the editor's authority—to hire and fire, to determine news content—the less likely the interpretive role is to be viewed as extremely important.

Two other studies have used Weaver and Wilhoit's modified scale to investigate the journalists' professional roles. One of these studies was conducted among Algerian journalists by Kirat in 1987. He omitted several statements from Weaver and Wilhoit's scale and added new ones to make the scale fit the Algerian journalists and their culture. Results of that study suggested that Algerian journalists did not support the investigative role. According to Kirat, "the Algerian media practitioner operates in an amalgam of organizational and institutional constraints that prevent him from performing the investigative role that he dreams of" (172).

The second study that used Weaver and Wilhoit's scale was conducted on Australian journalists by Henningham in 1996. Results of that study showed that Australian journalists were more inclined than U.S. journalists to support both the news disseminating and the investigative roles of the news media. As was the case among U.S. journalists, Australian reporters gave the lowest rankings to the adversarial role (Henningham, 1996).

CONCLUSION

Based on the studies cited in this chapter, it can be concluded that correspondents' demographic characteristics might have an effect on the way those
correspondents approach the news and operate in the field. More important,
the journalists' demographics might determine their professional roles, especially neutrality versus investigation.

Studying the demographic backgrounds of Western correspondents in the
Middle East might serve as an indication of the techniques of reporting on the
Middle East conflict.

In the next chapter, I discuss the details of the survey I conducted among
Western correspondents in Israel and Egypt. I also present the hypotheses and
research questions I used for this study.

8

Hypotheses for Analyzing the Recent Reporting and Views of Western Journalists for the Arab-Israeli Conflict

In order to approach the recent reporting trends of the Western journalists in Israel and Egypt within the context of the government–news media relationship, I developed several hypotheses and research questions. Then, to address these hypotheses, I designed a survey, and I traveled to Israel and returned to Egypt in the fall of 1998 to conduct personal interviews with Western journalists operating in these two countries.

WHY ONLY WESTERN JOURNALISTS?

This study is limited to Western journalists because their reporting and the prestige of the news organizations to which they belong have the greatest influence on international relations. Moreover, the international news scene is still overwhelmingly dominated by major U.S. and Western European news media. Furthermore, English is the dominant language for almost all Western journalists.

Moreover, the cultural differences between Israel and Egypt are perhaps more obvious to correspondents from the West than to correspondents from other regions of the world. I hypothesized that although Western correspondents might be familiar with the Westernized culture of Israel, many of them might encounter a "cultural shock" in Egyptian society with its Arabic and Islamic heritage.

In this context, Georgie Anne Geyer mentioned in her memoirs about serving as an American correspondent for the *Chicago Daily News* in the Middle East: "I recall with total vividness the dialectic of shock upon shock that went on inside me quite literally for months as I sought to understand and absorb this tempestuous region. I had previously covered Latin America, the Soviet Union, Asia, and Europe. In none of these extremely complicated places did I have comparable inner difficulties. The Middle East involves a special confrontation with oneself and one's previous prejudices, as well as with a new and ever fascinating culture" (1980, 65).

THE SURVEY

I administered the survey using a paper questionnaire that included questions used to assess the correspondents' reporting roles and techniques, their access to government officials, their reliance on formal and informal news networks, and their familiarity with the cultural contexts (mainly language and religion) in which they operate. The questionnaire also included demographic questions about age, years of stay in the Middle East, educational level, religion, current nationality, and professional title of the correspondents. It also included the journalistic roles scale developed by Johnstone, Slawski, and Bowman in 1972 and modified by Weaver and Wilhoit in 1986 and 1996.

The survey included close-ended and open-ended questions. The open-ended questions identified elements not specified in the close-ended questions and yielded information in much greater detail than did the close-ended questions. The close-ended questions provided greater uniformity of responses, however, and allowed more direct comparison and quantification of the answers. The data collected provided a one-time snapshot of the Western correspondents operating in Egypt and Israel at the time the survey and interviews were conducted. A copy of the questionnaire is included in Appendix B.

CENSUS

This study included a census of all the Western correspondents who operated on a permanent basis in Egypt and Israel at the time the study was conducted (between September 20 and October 31, 1998, in Israel, and between November 1 and December 24, 1998, in Egypt).

To locate this population, I obtained the lists of foreign correspondents from the Foreign Press Association bureaus in Egypt and Israel. The census included only foreign nationals from Western countries working as correspondents on a permanent basis and who are permanent members in the Foreign Press Association bureaus in either Egypt or Israel. Those who did not belong to the Foreign Press Association, who had a temporary accreditation, or were found to be Egyptian or Israeli citizens were excluded. The Foreign Press Association is the organization responsible for issuing permanent or temporary accreditation to foreign correspondents. To locate this population before leaving the United States, I called the Foreign Press Association bureaus in both Israel and Egypt and asked to be sent by mail inclusive lists of all foreign correspondents operating in the country. After receiving the two lists, I generated a population list of exclusively Western correspondents. This preliminary list included 96 correspondents in Egypt and 159 in Israel. Most Western correspondents in Israel were in Jerusalem, but a few were in Tel Aviv. All correspondents in Egypt were in Cairo. Arabic and Israeli names were excluded from the lists because Western correspondents were the target members for this study as previously mentioned.

As an Egyptian, my familiarity with the Arabic names made it easy to exclude them. The Israeli names were harder to identify because of my more limited knowledge. A filter question ("What is your current nationality?"), which I addressed to the correspondents when scheduling interviews allowed for exclusion of any person on the population list who was either an Egyptian or an Israeli citizen.

Once in Israel, I discovered that 53 of the 159 correspondents originally listed were Israeli citizens. The list was therefore reduced to 106. Similarly, once in Egypt, I discovered that several correspondents had left the country for good. Hence, the list of Western correspondents was reduced from 96 to 85. Therefore, the final lists included 106 Western correspondents in Israel and 85 in Egypt.

PILOT STUDY

After designing the initial version of the questionnaire, I conducted a pilot study (pretest conducted before the actual study) to detect questions that were poorly written or that failed to provide sufficient response options or did not contribute meaningfully to the purpose of the study. I also checked for errors in the questionnaire (e.g., spelling, punctuation, grammar, incorrect skips, or branching) and for questions likely to have been misunderstood by the respondents or to which they might have taken offense.

The pilot study included one former and two present American correspondents. One was Abdullah Schleifer, former NBC bureau chief in Cairo, Egypt. I interviewed Schleifer in person during the Broadcast Education Association conference in Las Vegas, Nevada. John Palmer, an NBC correspondent stationed in the Middle East during the 1970s, and William Blakemore, an ABC correspondent who also served in the Middle East during the late 1970s were interviewed by telephone.

I contacted the intermediaries of Peter Jennings, a national news anchor for ABC, who served in the Middle East as a foreign correspondent, and Georgie Anne Geyer, a former correspondent for the *Chicago Daily News* and syndi-

cated columnist who has served in the Middle East, but both refused to participate in the pilot study.

I introduced several modifications to the questionnaire as a result of the
pretest. The three journalists I interviewed emphasized that accessing foreign
correspondents would be a very difficult task. I understood this because I had
a hard time making contact with those three for the pilot study. In one case,
more than five long-distance phone calls were necessary to obtain a telephone
interview. Some of the correspondents did not return calls after I left messages
on their answering machines. Even after granting an interview, they were reluctant to give more than fifteen minutes of their time to this study.

RESPONSE RATE

Low response rate was a major concern in this study because of the nature of
the population. Generally, foreign correspondents are hard to locate because
of the nature of their job, which requires them to move around and cover unexpected events at various places in various times. In this context, Hess (1996)
said most foreign correspondents are "nomadic" in that they have to cover
more than one country and spend too much time away from their home base.

In this study, I interviewed 94 of a total of 106 Western correspondents in
Israel (88.7 percent) and 74 of a total of 85 Western correspondents in Egypt
(87.1 percent) (see Table 1).

Table 1
Number of Correspondents Interviewed in Egypt and Israel

Country	Total Number of Correspondents	Correspondents Interviewed	Percentage
Israel	106	94	88.7%
Egypt	85	74	87.1%
	191	168	88%

Many correspondents I contacted were amazed by the response rates, and several could not believe I succeeded in locating and interviewing so many correspondents.

One of the main reasons for this high response rate was the correspondents'
great interest in the research topic. Most of the correspondents expressed to
me their admiration and encouragement for studying the Arab-Israeli conflict
coverage and for making comparisons between two countries with as long a
history of animosity as Israel and Egypt. The majority of the correspondents I
contacted expressed great interest in knowing the results of the study.

Another reason for this high response rate is that I was physically in Israel
and Egypt interviewing correspondents face to face. Many correspondents

told me that they always throw away questionnaires they receive by mail because they do not have the time to answer them. They said a personal interview is the only method that could generate such a high response rate. Moreover, the face-to-face interview helped me establish a strong rapport with the correspondents that engendered trust. Such trust would not have been established by mail or in telephone interviews.

Finally, my persistence in contacting the correspondents helped in increasing the response rate. In several cases, I had to call the correspondents more than five times to schedule an appointment.

RESEARCH QUESTIONS

This study was designed to answer the following research questions.

1. Do Western correspondents in Egypt take on the same newsmaking role in their relationship with the government as do Western correspondents in Israel?
2. Does the government public relations apparatus in Egypt have the same level of credibility with Western correspondents as the Israeli government information establishment has with Western correspondents?

The importance of answering these research questions stems from the fact that they partly deal with the nature of the relationship between government and news media in Israel and Egypt. Moreover, they highlight the differences, if any, between the professional roles undertaken by Western journalists in both countries.

HYPOTHESES

The study addressed the following hypotheses:

H1. The culture will determine the correspondents' access to information.

a. Western correspondents in Israel are more familiar with Israeli culture than their counterparts in Egypt are with Egyptian culture.
b. Language is perceived by Western correspondents in Egypt as more of a barrier to their access to information than it is to their counterparts in Israel.
c. Religion is perceived by Western correspondents in Egypt as more of a barrier to their access to information than it is to their counterparts in Israel.
d. The longer correspondents have lived in either Egypt or Israel, the more familiar they are with that country's culture.

Based on my investigation of the relationship between journalists' demographics and their organizational roles, it can be hypothesized that:

H2. The higher the correspondents' educational level, the more supportive they are of the investigative role of reporting.

Based on the literature describing the governmental public relations machinery in Egypt and Israel, the following hypotheses can be developed:

H3. Western correspondents in Israel will perceive having more access to government sources than will their counterparts in Egypt.

H4. Western correspondents in Israel will report more government leaks (information secretly disseminated by officials to reporters) on the Middle East conflict than their counterparts in Egypt.

After presenting the literature emphasizing the importance of the security issue in Israel and how this issue affects the government-press relationship, it can be hypothesized that:

H5. Western correspondents operating in Israel will cite security as a legitimate reason for the government withholding information on the Middle East conflict more than their counterparts in Egypt.

H6. Correspondents will report that the security issue is used more by the Israeli government than by the Egyptian government as a justification for withholding information on the Middle East conflict.

Based on the literature discussing the significance of the informal networks as sources of information for foreign correspondents, it can be hypothesized that:

H7. Western correspondents in Israel will perceive themselves as having a better network of informal social and professional sources than will their counterparts in Egypt.

a. Western correspondents in Israel will perceive themselves as having more friends and acquaintances than will their counterparts in Egypt.

b. Western correspondents in Israel will perceive themselves as having more informal sources for verifying government claims on controversial issues with regard to the Middle East conflict than will their counterparts in Egypt.

The definitions of some of the terms used in the research questions and hypotheses and how these terms were addressed in the questionnaire distributed to the Western journalists in Israel and Egypt are presented in Appendix C.

CONCLUSION

This chapter gave a brief overview of the survey I used to collect data from the Western correspondents stationed in Israel and Egypt, how I located those correspondents, and the response rate I had in the study. The chapter also explained how I developed the research questions and hypotheses.

In the next chapter I discuss the interview procedures and the obstacles I encountered in contacting the Western correspondents. The chapter also sheds some light on the news media scenes in Israel and Egypt.

9

THE INTERVIEW PROCESS AND THE NEWS MEDIA SCENES IN ISRAEL AND EGYPT

Before undertaking this research project, I expected to face greater difficulties and obstacles contacting correspondents in Israel than in Egypt. Because I am Egyptian, I reasoned that I might be regarded with suspicion in Israel, where people are not used to meeting Egyptians conducting academic research. Moreover, I initially thought that an Arab being in Israel would raise suspicion, and therefore correspondents would be reluctant to trust me or share with me any information about such sensitive issues as security, government public relations apparatus, the quality of formal and informal sources, or the accessibility levels of government officials. I expected less difficulty in Egypt because I was more familiar with the culture and where I could find my way around easily.

However, the exact opposite occurred. I discovered that my Egyptian nationality served me well and worked to my advantage in Israel where most correspondents were pleased to see an Egyptian scholar undertake such a sensitive study on the Arab-Israeli conflict. One American correspondent I contacted even asked me if he could interview me for his newspaper as the first Egyptian scholar he had met conducting academic research in Israel. Other correspondents in Israel told me that they would like to see more researchers studying the Arab-Israeli conflict from this perspective.

OBSTACLES IN CONTACTING CORRESPONDENTS

During my stay in Egypt, I faced several problems in contacting the corre-spondents. One of the problems was that many correspondents were highly suspicious of me, and they thought I was spying for the Egyptian government. Many correspondents were reluctant to schedule appointments for interviews with me out of fear that I would convey the information they released to me to Egyptian government officials. Some correspondents accused me outright of working for the Egyptian intelligence service. So unlike their counterparts in Israel, correspondents in Egypt were more concerned and worried that the government might be investigating them. One correspondent in Egypt went so far as to telephone my academic adviser who was supervising my study in the United States to verify my authenticity.

I tried to overcome this problem by mentioning to the correspondents in Egypt that I had already conducted interviews with their colleagues and coun-terparts in Israel. This greatly reduced the correspondents' suspicion and gave me legitimacy in the eyes of the Cairo correspondents.

Another major problem was that most of the correspondents stationed in Cairo were also covering the rest of the Arab world. This meant that they had to travel to other Arab countries whenever a major incident took place. For ex-ample, during the Desert Fox military mission, which took place in Iraq in De-cember 1998 while I was conducting interviews in Cairo, most of the correspondents in Cairo left for Baghdad, the Iraqi capital, to cover the mis-sion there. This had a direct negative impact on my interviewing process, as it delayed conducting interviews with a dozen correspondents in Egypt.

INTERVIEW PROCEDURES

Whenever possible, I met personally with correspondents. This helped gen-erate a high response rate and ensured that, in most cases, all the questions were answered. I took notes and used a tape recorder to record the correspon-dents' answers. A cover letter was attached to the questionnaire. It included in-formation on confidentiality, informed consent, and some instructions for answering the questionnaire.

The process of pursuing the interviewees was conducted on a systematic rather than a random basis. The prestige of the news organization, the title of the interviewee, and the interviewee's home country determined the order of contacting the correspondents to be interviewed. Bureau chiefs working for prestigious news organizations and coming from the United States, Britain, France, or Germany were prioritized in the contact process. This prioritization was done to ensure that correspondents for the most influential news organi-zations were contacted should time constraints preclude contact with all cor-respondents on the list.

Initial contact with the correspondents was done by telephone. I called the correspondent to schedule an appointment for a personal interview. Most of the correspondents in Egypt and Israel had their home or office telephone numbers listed with the Foreign Press Association (FPA). The initial contacts were easier in Israel than they were in Egypt because almost all the correspondents in Israel had cellular phones that they carried wherever they went. Far fewer correspondents in Egypt had cellular phones. In most cases, I left messages on the correspondents' answering machines, but many of them never called back. In these cases, I had to go directly to their offices to schedule appointments with them.

Most of the interviews were conducted face to face. However, in very few cases (less than 10 in both countries) I had to leave the questionnaire at the correspondent's office and pick it up later without getting a personal interview. In one case, I had to fax the questionnaire to the correspondent, who faxed it back to me.

Most correspondents agreed to be interviewed at their office, which was sometimes in their homes. On several occasions, I inquired about the public places (coffee shops, hotels, pubs, and restaurants) correspondents frequented on a regular basis and met them there. It was much easier to interview correspondents at these public places than at their office or home because they felt more at ease and they were less distracted or interrupted by phone calls. However, it was harder for me to tape the interviews at these public places because of the ambient noise. Many correspondents had to cancel their appointments with me at the last minute because they were sent to cover a story. This required scheduling another appointment. The average duration of the interview was 25 to 30 minutes, but many correspondents showed a great interest in the questions and agreed to be interviewed for more than an hour and a half or two hours.

At the beginning of an interview, I briefly explained the research project, why I had selected the topic, and why I felt it was essential to contact the Western journalists in Israel and Egypt. I asked the correspondents about their social and professional lives in Israel or Egypt in general terms and the way they viewed the people in either country. This helped establish a rapport with the correspondents before I began asking the open-ended questions.

The questionnaire first asked whether the correspondent wanted his or her responses to remain confidential. I promised those who did not consent to being quoted by name that their answers would remain confidential.

In many cases, I also asked the correspondent if he or she knew other correspondents personally or had friendships with them. If they answered yes, I asked the correspondent to mention the project to them. This process facilitated my job, especially during the initial stages of the interviews, by making later interview scheduling easier. Later interviewees mentioned having heard about the project from their colleagues, and this led to locating several more correspondents to interview.

THE NEWS MEDIA SCENE IN EGYPT

Egypt has the highest number of Western correspondents among the Arab countries because it is considered by the West to be the heart of the Arab world, and the country where the Western journalists can get to know the pulse of the Arab street. All the foreign correspondents stationed in Egypt are in its capital, Cairo. They are scattered all over the city. Most of the Western news organizations, such as the Associated Press and Reuters, rent three-room apartments in tall buildings overlooking the Nile River.

Foreign correspondents stationed in Egypt do not have a specific place where they like to get together and socialize. They tend to spend most of their time at their offices or at home. I think that the main reason behind this trend is the transportation problem. The traffic in Cairo is very congested all week-days, and transportation is so bad that many people prefer not to go out once they go home after work. This made it hard for me to schedule appointments for interviews with Western journalists in Cairo outside their offices because most of them were very reluctant to go out and get stuck in traffic.

Cairo has a Foreign Press Association (FPA) office, which functions as a kind of ombudsman for the foreign correspondents, making sure that they are not ignored during press conferences and on tours to the offices of high-ranking Egyptian officials. Occasionally, too, the FPA facilitates scheduling interviews for the foreign correspondents with the hard-to-reach Egyptian officials.

Foreign correspondents in Cairo like to read Egypt's English publications, especially *Al Ahram Weekly* (government owned and operated) and the *Middle East Times* (privately owned) to get a "feel" for the daily and weekly events on the political and social scenes.

Egypt has an official office named the State Information Service (SIS), whose director is the official spokesperson for the Egyptian government. This office arranges meetings and outings for foreign correspondents and facilitates their job in Egypt. During my stay in Cairo, I interviewed SIS Director Nabil Osman, who viewed himself as the conveyer of government information and the mediator between the government and the foreign news media: "We act as the liaison between foreign correspondents and life at large in Egypt; my mandate is to facilitate, not to restrict. I am here to serve the correspondents if the need arrives."

The SIS director is the only official spokesman of the Egyptian government when it comes to dealing with foreign correspondents. Osman told me, "I am the spokesman for Egypt vis-à-vis foreign correspondents. I speak on behalf of all the ministries. And if I don't have the information, I seek it from the concerned departments. I proposed several times that there should be a spokesman's office in some ministries, but up till now it has not been implemented."

The SIS office provides public relations services to correspondents. "I am available to correspondents 24 hours a day. Whenever they wish, they can call me to decipher anything for them or to get information from other sources. If they want to do a field visit, initiate contact, or take photos in an area that requires permission, they come to me or they go to the Press Center," said Osman.

THE NEWS MEDIA SCENE IN ISRAEL

Israel has one of the highest densities of foreign correspondents in the world because of the continuous Arab-Israeli conflict. Moreover, after the Holocaust, the continuing history of the Jewish people has been a matter of special concern to a large number of people, especially in Europe and North America, and Israel is the focal point of this concern.

Most of the Western journalists stationed in Israel are located in Jerusalem. One Jerusalem hotel has a reputation as a correspondent gathering spot: The American Colony Hotel in East Jerusalem. Many Western journalists like to socialize at that hotel. I used to go there every afternoon during my stay in Israel to catch the Western journalists, who were hard to reach.

Some foreign media organization offices are clustered in a couple of buildings, so that the correspondents working from them are more likely to run into one another and become more or less closely acquainted. The Jerusalem Capital Studios (JCS) building in downtown West Jerusalem houses many television and radio organizations. They have been coming together because of the advanced technical facilities available there.

Closer to downtown West Jerusalem is the Beit Agron building, named after Gershon Agron, founding editor of the *Jerusalem Post*, Israel's main English-language newspaper. Beit Agron houses the Government Press Office, the spokesman of the Israeli Defense Forces, and the office of the Military Censor. Along its corridors, one also finds the small offices (mostly a couple of rooms each) of a number of foreign newspapers, such as the *London Times*, the *Guardian*, and the *Independent*.

There is a Foreign Press Association, office in Jerusalem. It provides the same services to foreign correspondents as its counterpart in Egypt.

Israel has an unusually news-conscious society. Almost all of the people who live there enjoy talking about politics and engaging in controversial political conversations. Many foreign correspondents in Israel rely on the Israeli radio, which has news bulletins every half hour, and as one of the correspondents remarked, "If you are in a city bus in Jerusalem and the driver has his radio on, you will notice that when the news comes on, everybody in the bus becomes quiet" (Ulf, 1998, 552).

The Government Press Office (GPO) gives accreditation to foreign journalists in Israel and helps organize workshops to help them beome familiar with life in Israel. The also provide several other services to foreign correspondents, such as providing them with telemeser (a telephone service that provides updates on a regular basis of what is going on in the world) and beepers (which alert the correspondents to ongoing news conferences) and organizing news briefings twice or three times a week.

During my stay in Israel, I interviewed the two top GPO officials: Jenny Koren, Director of the Tel Aviv GPO Branch, and Moshe Fogel, General Director of the GPO in Jerusalem. "The head of the GPO has a mandate to give interviews and to represent the government's position," said Fogel.

Unlike the Egyptian government, which provides one official spokesperson for the foreign news media, the Israeli government provides several government spokespersons. "Every ministry in Israel has its own specialized spokesperson; however, the GPO is a representative of the government's points of view in general," said Koren.

CONCLUSION

This chapter focused on the interview process and the description of the Israeli and Egyptian media scenes. The next chapter describes the nature of the relationship between the government and the news media in general and in Israel and Egypt in particular, and how this relationship affects access to information about the Arab-Israeli conflict.

10

GOVERNMENT-MEDIA RELATIONSHIPS AND DIRECT CENSORSHIP IN ISRAEL AND EGYPT

The political, military, and cultural aspects of any conflict provide the necessary context for an investigation of the relationship between governments and the news media generally. Many communication scholars have highlighted the role of the news media in shaping and formulating political decisions. Politicians who recognize the significance of the news media in affecting public opinion try to use these media to promote specific policies.

GOVERNMENT-MEDIA RELATIONSHIP AND ACCESS TO INFORMATION

According to Boulding and Senesh (1983), "knowledge is power" in the sense that there is a close relationship between those who wield political power and those with superior knowledge. "The interactions between the political system and knowledge system can lead to decisions and actions that increase the chances for creating and sustaining a humane and satisfying social order" (274). Based on that argument, political systems always attempt to enhance the knowledge process by communicating their decisions to all the interested parties through the news media.

Max Weber observed that the availability of knowledge about any conflict can help individuals clarify facts and understand the implications of their values. Similarly, James Rule assessed the availability and utilization of knowledge by the political system, and concluded that knowledge can provide insights about how to achieve "social betterment" and how to resolve conflicts. Boulding and Senesh maintained that political systems should facilitate the knowledge process, by communicating their knowledge bases and decision premises to all interested parties in a pluralistic competition, outside scrutiny and public accountability.

Decision-making theory is closely related to negotiating strategy because the interactions among states are consequences of decisions their governments make. The most important link between intergovernmental negotiations and decision-making is the flow of information through the news media. "A large part of negotiations between governments consists of the emission of signals designed to influence the other party's perceptions. The perception of such signals is in turn a crucial part of the decision making process" (Snyder & Diesing, 1977, 28).

Communication and information processing mediate between state-to-state bargaining and the internal decision-making process. Bargaining is essentially a process of communication intended to influence the other party and gain information about that party. Decision makers need information to make decisions about bargaining strategies and moves. "The nature of com-munication channels within the decision-making unit and the images and expectational biases of the individuals who transmit and receive information will strongly affect the interpretation of information" (Snyder & Diesing, 1977, 480).

The dynamics of the relationship between the news media and policy mak-ers are clear in several ways. "The making of foreign policy is a marathon, not a sprint, and news coverage is one of many factors affecting its outcome. . . . News reporting may speed up decision-making or make a small matter sud-denly loom large" (Seib, 1997, 151).

Information is not merely a matter of developing and satisfying the public's intellectual curiosity. In ventures such as the Middle East conflict, public sup-port or disapproval of government policies should be based on information from diverse sources, including both journalistic and governmental ones. In-formation should not be controlled by politicians who then manipulate con-stituents' ignorance. The democratic process is undermined by inadequate knowledge.

Journalists help shape policy, not just report about it. They have consider-able influence on whether the decision makers and politicians reach a decision. In their role as information providers, the news media are not entirely neutral. They make important choices regarding what to cover and what to ignore; what resources to expend in coverage; how to present stories; and whether to do follow-up reports. "Journalists might throw their news-gathering net far enough to reach events that otherwise would go undiscovered" (Seib, 1997, 142).

Commenting on the relationship between news and policy, Walter Lippmann (1922) said, "the press is like the beam of a searchlight that moves restlessly about, bringing one episode and then another out of darkness into vision. . . . When this light is turned upon men, it reveals a situation intelligible enough for a popular decision."

Huth (1988) argued that the news media role in foreign policy should be "to facilitate coherent decision in an incoherent environment" (2). According to Huth, the lack of reliable information about an adversary in any conflict might lead to more complications. "Policy makers do not know exactly which points and messages need to be emphasized and which need to be clarified when communicating with the adversary," he said. It is the role of the news media to highlight such points (2).

In many situations, uncertainty is a result of scant information about the attitudes and beliefs of key decision makers within an opposing state and the nature of policy debates at the highest level of that government. For example, in the Middle East crisis of 1967, the initial buildup of Egyptian military forces along the Israeli border was intended to deter a potential attack by Israel against Syria. But Israeli leaders quickly perceived the potential for an offensive strike by Egypt and mobilized their own forces to strike first if necessary. This led to the start of a war between the two sides. Therefore, the policy makers' unsuccessful policy, resulting from a lack of information about their adversaries' intentions, "not only [failed] to deter the use of military force but [provoked] armed conflict [and made] it more likely in the future" (Huth, 1988, 11).

Political scientist Patrick O'Hefferman (1994) surveyed 483 high-level officials and senior policy makers serving the U.S. federal government between November 1977 and March 1988 about their perceptions of the role of the news media in making American foreign policy. Results of this survey showed that 87 percent of the respondents could recall cases when the news media were the only source of information available for decision making, and 65 percent agreed that the news media were frequently the fastest source of information for policy making.

A significant aspect of the news media role as a rapid information source is the degree to which it is used at the earliest stage of the policy cycle, the "problem identification stage." Seventy-four percent of the foreign policy respondents to O'Hefferman's survey indicated that the news media have some impact at this stage, compared to 26 percent who indicated no effect. More than 80 percent of the foreign policy officials said they rely heavily on the news media in formulating foreign policy.

The political system is interested in how knowledge is utilized by individual citizens and groups. Therefore, the state intervenes in knowledge creation and diffusion, believing its actions will affect knowledge in use which, in turn, will produce behavior supporting state goals. In doing that, the state can either allow a free flow of information with minimal restrictions or it can exercise considerable control over the news media by direct operation censorship, restrictive codes, and control of materials.

Some political regimes allow for a high degree of transparency, accountability, and information exchange. These regimes exercise little direct control over the news media and the flow of available information. Other regimes directly manipulate the entire media system by way of censors and content legislators. Both Israel and Egypt have some degree of government censorship over their news media. A discussion of the history of direct censorship practiced by the Israeli and the Egyptian governments over the news media will help readers understand the nature of the government-media relationship in both countries.

DIRECT CENSORSHIP IN EGYPT

When President Gamal Abdel Nasser took over the regime following the 1952 revolution that ended the British occupation, he soon became convinced that the press and the flow of information should be brought under control as closely as possible. Criticism tended to be directed only at low-level employees, and the "semi"-official press became increasingly loaded with propagandistic material on Arab socialism, nationalism, and unity.

For resident foreign correspondents, it was extremely hard to obtain information during Nasser's reign. Access to ministries was restricted and officials were reluctant to take on the responsibility of imparting facts. "Secrecy became the watchword—secrecy for its own sake, and invoked as part of the strategy for the battle with Israel. The avoidance of anything but a disparaging mention of Israel was carried to ridiculous lengths. It had the dangerous effect of sealing Egyptians off from worlds other than those of the Arabs" (McDermott, 1988, 242).

Several measures of direct censorship were introduced. The May 1960 legislation ruled that no newspaper could be licensed without the permission of the ruling party. Government control was exercised partly by the presence of censors in newspaper offices and partly through self-censorship. "The big stick loomed over all this in the form of the unpleasant threat of jail, a threat which Nasser did not hesitate to use" (McDermott, 1988, 243). Nasser maintained extensive oversight of the press from 1953 on, through frequent personal contact with the major papers' editors, direct and personal editing of the papers' contents, and tight coordination with the Ministry of Information. That ministry housed the Bureau of Censorship, which was regularly informed of black-listed topics. "The bureau scrupulously blocked stories on government-related corruption, while the government papers remained at the beck and call of key regime elites" (Beattie, 1994, 137).

The regime's relationship with the Journalists' Syndicate (a government-owned but independently operated organization that organizes journalists' work at newspapers) underlined its "interventionist" policy. The syndicate's executive council was dissolved in 1954 and a new pro-government council was appointed.

Nasser was highly suspicious of journalists and intellectuals. "As with his treatment of a succession of experiments with single-party political organizations, he feared that anything which might become established could use its power to foment hostility against him" (McDermott, 1988, 244).

The nationalization of the press in 1960 has been described by many observers as the most drastic measure affecting press freedom in Egypt since at least 1900. Due to the absence of any criticism of Nasser and his regime, the press acquired the reputation of being dull and predictable in handling domestic affairs. Even after Egypt's defeat in the 1967 war against Israel, the press lacked the moral courage to initiate serious criticism. Journalists were unwilling to risk their only means of livelihood by voicing criticism that might have been interpreted as anti-revolutionary. This situation continued until Nasser's death in 1970 (Almaney, 1972).

There was no major transformation in the political role of the press from the Nasser to the Anwar Sadat periods. Sadat, who took over power in Egypt in 1970, regarded the press as an instrument for shaping public opinion in the government's interest. Like Nasser, Sadat continued to appoint trusted editors who were expected to self-censor their articles, and when they did not, they were removed. The Ministry of Information was abolished in 1977, but by 1980, a Higher Press Council charged with implementing a code of ethics on journalists had taken its place.

After the 1973 war, the government announced a new era of press freedom, and conservative journalists proscribed under Nasser began to reappear. But the removal of the editor in chief of one of the major national papers for allegedly trying to turn the paper into a "center of power" showed the regime was "unprepared to tolerate a major journalistic voice at variance with its basic policy" (Hinnebusch, 1985, 181). Sadat did permit the press a greater autonomy than it had enjoyed under Nasser. But it continued to take its cues from the regime. "The biggest change in the press under Sadat was not so much in the degree of freedom to write as in who enjoyed this freedom" (182). One of Egypt's most renowned journalists emphasized the paradox of the Nasser and the Sadat eras: "It is very strange, because Nasser would not interfere with our writing; he would imprison us. Sadat suppressed writing but did not imprison" (McDermott, 1988, 252).

A new era of democracy and lack of direct censorship over the press started when Hosni Mubarak succeeded Sadat in 1981. "Mubarak had no instinctive interest in the press beyond broad liberal ideas and a desire that neither the state, the Presidency, nor the armed forces should be insulted or undermined by criticism" (McDermott, 252). The result was that he did not intervene as Nasser and Sadat had done.

What has happened under Mubarak has produced perhaps the most stimulating period in the press since the 1920s and 1930s. The censor in the Information Minister's office in the Television Building remains, and consultation at the editorial level continues, however, there is far less presidential direction. The parties do apply some censorship on their own publications, mainly in the interest of self-preservation. But otherwise, "even traditional foes of the predominant authority of the Presidency have welcomed Mubarak's era. The greater freedom has allowed some thoughtful and lengthy criticism of government policy" (McDermott, 1998, 252).

DIRECT CENSORSHIP IN ISRAEL

News media in Israel are closely related to the structure of the political system on two levels: the direct link between particular news organizations and their sponsoring bodies and the indirect influence of the center on the distribution of information in the nonaffiliated media (Galnoor, 1982). However, regardless of their political affiliations, all the news media in Israel have a self-imposed constraint on their autonomy: state security. Throughout the state period, security and foreign affairs remained such sensitive matters that there was widespread agreement that the news media should be restricted in these matters. Thus, most newspapers operated within the boundary of the national consensus, especially in security affairs.

In this context, Peri (1993) noted that "the history of the Jewish people and the Zionist movement have left a deep imprint on Israeli perception of security. Israeli views on the subject rest on a deep foundation of beliefs and fundamental presuppositions regarding basic issues of Jewish collective existence: Is the world essentially hostile or not? . . . . Is national existence guaranteed. . . . or does the threat of annihilation constantly hover over us" (346)?

Secrecy and publicity laws in Israel prescribe everything official to be secret unless disclosure is specifically permitted. The widely shared agreement about the necessity to withhold information concerning security and foreign policy contributes to general government control of information. According to Karl (1983), there are three kinds of censorship in Israel: Censorship at the source, where the journalists are not given correct information, or they know half of the truth, but the other half may be much more important; military censorship, to which all domestic and foreign dispatches on military matters are subject; and voluntary censorship, where the reporters themselves abstain from criticizing the government or directing unpleasant questions to the official sources.

The Military Censor is authorized to prevent the publication of any material that in his opinion would be, or be likely to become, prejudicial to the defense of Israel or to the public safety or to public order. Such measures enable the political regime to suppress legally the publication of all information. "More important perhaps, they enable the release of information to carefully chosen people and at selected times. This created an effective system of cooptation according to which information is released only to those who are 'reliable' " (Karl, 1983, 230).

The authority of the military machine in Israel extends to include all other bodies, including the press. "The military organization is motivated to play a key role, if not to supersede other groups in the making of national security policy" (Perlmutter, 1978, 201). In this way, the Israeli state radio was subject to direct government control; and the newspapers accepted as a natural situation their complete dependence on official sources for information about security and foreign affairs. They seldom question the content of an official release on these matters. On security issues, such as raids across the borders, Israelis knew only the official version of the story (Galnoor, 1982).

An example of an event in which the state tried to withhold "sensitive" news concerned the Israeli invasion of the Suez Canal in Egypt in 1956. Publication of foreign reports discussing Israeli collaboration with France and Britain in this invasion were banned in Israel and denied through the news media.

Another incident that witnessed direct censorship by the Israeli government was the Israeli invasion of Lebanon on June 6, 1982. During that invasion, Israeli troops were relying entirely on Lebanese radio for their information on the war, and they found these reports more accurate than their own army's announcements. . . . A combination of heavy censorship and misinformation by an army spokesman had allowed the war to expand without the country's realizing it. The untruths dispensed by the army undermined the commanders' credibility among the troops.

Karl (1983) cited a *Time* article of June 21, 1982, describing the problems of foreign correspondents covering the Israeli invasion of Lebanon from Israel. During transmissions of stories, telephone lines were cut and film was confiscated at the Tel Aviv airport. David K. Shipler, *New York Times* bureau chief in Jerusalem during that time, complained of military censorship: "It is pretty frustrating," he said. "We can go in and ask the military spokeman what is going on, but we will not get very much" (297).

Despite this strict censorship, when it came to security issues, many political parties used their newspapers to initiate campaigns for or against the government and to publish official information that could support their positions. On several occasions, damaging information in Israel has been published in one newspaper or another. The margin of independence of all the news media in Israel grew considerably after the 1973 war. "As the boundaries of the national consensus grew problematic, there was less self-restraint and a growing emphasis on the people's right to know" (Galnoor, 1982, 231).

CONCLUSION

It is clear from this chapter that there are major differences between Israel and Egypt regarding the nature of the relationship between government and the news media. As the chapter highlighted, both countries have different forms of direct censorship, but they differ in the way they practice it.

In the next chapter I further explain the government-media relationship by using the newsmaking model—one of two models used in this study to describe how the government deals with the news media.

11

THE NEWSMAKING MODEL FOR THE ANALYSIS OF GOVERNMENT-MEDIA RELATIONSHIPS IN ISRAEL AND EGYPT

Several theories and communication models have tried to address the nature of the relationship between the government and the news media. However, the two models that have best described the government-press relationship with all its complexities and that are best suited for this study are the newsmaking model and the two-way asymmetric model. Although these models seem to be similar in that they highlight the role of the government bureaucracy and the news organization in the exchange of information about public events, there are major differences between them.

In this chapter, I present a detailed examination of the newsmaking model, how it developed, who the major contributors were, and how it approaches the relationship between the government and the news media. I will also use the newsmaking model to describe the nature of the government-press relationship in Israel and Egypt.

NEWSMAKING MODEL

The newsmaking model was introduced by Richard Ericson, Patricia Baranek, and Janet Chan (1987), who argued that "news can be seen as the product of the interaction of two bureaucracies—one composed of newsmen and the other of officials . . . The reporter and the official use each other to advantage their own organization: the former exploits his contacts in the government to obtain exclusives; the latter exploits the need for news to deliver messages to key audiences" (40).

This model is a development of the early gatekeeping concept that originated in work carried out by Kurt Lewin (1947) dealing with housewives' decisions about household food purchases. Lewin argued that food reaches the family table through "channels," which start with the grocery store, where food is purchased. He concluded that not all members of the population are equally important in determining what is eaten, and that social change could best be accomplished by concentrating on those people with the most control over food selection for the home (Shoemaker, 1991).

Lewin's concept was taken up and applied by White (1950) in a study of a wire editor on a small-city newspaper, whom White called "Mr. Gates." The study showed that the editor's selection decisions were based on his subjective opinions and on his personal evaluation of the merits of the story's content. "Mr. Gates" also acted on behalf of his organization and profession (routine level). For example, he rejected some of the stories because there was not enough space for them or because other similar stories had run or were already running (385). White's gatekeeping concept was criticized for being limited in that it does not recognize that multiple gatekeepers may each have their own role conceptions or positions in the gathering, shaping, and transmission of news (McQuail & Windahl, 1993).

Bass (1969) refined the gatekeeping model by introducing a new concept in which the gatekeeping activity is the result of a "double-action internal news flow" involving news gathering and news processing. News gatherers (reporters and writers), according to Bass, make raw news (events and speeches) into news copy or news items. News processors (editors and copyreaders) modify and integrate the items into the "completed product" that can be transmitted to the audience.

Galtung and Ruge (1965) said gatekeeping involved successive selections of news events according to a number of news values or criteria that affect the perception of these events. They said that these criteria are shared by gatekeepers, and, therefore, they are systematic and predictable. According to Galtung and Ruge, the nine criteria determining the selection of news events are as follows:

1. Time span (events coinciding with the time frame of the media are more likely to pass through media gates)
2. Intensity of threshold value (events of great magnitude are more likely to pass through media gates)
3. Clarity/lack of ambiguity (events whose meaning is in doubt have less selection chances)
4. Cultural proximity or relevance (events of close cultural relevance for the intended audience have good chances of being selected)

5. Consonance (events' congruency with expectations are preferred by gatekeepers)
6. Unexpectedness (unusual events are most likely to be selected)
7. Continuity (selecting an event once gives it more chances for being selected in the future)
8. Composition (some news events are selected because they are different from others in the entirety)
9. Sociocultural values (values of both gatekeepers and their societies can influence selection above and beyond the other eight factors).

These news criteria have been integrated into Ericson, Baranek, and Chan's (1987) newsmaking model, but with some major modifications as was mentioned.

They argued that news brings to mind events in the world through the accounts of journalists and their sources. Using their sources, journalists offer their own versions of events as they think they are most appropriately visualized. They believe that deviance is the defining characteristic of what journalists regard as newsworthy, and they defined deviance as "the behavior of a thing or person that strays from the normal." "Visualizing deviance . . . allows journalists to act as watchdogs, policing organizational life for deviations from their conceptions of the order of things. In turn, this watchdog role allows journalists to bring into relief the normal or expected state of affairs" (5).

According to Ericson and his colleagues' model, bargaining along bureaucratic lines within the newspaper determines who covers a story, what changes editors make in the copy a reporter files, and how much play a story gets. Officials, in turn, disclose information as a by-product of their own bureaucratic politics—in an effort to initiate support for a particular course of action.

The model portrays a two-stage process involving source organization and news media. The source organization transforms a specific occurrence into an event that is potentially available to the reporter as news. The source's preselection of this occurrence is filtered according to a set of news factors, including timing, freedom of information, organizational visibility, and ability to give an account that satisfies news-media criteria of rational acceptability.

Communication between source organizations and the news media can take place through a variety of channels, from the highly structured (official reports, news conferences, news releases) to the less structured (telephone or personal interviews) to the unstructured (reporter learns of an event by chance or on proactive initiative within the source organization). News organizations apply other sets of news criteria (timing, space, material, and technical constraints) before choosing what finally enters the medium in the form of news event accounts.

Journalists and their sources use social and cultural resources together as they turn occurrences into events for public use. "In this respect, sources join with journalists as newsmakers, transforming amorphous happenings in the world into a meaningful structure that has potential as a news event" (Molotch & Lester, 1974, 102).

News organizations and source organizations overlap, and in some respects become part of each other. Reporters develop regular relationships with sources, share in their organizational cultures, and even occupy space within the walls of the organizations they report on. Sources reciprocate in various ways, are invited to meet with editors and management, and are asked to write or produce features or columns for the news organization. "A fluidity develops across organizational boundaries, as the reporter finds a niche within the source organization" (Weick, 1979, 88). The news organizations, in their coverage of events at political and governmental institutions, act as a crucial link between culture and politics in a way that is seen as indispensable to democratic government.

The news media are important players in the political arena, helping to construct the ideology that makes autonomous politics possible. "Politicians and journalists share in the construction of ideology by framing the public culture . . . This is the culture of investigation of adversaries, of policing organized life" (Ericson, Baranek, & Chan, 1987, 40).

Graber (1997) identified four models of the news-making process. First among these models is the "mirror model," contending that news is a reflection of reality and that newspeople observe the world around them and report what they notice as accurately and objectively as possible. Critics of the mirror model pointed out that this conception of news making is unrealistic, as journalists choose what they wish to observe and report in a way that matches their own ideologies. In this context, Ericson, Baranek, and Chan (1987) said "a newspaper is not a mirror of reality, but a 'mobile spotlight' focusing on particular people, organizations and troubles" (22).

Second among Graber's models is the "professional model," in which news making is viewed as "an endeavor of highly skilled professionals who put together [an] interesting collage of events selected for importance, attractiveness to media audiences and balance among the various elements of the news offering" (1997, 23). The third is the "organizational model," which contends that determination of what items will become news emerges from the pressures inherent in the organizational processes and goals. The final model is the "political model," which rests on the assumption that news reflects the ideological biases of individual newspeople, as well as the pressures of the political environment in which the news organization operates. "High-status people and approved institutions are covered by the media; people and events outside the dominant system or remote from the centers of power are generally ignored" (24).

REPORTERS' BEATS

Roscho (1975) pointed out that one of the fundamental aspects of news making is reporters' beats. According to Roscho, assigning reporters to beats is essential for establishing and maintaining a functional relationship between sources and reporters through which they routinely exchange news for publicity. He defined beats as "locations likely to offer a steady stream of timely information—that is, recent events of broad current interest that can be reported with the requisite immediacy. . . . On those beats, the reporters' ability to observe the sources' visibility and the information's timeliness are optimal" (72). By routinizing the seemingly nonroutine, these beats help the press in managing uncertainty and meeting its organizational requirements.

On most beats, the source symbolizes incorporation of news reporting into the organization by providing office facilities for journalists. On beats, journalists become part of the source organization, not only physically, but also socially and culturally. In this context, Ericson, Baranek, and Chan et al. (1989) argued that journalists "become socialized into the occupational culture of sources on the beat to the point where the relation between their understanding and values coheres with that of their sources. This level of socialization means that the signwork done by sources does not conflict with what the journalist finds agreeable" (7).

According to Ericson, Baranek, and Chan, reporters and sources on the beat become involved in a process of ongoing reciprocity through which sources are able to refine their accountability in terms of news discourse, which in turn allows them to achieve organizational accountability to the publics that concern them. The reciprocity on news beats includes knowledge being passed from journalists to sources. The journalist can offer a source knowledge about upcoming plans or events of other organizations that are of strategic relevance to the source. Reporters can also inform the source about other people in the source organization, whose activities might have a bearing on those of the source. Most significantly, the journalist can provide guidance to the source regarding how to formulate news accounts in a manner that will ensure access to the news media.

REPORTERS AND OFFICIALS

Most of the information on which reporters rely in covering news events comes from officials and government sources. "Official viewpoints are likely to be particularly dominant when reporters must preserve access to their special beats, such as the Pentagon or Justice Department, or when story production requires government assistance in collecting or gaining access to data" (Graber, 1997, 124).

For the reporters, most news is not what has happened, but what someone says has happened. This makes the choice of sources crucial. "Who the sources are bears a close relationship to who is news" (Manoff & Schudson, 1986, 25). One academic study found that as a consequence of reporters' news-gathering routines, which favor government officials as news sources, nearly half of the sources for all national and foreign news stories on page one of the *New York*

Times and the *Washington Post* in 1985 were officials of the U.S. government (Manoff & Schudson, 1986).

Gans (1979) argued that there are several criteria for the selection of government sources by news reporters. Gans said reporters, in applying these criteria, have only a short time to gather information and must therefore attempt to obtain the most suitable news from the fewest number of sources as quickly and as easily as possible, and with the least strain on the organization's budget.

First among these criteria is past suitability. If sources have provided information leading to suitable stories in the past, they are apt to be chosen again, until they eventually become regular sources. However, some regular sources are liable to supply repetitious information over time, and in this case, journalists become "bored" with some of them. Sources representing single-purpose organizations, who continually deal with the same issue are likely to be dropped from the news.

Another criterion for reporters' selection of official sources is productivity. Sources are judged by their ability to supply a lot of information without undue expenditure of reporters' time and effort. In their news-gathering process, reporters try to minimize the number of sources to be consulted. This accounts for the predominance of high public officials in the news. As spokespersons for their agencies, those officials can spare journalists' time and effort by eliminating the need to interview other agency members.

Third among the criteria for selection of sources is reliability. Reporters look for reliable sources whose information requires the least amount of checking. However, if a story is controversial, reporters are expected to gather proof from at least two separate and independent sources.

The fourth criterion is trustworthiness. When reliability cannot be checked quickly enough, story selectors look for trustworthy sources who are known for their accuracy and honesty. Journalists often have difficulty in judging the trustworthiness of their sources. This is because most journalists have a natural distrust for politicians, who are deemed to be inherently "two-faced" and inconsistent. Journalists believe that many politicians "come to them with self-serving motives that they are not always inclined to be completely honest." Officials who cooperate with journalists and treat them cordially are likely to be trusted more than others. Moreover, sources in positions of formal authority are considered more trustworthy than others.

Authoritativeness is the fifth of Gans' criteria for selecting sources. "All other things being equal, journalists prefer to resort to sources in official positions of authority and responsibility." When stories become controversial, journalists can defend themselves before news executives by having relied on authoritative sources. Moreover, story suggesters can sell stories from these sources more easily than from other sources. Newspeople naturally go after the official who is given discretion by his governmental organization in publicity matters and who is kept informed of organizational decisions as they are reached. Therefore, reporters tend to regard the official as important to them only after he is assigned critical tasks of responsibility within his agency or department. An official without discretion is expendable by reporters.

Government officials also have their own criteria for selecting the news reporters to whom they can release information. The distinctions that determine preferred treatment on the part of the officials are primarily defined by the status of the reporters and the media strategies of their news agencies. Reporters' status depends on location, assignment, seniority, ability, and employer. Most U.S. officials prefer to deal with reporters from Washington. Those officials believe that Washington reporters are more knowledgeable and easier to deal with than those from other parts of the country (Hess, 1984).

Officials, well aware of reporters' needs, are not above turning these needs to their own advantage. The reporter's urgent need to have access to a specific official gives that official a measure of control. In his comment on this situation, George Reedy, former White House press secretary, said, "It is impossible to grant everyone access and therefore, the access that can be granted must be carefully and painstakingly determined" (cited in Sigal, 1973, 53).

Nimmo (1964) mentioned that there are three basic patterns of relationship between government sources and news reporters. The first pattern is cooperation, in which the reporter and the government official are in regular contact. Each is a primary source or channel for the other. They cooperate to communicate to the citizen. In this case, reporters share views of their personal responsibilities with their sources. The second pattern is compatibility, which occurs when officials and reporters utilize each other's services less consistently and not to the exclusion of using other sources or channels. There is less harmony between actors in this relationship than in the cooperative type, but enough remains to resolve the conflicts that might disrupt relations entirely. Such harmony stems from similar, although not identical, views held by reporters and their official sources.

The third pattern characterizing the relationship between officials and reporters is competition. In this pattern, there is minimal contact between officials and reporters. "Divergent views of their roles as political communicators make this relationship basically competitive" (Sigal, 1973, 106).

Graber (1997) argued that the government-press relationship can be classified into three types. First among these types is the fear of adverse publicity. In this situation, newspeople bully politicians and other public figures into action by threatening to publicize stories that these people would prefer to conceal. Unlike overt threats, which are rare, implied or anticipated threats can have major political consequences. Politicians often act or refrain from acting because they know that newspeople might publish damaging information. Politicians particularly fear adverse publicity from influential columnists.

Policy makers also fear premature publicity, through which they are forced to take a public position on a policy during the formulation stage, making this position different from what it would have been at a later stage, after negotiation and compromise. This premature publicity hardens positions, reduces flexibility, and lessens bargaining room because once a position has been publicized, it becomes difficult to change (Dunn, 1969).

Another type of government-media relationship is that of news personnel acting as surrogates for public officials by actively participating in an evolving situation, such as diplomatic impasse. The solution, developed with the assistance of news personnel or at their initiative, may shape the government action. Walter Cronkite's impact on relations between Israel and Egypt, by serving as a go-between, is a famous example of diplomacy conducted by journalists.

A third type of interaction between the news media and government occurs when the reporters become mouthpieces for government officials, either because of belief in their causes or in return for attractive stories and other favors. This type of interaction often involves leaks. "Government officials who are disgruntled with current policies or practices for personal, professional or political reasons may leak information to sympathetic journalists to enlist their support" (Graber, 1997, 167). Journalists may cooperate and publish the allegations, or they may investigate the situation with the cooperation of the official sources who leaked the information.

INFORMATION LEAKS

Hess (1984) defined a leak as "a premature unauthorized partial disclosure of informative material by a public official, whose domain is the formal channels of information" (75). The primary reason officials try to stay away from leaks, according to former presidential press secretary George Reedy, is that since manipulation of the press involves favoritism to some newsmen, it inevitably creates antagonism among others. According to Hess, there are several types of leaks made by public officials. First among these types is the "ego leak," which involves giving information primarily to satisfy a sense of self-importance. "This type of leak is popular with staff who have fewer outlets for ego tripping." Another type of leak is the "goodwill leak," which is "a play for a future favor." The primary purpose of this leak is to "accumulate credit with a reporter, which the leaker hopes can be spent at a later date." This type of leak is often on a subject with which the leaker has no personal involvement (76).

A third type of leak is the "policy leak," which is "a straightforward pitch for or against a proposal using some document or insiders' information as the lure to get more attention than might otherwise be justified." Famous leaks, such as the Pentagon papers in 1971, fit in this type. Another category of leaks is the "animus leak used to settle grudges." In this leak, information is disclosed to embarrass another person (76).

The last type of leak is the "trial-balloon leak," which involves revealing a proposal that is under consideration in order to assess its assets and liabilities.

"Usually proponents have too much invested in a proposal to want to leave it to the vagaries of the press and public opinion" (Hess, 1984, 77).

In his comment on the government's "leaking" policy in dealing with the press, Wise (1973) said:

In the years following World War II, government and the press in Washington played a game of cat and mouse. The rules of the game were never articulated, but they went something like this: government officials would leak classified information to reporters when it suited their purposes, and reporters understood that they were free to use this material. But reporters who obtained access to embarrassing government secrets on their own, perhaps from dissident officials within the government, or who delved into the operations of the Central Intelligence Agency could never be entirely certain what actions the government might take against them. (145)

Wise maintained that leaking official secrets by government sources to reporters is part of a political game played by the government to achieve certain political ends. "The government hides what it can . . . and the press pries out what it can. . . . Each side in this game regularly 'wins' and 'loses' a round or two" (1973, 106).

REPORTERS' ASSIMILATION

Reporters and their official sources can collaborate and develop an intimate relationship in which "the boundary between ordinary reporting and manipulative journalism can become blurred" (Gieber & Johnson, 1961, 294). In this situation, politicians try to "co-opt reporters for their own purposes, wining and dining them, giving them exclusive stories, or plying them with secret information they cannot publish" (295). This leads to assimilation, which involves the existence of a mutual benefit between reporters and their sources, reaching a point in which it conflicts with the reporters' independence and professional norms. Assimilation can lead to the suppression or the manipulation of information in the interest of politicians. This is because regular contact between journalists and their sources may lead to some degree of personal identification and friendship, which may result in a hesitancy on the part of the journalists to reveal information that might harm or create a barrier between them and their sources. "Experienced reporters seem to be able to escape co-optation, even while they enjoy being flattered with invitations and leaks; and they learn to endure a politician's wrath when his or her flattery does not stave off a critical story" (Gans, 1979, 134). Murphy (1976) pointed out that there are several stages involved in the interaction between reporters and news sources at the local level. The first stage is making contact, and it refers to the initial step in which the reporter locates the news source or the news source locates the reporter. Identification is the second stage, and it refers to stating one's own purpose and use and finding out the purpose and use of the other actor. The third stage is bargaining, and it refers to the competitive-cooperative process by which journalists attempt to get information from their sources and by which the source gets favorable publicity out of the journalist or attempts to prevent him from publishing something the source does not like. The final stage is the collection of data. The data that are collected are related to both the intentions of the source and the preconceptions the journalist brings to the story.

Sigal (1973) argued that reporters pay a price for access to official sources: they become dependent on their official sources. Dependence includes reluctance to offend news sources in the stories they write; considerable willingness to print whatever their sources tell them; and little or no insistence that officials take responsibility for the information they pass along. "The pressure to get news makes reporters reluctant to reject information provided through routine channels, lest they jeopardize their access through less formal channels" (54).

WHO HAS THE UPPER HAND: REPORTERS OR OFFICIALS?

Government officials try to centralize the distribution of information through routine channels, thereby guaranteeing a means of influencing governmental outcomes. Senior officials employ a variety of tactics against reporters on the beat to restrict news gathering to routine channels. One tactic is to keep the reporters busy with a steady stream of information through these channels "on the premise that the best way to keep the press from peering into dark corners is to shine a light elsewhere" (Sigal, 1973, 54). Another set of official tactics involves criticizing reporters or complaining to editors and publishers.

In the bargaining process, reporters also have resources and tactics at their disposal. "Like bees cross-pollinating in a garden, they do get around their beat and usually have tidbits of information to trade with understanding officials." Most officials want their side of the story told, especially if they know that the reporter intends to write the story, with or without using them as the source. "Reporters must bargain for news with sources who hold most of the chips, and newsgathering turns into a series of compromises with the principle of telling everything they know" (Sigal, 1973, 55).

Many scholars agree that official sources have the upper hand in their relationship with reporters. Gans (1979) argued that sources have somewhat more power than reporters, because they can punish reporters by withholding information, thereby putting them at a disadvantage with their peers from competing news media. Roscho (1975) mentioned that one of the most frequently used techniques by government officials to control the reporters dealing with them is providing those reporters with "off-the-record" information. In dealing with such information, "the reporter is saddled with the responsibility of implicitly claiming a degree of knowledge about matters he has only some acquaintance with. The actual source, if he becomes known, may disclaim responsibility for disseminating the information and even reverse his intended policy, leaving the reporter unable to prove the 'truth' of what he had reported" (89).

According to Roscho, many senior government officials prefer to remain anonymous, especially when conveying information regarding a controversial issue. The more highly placed a reporter's sources, the more likely that they will prefer to conceal their identity, even when their information is wholly accurate. The reporter who insists on not using unattributable or unverified information may find himself uninformed about highly newsworthy matters. "Would-be sources seeking to manage the news for their own political ends, would turn to more amenable reporters, willing to publish anonymous information for their own professional ends" (1975, 90). Roscho also stated that "the most overt form of news management by government is censorship, which may take varying degrees of severity as the censoring source seeks to assure the invisibility of certain data" (91). An example that would illustrate a form of censorship practiced by American public officials is the censorship imposed by the CIA on former employees who try to make money by selling stories about their work at the CIA to the press.

INFORMATION SUBSIDIES

Gandy (1982) pointed out that a far more popular technique used by governments to control their news sources is the information subsidy (press releases, official reports, etc. issued by government agencies). He also pointed out that an information subsidy is an attempt to produce influence over the actions of others by controlling their access to and use of information relevant to those actions. This information is characterized as a subsidy because the source of that information causes it to be made available at something less than the cost a user would face in the absence of the subsidy.

Subsidy givers have an incentive to hide or disguise their relationship to the information they provide, in order to maximize its use by the relevant others. The delivery of an information subsidy through the news media may involve an effort that reduces the cost of producing news faced by a reporter. Faced with time constraints and the need to produce stories suitable for publication, journalists find themselves obliged to use the governments' subsidized material. "By reducing the costs faced by journalists in satisfying organizational requirements, the subsidy giver increases the probability that the subsidized information will be used. The journalist receives a direct information subsidy, and the target in government receives an indirect subsidy when the information is read in the paper or heard on the news" (Gandy, 1982, 62).

According to Gandy, the quality of the information subsidy is determined by the credibility of the information source. If the source's credibility is low because of his obvious interest in the outcome of a decision, that source has an incentive to present the information through a more credible, disinterested source. "Journalists, garbed in a cloak of objectivity, are valued as channels through which to deliver an information subsidy without having to pay a credibility tax" (1982, 198).

Because of these control techniques practiced by government sources over reporters, it is argued that journalists are "conduit pipes" and "secondary definers" in relation to their sources.

THE PRESS HAS POWER OVER OFFICIALS

Ericson, Baranek, and Chan (1989) argued that news media are very powerful, in possession of key resources that frequently give them the upper hand. According to Ericson and his colleagues, there is considerable variation with regard to who is in control, depending on the context, the type of sources and news organizations involved and what is at issue. Some source organizations are more powerful than others in routinizing news access and shaping the public conversation. In the meantime, some journalists are more powerful and influential than others in dealing with people in authority.

Ericson and his colleagues stated that "all news outlets have some fundamental assets that put them in a powerful position: the power to deny a source any access; the power to sustain coverage that contextualizes the source negatively; the power of the last word (the news outlet can choose to exclude additional comments from the aggrieved source, to edit those comments as it sees fit, or to juxtapose those comments in its own commentary in order to undercut them); and the power of translation of specialized and particular knowledge into common sense" (1989, 378).

Sigal (1973) followed the same line by saying that most people have been concerned about "access for the press," and how the governors exercise control over the information released to the governed, but very few people have expressed concern about "access to the press," and how the news media can control which sources can have access to them. According to Sigal, government officials go after the news media because they want to increase their publicity and enhance their public image. Moreover, the existence of rival government bureaus with alternative information can increase the efforts of these bureaus to access reporters and reduce the likelihood of control over those reporters.

One of the reasons that makes the press powerful in its relationship with the government, according to Sigal, is that the press is a source of much of the important information that the government gets about itself and its own parts. "The significant impact of the press upon the President," argued George Reedy, "lies not in its critical reflections but in its capacity to tell him what he is doing as seen through other eyes . . . Virtually all other communications that reach him will be shaped either directly or indirectly by people who wish either to conciliate or to antagonize the Chief Executive" (cited in Sigal, 1973, 186).

According to Sigal, "the press, in amplifying some political voices and muting others, in distorting some messages and letting others come through loud and clear, affects the nature of governance" (187).

REPORTERS' CRITERIA IN SELECTING INFORMATION

As I mentioned earlier, a significant aspect in the newsmaking model is the criteria set by reporters and news organizations in their selection of which information is to be transformed into news stories. According to Ericson, Baranek, and Chan (1987), these criteria are based on the journalists' working and occupational ideologies, and they serve as a means for justifying the news product publicly to achieve and sustain legitimacy. Setting these criteria contributes to journalists' claim to authority and allows them to avoid offending important segments of the mass public.

Murphy (1976) stated that journalists' occupational ideologies are not just psychological or individual characteristics, but they are social and organizational contexts that provide journalists with the means "to perceive and construct reality in a way which legitimates their own positions vis-à-vis the distribution of power, wealth, prestige and other values" (47). According to Murphy, a journalist's formulation of occupational ideology is a combination of local values, which he has attained through living and working in a specific society, and his preconceived views as to what constitutes a good story—which he has acquired through his contacts with co-professionals. Murphy argued that there are four dominating constraints in a news organization: time, space, money, and circulation. The newspaper's continuous concern with an up-to-date coverage of events requires the ability to introduce last-minute changes to stories. It also demands a large journalistic staff and means maximizing the editorial content of the paper. All this involves additional expenditure of money and space.

Graber (1997) mentioned that the criteria newspeople use in story selection relate primarily to audience appeal rather than to the political significance or the educational and social values of the stories. According to Graber, newsworthiness is the main criterion used by editors in selecting stories for publication. There are five elements included in newsworthiness. First, stories must be likely to have a strong impact on readers or listeners. The more effect a story has on people's lives, the more likely they will be attracted to it. Second, the natural or man-made violence, conflict, disaster, or scandal make a story newsworthy.

The third element of newsworthiness is familiarity. News is attractive if it pertains to well-known people or involves familiar situations of concern to many people. Proximity is the fourth element of newsworthiness. People are more interested in local stories than they are in national or international stories. The fifth element is that news should be timely and novel in the sense that it has just occurred or it does not happen all the time.

NORMS AND PRACTICE IN JOURNALISM

The search for values, norms, and rules has been the dominant approach in the study of journalists' decisions. This approach was exemplified in the work of Chibnall (1977), who argued that journalists, in their news judgments, are guided by a normative paradigm, which includes a list of personal values and professional norms and rules. Chibnall referred to these rules as "the professional imperatives of journalism" (22).

Ericson, Baranek, and Chan (1987) pointed out that the normative approach in studying journalists' decisions and news judgments is problematic for a number of reasons. First among these reasons is that in news making, as in the case of other occupations, "there is a significant disjunction between the professional norms professed in the public culture and the degree of commitment to them by members of the working culture" (130). They believe that many academic researchers tend to accept the public-culture values and norms of journalism at face value, regardless of whether journalists are actually following their normative obligations in their everyday activities.

An example cited by Ericson and his colleagues that illustrates journalists' deviation from normative paradigm is the norm of objectivity and the high probability that it might not be applied by journalists. Within journalism, it is possible to act outside the strategic ritual of objectivity by using deceptive techniques of questioning and deceptive technologies of recording, or by using sources other than the authorized knowers of official bureaucracies.

Another problem involved in applying the normative paradigm to journalism as mentioned by Ericson and his colleagues is that there is a level of action that cannot be explained in terms of norms or rule-following. "It is commonplace in journalism, as in other occupational cultures, for its practitioners to say that their judgments do not entail following rules." It is common that many journalists engaged in a particular activity are unable to articulate the rules about it. Journalists' argument that news judgments are not rule-governed should be taken seriously as part of the recognition that it is not just norms and values that govern an organizational order.

According to Ericson and his colleagues, many journalists oppose the idea of following a written manual or a guidebook for journalistic practice. Reporters, in the course of preparing stories, do not consult the style manual regularly. Therefore, this style manual is impractical in the actual news-making process. "Learning the craft," they argued, "does not involve consultation of such authoritative texts. It comes from consulting news texts, being scrutinized by editors, talking to more experienced colleagues and doing the work" (1987, 132).

Journalists emphasize that they learn about their craft in a subtle way through daily interactions with reporters, sources, and editors. What is learned through experience is "recognition knowledge" (e.g., how to recognize an event or a source who is appropriate for a story); "procedural knowledge" (e.g., how to develop a story and to operate within time and resource constraints); and "accounting knowledge" (e.g., how to justify actions taken if someone questions what has been done). The "vocabulary of precedents," learned from colleagues, editors, sources, and content, is the stock of knowledge that enables journalists to make news judgments. This stock of knowledge is available only through on-the-job experience, and not written in copybook form (Ericson, Baranek, and Chan 1987).

GOVERNMENT-PRESS RELATIONSHIP IN EGYPT

There are strong incentives for Egyptian journalists to support the ruling regime and its policies, at least on issues about which the regime is sensitive. All of the editors in chief of the government-owned newspapers in Egypt are appointed by the president, who is also the head of the ruling National Democratic Party. This makes those editors loyal to the regime in their columns. Without an organized opposition party or group, there is no public criticism of the regime to report in the newspapers' columns, and the psychological atmosphere makes it very difficult for the newspaper columnist independently to voice criticism of the government (Rugh, 1987).

The press-government relationship in Egypt has witnessed several permutations of information control and management from Nasser's era until the present regime of Mubarak.

Information control took a variety of forms under Nasser and Sadat. Direct censorship procedures included press laws, codes of ethics, dismissal of journalists, seizures of papers and books, and withholding of newsprint from opposition papers. Subtle forms of censorship ranged from self-censorship to scare tactics against dissidents to public criticism of government opponents by the president (Nasser, 1982).

However, the Egyptian press is not "a dull, completely predictable and slavish mouthpiece of the regime" (Rugh, 1987, 43). It has its own character, style, and vitality. It is not just a "government publicity sheet." There is some room for expression of opinion without strict censorship. Even during the times when government censors were assigned to sit in newspapers' offices, there was some give-and-take policies between censors and editors, the latter sometimes arguing against specific orders with which they disagreed.

The Egyptian regime now influences the press primarily through its control over personnel. Editors in chief of government newspapers are aware, without being told explicitly, that they are expected to promote the government's policies. The ruling party, in appointing people to key editorial positions, makes sure that those people are going to be supportive of the government.

The Egyptian government, in its dealings with journalists, adopts the policy of "the stick of legal sanctions and the carrot of inside information." Under this policy, the ruling group can be coercive by using state powers, such as arrest and detention of journalists, to help enforce conformity with the regime's basic policies. Serious deviations from these basic policies by journalists can be used as a reason for arrest and punishment of offenders. In the meantime, the rewarding of "helpful" newspapermen by providing them with inside information that enhances their role as journalists is a technique used by the government. This technique reflects the political affinity between the ruling group and most of the leading journalists.

The most famous example of the symbiotic relationship between an Arab leader and a journalist is that of late Egyptian President Nasser and Mohammed Haykal, one of the most renowned Egyptian journalists. "Their thinking was similar; Nasser found him a useful sounding board for ideas while Haykal gained insights into the Egyptian leader's planning which made his columns more interesting" (Rugh, 1987, 41). Haykal's role as Nasser's adviser and participant in the decision-making process far exceeded that of a White House press secretary in the United States. "His power and influence resulted from several factors, including his eloquent style, fluent pen, and strong sense of news value. He introduced a new style in Arab journalism different from the sensationalism of other writers" (41). Several Egyptian government officials maintain personal ties and informal connections with key newspapermen, which they use to convey political guidance (42).

The marriage between politics and the press was vividly illustrated in Egypt under Nasser's regime during which the press was more supportive than critical of the political establishment. The period from 1952 to 1960 was marked by an unstable relationship between the political leaders and the press. During this period, censorship was imposed and lifted several times, and censors were appointed for every newspaper (Dabbous, 1994).

The first confrontation between government and the press took place in 1954, when Nasser briefly lifted press censorship. Nasser's critics took advantage of this opportunity and attacked him for failing to allow democracy in the country. This prompted the government to reimpose censorship one month later and to warn journalists against spreading doubts about the revolution.

Moreover, several measures were taken by the government to integrate the press into the regime. In 1956, a new constitution was issued, stating that "freedom of the press is safeguarded in the interest of public welfare and within the limits of law." In 1960, the Egyptian press was nationalized under the Press Organization Law, and a board of directors was appointed by the government to control and manage the press organizations (Dabbous, 1994).

Despite the government's tight control of the press under Nasser, the press-government relationship in Egypt was more relaxed than in other Arab countries. Egyptian papers were allowed to criticize government officials, but this criticism usually came in the wake of critical remarks already made by the president himself.

The 1967 war shook the foundation of Nasser's regime and exposed the flaws in the political system. Many critics started calling for press freedom. In 1968, the government signed a new law that would guarantee freedom for journalists in carrying out their journalistic mission.

After assuming power in 1970, Sadat began to relax press controls by opening news sources to reporters. However, press censorship continued, and all newspapers had resident censors to whom all copies were submitted. These censors were civilian government officials answerable to the Ministry of Information. The same direct censorship procedures (press laws, codes of ethics, dismissal of journalists, seizures of papers and books, and withholding newsprint from opposition papers) that were applied by Nasser's regime continued under Sadat's regime. These censorship procedures were used as a means to silence the government's critics.

In 1973, Sadat accused several Egyptian journalists of making contact with foreign correspondents with the aim of spreading unrest and tarnishing Egypt's reputation by supplying foreign mass media with false information. As a result, 64 journalists were fired. Moreover, Sadat accused the foreign correspondents in Cairo of distorting news coverage of Egypt, and he expelled some of them from Egypt for interviewing his outspoken critics. Sadat also closed publications of the Islamic opposition in Egypt for criticizing his peace treaty with Israel.

On February 2, 1974, Sadat issued a decree abolishing censorship except for military matters. This was seen as a trend toward more freedom for the press. In 1975, Sadat issued another decree establishing the first press council in Egypt with powers to approve the publication of newspapers and licensing of journalists.

In 1978, the Egyptian parliament added a new article to the Constitution saying that the press is "a fourth power of the people," and that "the people shall exercise their powers over the press as stipulated in the Constitution and the law" (Nasser, 1990, 16). In 1980, Law 148 was issued, dealing with the authority of the press and the rights and responsibilities of reporters. This new law conceived the press as "a fourth power of the people" after the executive, legislative, and judicial branches of the government. According to this law, "the people shall exercise their powers over the press as stipulated in the Constitution and the law . . . Freedom of the press shall be guaranteed, and press censorship shall be prohibited" (Nasser, 1990, 16). However, Sadat failed to make the democratic atmosphere prevail, and in September 1981, all the opposition papers were closed, and many leaders of the opposing parties were imprisoned.

When he took power in 1981, Mubarak showed more tolerance of criticism, and he was willing to allow more press freedom. He set free all the dissident journalists and gave the opposition parties the freedom to operate.

Although there is no direct censorship of the press, opposition papers suffer from another problem: all party papers must print at the national government-owned printing plants, thus giving the national press an advance look at any criticism directed at the government and a chance to respond promptly. "The present situation of the Egyptian press shows a substantial improvement in freedom, but not an unlimited one . . . However, Mubarak has restored to the press a moderate code of liberation that can be seen as the starting point for a long-term perspective on media development in Egypt" (Dabbous, 1994, 72).

GOVERNMENT-PRESS RELATIONSHIP IN ISRAEL

Since the establishment of the state of Israel in 1948, situational factors, Arab hostility, military considerations, and foreign interest in Israel have shaped and slanted the framework of the government-press relations. Given the continuing threat to Israel's national existence, there is a long-standing consensus among the Israeli journalists on the need for a tight secrecy policy that would prevent publishing certain matters that have to do with security (Goren & Rothman, 1982).

Arguments over what is really security information extend not only to military and foreign affairs or the strategic and economic capacity of the country but also to information that would be published without question in other countries, such as transportation routes, water resources, commercial links with other countries, and immigration. "The legitimacy of withholding information about security and foreign policy contributes to general secrecy and creates opportunities for governmental manipulation of information" (Galnoor, 1977, 178).

Foreign correspondents operating in Israel were as ready as Israeli journalists to recognize the existence of a national emergency that would legitimate the censorship of security information.

Because of the ongoing serious security problems in Israel, an "army censorship apparatus" has the authority to censor national security–related material, for by law all editorial matter must be sent to the censor prior to publication. "However, distinct evolution over time in the press' relationship to the governing authorities is discernible" (Lehman & Schejter, 1994, 110).

Israeli journalists with a deep commitment to the Zionist endeavor accept censorship as a choice, not an imposition by the government. In this context, Jim Lederman, a foreign correspondent with 25 years experience in the Middle East, claimed that Israeli journalists are co-opted by government officials and serve as functionaries of the state. Seen from his perspective, "Israeli journalists agree to a voluntary, self-policing type of censorship because the alternative, confrontation and ultimately control, is far less appealing" (cited in Liebes, 1997, 31).

In Israel, there is an internalizing hegemony among many editors and journalists who regard the censors' role as "legitimate, even crucial." For those journalists, the chief military censor is personally respected as a professional, "like a doctor who knows what is causing damage . . . It is almost as if the journalists are relieved of the burden of responsibility for deciding where the lines of free speech should be drawn" (Liebes, 1997, 34).

The Israeli newspapers used to be affiliated with and subsidized by the factions of the Zionist movement. This partisan press system gave politicians an effective weapon to fight press independence. The Israeli government used to set sanctions, including preventing access to government sources and applying economic pressures, on the newspapers that did not abide by the government's interests. In the years between 1948 and 1976, there was severe attrition of the partisan press, and many newspapers became politically independent.

At present, the performance of political reporters is only marginally constrained by the government. These reporters receive information through the organizational framework from official sources who provide both on-the-record and off-the-record briefings. Commitment to preservation of the state still defines the boundaries of the government-press relationship, but there is more elasticity in applying the commitment as a criterion of press performance (Goren & Rothman, 1982).

Military correspondents, on the other hand, are subject to more rigorous organizational constraints than their colleagues. Most journalists, even those who cover nonmilitary subjects, are members of the army spokesman's unit. In case of war, they become military correspondents, but in peacetime they are not in direct contact with the army. The military correspondent formally undertakes to comply with certain secrecy and censorship regulations. Military correspondents also receive a considerable amount of classified background information, which, because it is available to all accredited correspondents, enhances the uniformity of their stories.

Israeli reporters representing the prestigious papers, such as *Maariv* and the *Jerusalem Post*, have personal contacts with important political figures. Leaks are a major component of an elaborate exchange system through which these reporters receive politically sensitive information.

Galnoor (1977) noted that in Israel, "government affairs are formally very sensitive, yet a great deal of confidential information gets into circulation, occasionally concerning sensitive matters of security and foreign relations and quite regularly concerning internal deliberations on domestic issues" (176).

The shock of Israel's defeat in the 1973 war dramatically lessened the government's credibility and shook the foundations of the government-press relationship. Many journalists started to realize "the government's tendency to use 'security' as a blanket for covering up blunders and politically embarrassing information" (Galnoor, 1982, 178).

Many Israeli journalists have accused the government of abusing security issues for internal political purposes; moreover, the leading foreign correspondents in Israel publicly regretted their former willingness to accept the government's view of defense and military matters at face value. The President of the Association of Israeli Journalists, during meetings of the Israeli Press Council in 1974, stated:

It seems to me that we were unduly ready to stand to attention whenever the word "security" was uttered . . . We accepted official assessments of the situation without question because in the defense sphere, we did not develop norms for criticism and the exercise of independent judgment. We automatically agreed that there were people on whom we could rely with our eyes shut. (Goren & Rothman, 1982, 268)

The 1982 Lebanon War marked another watershed with extremely critical reports appearing in the Israeli press. The start of the Palestinian *Intifada* in late 1987 made Israeli journalists feel more of a need to publicly discuss all issues; and the rising economic competition between the mainstream daily newspapers heightened this trend.

Protest and intense criticism on the part of the Israeli journalists failed to introduce major alterations in the framework of government-press relations. "The task of reconciling legitimate security needs with the commitment to a free press and frank and open coverage of governmental policy and actions remains as formidable as ever . . . The core of the relationship turns on the continued willingness of the press and the government to maintain democratic values in a society that, since its inception, has been at war with its neighbors" (Goren & Rothman, 1982, 268).

The Israeli printed press is still regulated by the 1933 Press Ordinance, which states that "no newspaper can be published without previously receiving a license signed by the Ministry of Interior Affairs." The ordinance authorizes the Minister of Interior to close a newspaper for publishing "either a news item that might jeopardize the public's safety or a false account that causes panic or despair" (Lehman & Schejter, 1994, 121). The right to close a newspaper is also granted to the military censor, who is also entitled to review all the material intended for publication (prior restraint), confiscate printing presses used for printing forbidden materials, and forbid publication of material endangering the state security.

In addition to the military censor, the Israeli press is controlled by a self-regulatory body known as the Editors' Council. The council is a joint body including all the Hebrew-language dailies. It operates under an agreement in which matters of national security are brought by the government for discussion in informal meetings and will not be published.

Another self-regulatory body is the Press Council, which was formed in 1963 by the National Organization of Israeli Journalists, the Editors' Council and the newspaper management union. The Press Council oversees the ethical conduct of Israeli journalists, and issues ethical codes that apply to both members and nonmembers of the council. Israel's Arabic-language press is not part of the Editors' Council. Because of Israel's sensitivity to its security situation, "the Arabic press is held to stricter standards of political 'incitement' and discussion of military-related issues" (Lehman & Schejter, 1994, 122). As a result, Arabic-language papers have either been closed temporarily or forced to go out of business permanently.

A more educated citizenry and a gradual reduction of national security tensions are increasing the pressure on Israeli authorities to lessen censorship and other communication regulations. In line with greater liberalization of economic policy, the Israeli media scene attitudinally, philosophically, and organizationally is steadily more open to greater freedom of expression among the print media.

CONCLUSION

This chapter explained in detail the newsmaking model, and how it is used to explain the nature of the relationship between reporters and officials. The chapter also presented some of the criteria used by government officials in selecting the news reporters to whom they can release information and the criteria used by news reporters in selecting government sources. The chapter posed the question: Who has the upper hand: reporters or officials? As was clear from this chapter, the answer to that question depends on the resources and tactics available for the government sources and the news reporters.

In the next chapter I describe the one-way asymmetric model, which is the other model I used in this study to explain the nature of the relationship between the government and the news media.

12

THE PUBLIC RELATIONS ASYMMETRIC MODEL FOR THE ANALYSIS OF GOVERNMENT-PRESS RELATIONSHIPS IN ISRAEL AND EGYPT

Much of the research on the relationship between governments and the news media emphasizes the tremendous advantages enjoyed by political leaders over other sources. Political leaders are considered newsworthy, and the "newsbeat" system ensures officials routine access to the press. The government also enjoys an extremely high level of organization and resources that facilitate the production of newsworthy events and provides a sophisticated public relations system.

Governments, in their relationship with the press, apply several types of public relations and "bureaucratic propaganda" to improve their image in the public eye, present official reports in favorable terms, and survive through the appearance of legitimacy (Altheide & Johnson, 1980). Many governments appoint specialized public relations experts to help deliver the "right" messages to the "right" audiences using the "right" news media.

Analyzing the nature of the relationship between the government and the press in Israel and Egypt requires the study of public relations patterns that are practiced by policy makers and politicians in their dealings with the press.

WHAT ARE PUBLIC RELATIONS?

Grunig and Hunt (1984) defined public relations as "the management of communication between an organization and its publics" (8). The news media can be used to promote the messages of a specific organization among its public. Communication in public relations can be of many kinds, ranging from one-way to two-way interactive processes.

PUBLIC RELATIONS MODELS

Public relations strategies can be described through four basic models. First is the press agentry/publicity model, which describes propagandistic public relations that seeks news media attention in almost any way possible. The main purpose of this model is propaganda. The organization's goal is control or domination of the environment, and public relations contributes to this goal through advocacy or promotion. This model came into use in 1850. An example illustrating this model is a newspaper claiming to its readers and advertisers to be the most popular or the best.

The second public relations model is the public-information model, which was developed at the beginning of this century. This model characterizes public relations as practiced by "journalists-in-residence," who disseminate accurate and truthful information about the organization but do not volunteer negative information. This model helps the organization achieve its goal of adaptation to or cooperation with the environment at large through the objective flow of information.

Both the press agentry and the public information models are one-way models in that practitioners who adopt them give information about the organization to the public but do not seek information from the public through research or informal methods.

A third model is the two-way symmetric model, which came into use in the 1960s, stressing mutual understanding between the sender and the receiver and involving an effort to exchange views and information through a balanced communication process between the organization and the public. It depicts a lasting communication relationship in which the sender and the public share power and initiative on equal terms to solve problems and to avoid conflicts (McQuail & Windahl, 1993). The major purpose of communication through the symmetric model is to facilitate the establishment of common goals between the source and the receiver. Persuasion of one person or system by another is less desirable.

The symmetric model includes the following presuppositions: Equality (people should be treated as equals, and anyone, regardless of education or background, may provide valuable input into an organization); autonomy (people are more innovative, constructive and self-fulfilled when they have the autonomy to influence their own behavior); decentralization of power (management should be collective, and authorities should cooperate rather than dictate); conflict resolution (conflict should be resolved through negotiation, communication and compromise, and not through force, manipulation, coercion, or violence); and responsibility (people and organizations should concern themselves with eliminating the adverse consequences of their behaviors on others) (Grunig & Grunig, 1989).

Finally, among the public relations models is the two-way asymmetric model, which describes a process in which the sender intends to persuade its public; the source's need for information about the communication needs of its public makes "feedback" and "feedforward" essential. Feedforward refers to the information a sender has about the audience before communicating. "In terms of power and initiative-taking, the source can be said to dominate the relationship" (McQuail & Windahl, 1993, 195).

The two-way asymmetric model best reflects the nature of the relationship between the government and the press in the Middle East. This is because most of the Middle Eastern governments, in their dealings with the press, not only try to exchange political views or convey information about specific issues but also organize systematic political campaigns through which they try to convince the press and the public of a certain policy. Moreover, in the Middle East, the government-press relationship is based on coercion and manipulation on the government's part rather than on mutual understanding and negotiation. The two-way asymmetric model is analyzed at length in the following section.

THE TWO-WAY ASYMMETRIC MODEL

This public relations model was developed by Grunig and Hunt in 1984 to describe a process in which the source or the sender uses available social science knowledge and audience research to construct a persuasive campaign. Therefore, it is "scientific persuasion" because the source uses research to identify the messages most likely to produce support from the public without having to change the behavior of the organization. The public's feedback is then used to help construct a better and more persuasive message. Effects are asymmetrical because the desired behavioral change benefits the source, not the public.

In this model, the source can be said to dominate the relationship and to have more power and initiative-taking than the public. In other words, this model suggests that the effects of the communication are imbalanced in favor of the source, who does not change as a result of public relations, but attempts to change public attitudes and behavior.

This model had its origins in World War I, during which propaganda played an important role in getting the United States into the war and then in convincing the people to support the war effort. After the United States entered the war, President Woodrow Wilson appointed a former newsman, George Creel, to head the Committee on Public Information, the U.S. propaganda agency. Creel was very successful in organizing a large-scale war propaganda campaign. The committee achieved great success because it made use of psychological principles of mass persuasion. The committee constructed messages that appealed to what people believed and what they wanted to hear.

"What the committee did was to codify and standardize ideas already current, and to bring the powerful force of emotions behind them" (Grunig & Hunt, 1984, 40). The Creel committee suggested to a new generation of public relations practitioners that mass persuasion was possible and that it could have its base in social science.

Among the new public relations' generation coming after the Creel committee was Edward L. Bernays, the practitioner whose work best illustrates the two-way asymmetric model. Bernays joined the Committee on Public Information as a way of providing patriotic service to the United States. Like other practitioners of the asymmetric model, Bernays tried to find out what the public liked about a specific organization and then he highlighted that aspect of the organization. Moreover, he determined what values and attitudes the public had and then described the organization in a way that conformed to these values and attitudes. Bernays called these strategies the "crystallizing of public opinion" and the "engineering of consent" (cited in Grunig & Hunt, 1984, 40).

Although most practitioners of the two-way asymmetric model stress serving the public interest, in practice, the model has been an effective tool used by established political and social groups and corporations to retain their positions in society. Grunig and Grunig (1989) pointed out that each organization in the society does what it does because a coalition of the most powerful people in that organization—the dominant coalition—chooses to do so. Strategic use of public relations reflects choices made by the dominant coalition.

The dominant coalition chooses a public relations strategy that it believes will be useful for dealing with the public that are most troublesome or constraining in its environment. And it chooses a strategy that suits the organization's ideology. Public relations practitioners with the knowledge, training, and expertise to practice the two-way asymmetric model of public relations are more likely to be included in the organization's dominant coalition.

Grunig and Grunig (1989) stated that the asymmetric model includes the following presuppositions: Internal orientation (members of the organization look out from the organization and do not see the organization as outsiders see it); closed system (information flows out from the organization and not into it); efficiency (control of costs is more important than innovation); elitism (leaders of the organization know best, and they have more knowledge than the public); conservatism (change is undesirable); tradition (it provides the organization with stability and helps it maintain its culture); and central authority (power should be concentrated in the hands of a few top managers, and employees should have little autonomy).

Grunig and Hunt (1984) argued that asymmetric model practitioners stage events or write press releases that have legitimate news value, in which they articulate the position of their organization. Moreover, they try to understand the behavior of journalists, so that they can tailor their messages to the communication habits of journalists. Conflict may still result from the asymmetric model because journalists frequently want to have access to an organization, something the asymmetric model may try to limit. Therefore, the asymmetric model does not work well in a democratic political system.

Politicians relying on the two-way asymmetric model both gather and disseminate information. Because their goal is to persuade or to control their audiences, including journalists and the public, they acknowledge the need to know as much about those audiences as possible. Then, armed with the results of opinion surveys or focus-group studies, they construct messages designed to appeal to the informational needs or attitudes of those audiences (Grunig, 1992).

Turk (1986) mentioned that public relations practitioners serve a proactive function by originating information and providing it to the media through press releases, news conferences, or official organization documents and reports. They also serve a reactive function, responding to requests for information from journalists. This reactive function includes routines and activities, such as making and returning telephone calls to answer journalists' questions or arranging for journalists to interview organizational experts for the information they seek. Together, these proactive and reactive public relations routines are the currency of information subsidization paid to the news media "in exchange for the privilege of reaching the public with a message that will reflect favorably on them and on the organizations they represent" (4).

According to Turk, the sources of information upon which journalists rely have more power over the media content than the selection processes of journalists themselves. This is because news does not happen until the source agrees to release information to the newsmen.

Grunig and Grunig (1989) argued that public relations practitioners try to exert symbolic control over certain aspects of the environment through the dissemination of persuasive messages. For those practitioners, "this process of seeking symbolic control—to reiterate, of preferring certain environmental outcomes over others—is a human necessity" (47). In this context, Turk pointed out that the asymmetric model is intended to be persuasive, even manipulative, in that feedback from the audience is used to guide the source in how to get the public to behave as the source wants them to behave.

PRESS CONFERENCE

One of the major public relations strategies adopted by government officials to attract journalists is to hold a press conference. This is an occasion in which the officials can speak to a number of reporters at one time on an issue of public concern and interest in an almost one-way format. A press conference offers journalists a good opportunity to get a public official "on the record" with regard to government policies. Moreover, the press conference saves time and energy. "It obviates the necessity of several hundred men running around for information which may just as well be given them collectively" (Rosten, 1937, 60).

However, the press conference format puts the reporter at a disadvantage, as he might not be able to ask a question or a follow-up question. This is because the news source generally decides who asks the questions, determines the length of questioning, and rephrases tough questions to his or her liking. In other words, the press conference gives the reporter little or no chance to challenge, clarify, or place in context information provided by the news source (Strentz, 1989).

According to Tunstall (1971), the press conference's environment, which allows for the attendance of many reporters may lead to irrelevant questioning. Moreover, anything said at a press conference becomes so widely available that it is somewhat devalued among journalists.

"BACKGROUNDER"

Another type of public relations on the part of government is the background briefing or the "backgrounder." This is a "quasi-routine" or informal channel of news gathering in which the news source does not necessarily initiate the exchange. Briefings do not require the elaborate preparation, the clearance procedures, and the commitment of formal authority that are involved in preparing for a press conference.

During a briefing, the reporters usually do not follow a transcript, and they have greater flexibility regarding the substance and format of their questions. Briefings can take several forms. Senior officials can conduct all their daily briefings on a background basis, or an official can call in a selected group of beat reporters for a briefing.

According to Wise (1973), reporters at background briefings could reject information with only vague attribution, such as "administration officials" or "government officials." Information attributable to officials of a specific department or unit of the government might be acceptable, because it allows the audience to know a more specific source of the story originating at a backgrounder and to draw their conclusions about its potential intention and accuracy.

PRESS RELEASE

Another public relations technique adopted by governments is the press release, which is an official handout distributed by the government to press organizations regarding the government's policy on an official matter. It is a simple, inexpensive, and direct method of bringing a given body of information to the attention of the newspeople. Once given to the press, the press release becomes a matter of public record, to be filed and integrated into the news organization's archives (Altheide & Johnson, 1980). Press releases have been criticized by journalists on the basis that they are misleading, full of routine and "flak," and are simply an instrument of government publicity "of utility to government but not to the press" (Nimmo, 1964, 149).

PUBLIC INFORMATION OFFICERS

The government, in undertaking all these public relations strategies, appoints special persons whose main job is to deal with the press and to convey the government's official viewpoints on political, economic, social, and other issues to the journalists and the general public. Those persons, who are called "public information officers" or, as Nimmo (1964) called them, "political servants," perform several tasks. They fulfill all information requests made by the public; supply information to the news media when requested, regardless of its nature; and explain everything without trying to propagandize. Nimmo argued that the function of the information officer is to publicize the government's real activities in a way that would maximize public support for its policies and minimize opposition to these policies.

According to Nimmo, "the information officer is an administrative specialist, skilled in the employment and manipulation of symbols. His expertise lies in mastery of the means of distribution which will make his audience aware of the agency's information policies and which will give a rationale for binding the citizens to the program in a spirit of sympathetic loyalty" (1964, 20).

In his comment on the role of the government's public relations personnel, Wise pointed out that the government, through its public relations machinery, can lie, withhold information, or classify it. It uses this machinery to distribute official information that it wishes the public to receive. According to Wise, "the PR man is much more than a mere transmission belt; he must sell truth within the limits of established policy. Often he is as much a part of the process of information distortion as the decision makers" (1973, 351).

GOVERNMENTAL PUBLIC RELATIONS IN EGYPT

The Egyptian government organizes frequent press conferences through which public statements of policy made by senior officials and their representatives are channeled to the news media to keep them updated on current policy initiatives and the regime's official view of events. The formal declarations, remarks, or explanations of policy made during press conferences are usually taken as guidance by the journalists (Rugh, 1987).

One of the main public relations tools used by the Egyptian government is the national news agency known as Middle East News Agency (MENA). This agency, which is subject to direct control by the Ministry of Information, not only conveys news of the regime's activities that the press is expected to carry but also provides occasional commentaries or backgrounders that reflect the regime's interpretation of events. Transmitted daily by teletype to all major newspapers in the country, this regular supply of information is also taken by reporters as guidance on what to publish and what interpretations are desired by the regime.

MENA publishes the *Cairo Press Review*, which provides a daily summary of the most important editorials, columns, and articles published in the Egyptian press. The review is published in English, which makes it possible for diplomats and foreign correspondents in Egypt to be up-to-date with the news published in the Egyptian press. MENA also publishes the *Party Press Review*, which translates into English the news published by the opposition party papers in Egypt (Dabbous, 1994).

When the regime wishes to convey specific guidance on a sensitive political subject, an information ministry official or a senior aide in the presidency telephones a responsible editor in every newspaper to indicate the government's position. This position is subject to discussion and modification of detail. According to Schleifer (1987), in Egypt, as in the rest of the Arab world, the government ministries lack a highly efficient public relations spokesman system. "It is nearly impossible to find a viable ministerial spokesman system anywhere in the Arab world" (349).

Commenting on this problem in the Arab world, Steve Bell, ABC's anchor in 1981, said: "We have a terrible problem of balance. The network has a very good bureau in Tel Aviv, and the ability to satellite news directly out of Israel. But there is a continuing problem of access in Arab nations" (cited in Schleifer, 1987, 315). Along this same line, Curtiss (1986) cited Sanford Socolow, one of CBS' correspondents to the Middle East in 1981, as saying: "The Arabs just do not give us access. And they pay the price for that—and they have never seemed to figure out that they would have a lot more people sympathetic to them if they had opened up to us over the years" (Curtiss, 1986).

GOVERNMENT PUBLIC RELATIONS IN ISRAEL

The Israeli government has created an official network for the dissemination of information. This network includes representatives of the ministries and their agencies, the Government Press Office, and the secretary to the government. Since the inception of the state, the secretary to the government has acted as the government's representative in dealing with the news media, although the prime minister has also had a representative of his own (Yaacobi, 1982).

The Government Press Office offers technical service to foreign correspondents. For example, correspondents must apply to this office for accreditation. The office also distributes communiqués composed by various ministries to local and foreign correspondents and provides translation services for the latter.

In the government formed after the 1973 war, a separate Ministry of Information was set up for the first time. The first minister of information was Shimon Peres, who also acted as the government's official spokesperson. He was in constant touch with journalists and attracted the attention of local and foreign news media.

The spokesperson of the Foreign Ministry meets with local and foreign correspondents on a regular basis. "Because diplomatic usage assigns definite connotations to his formal statements, many of his briefings are not for attribution" (Goren & Rothman, 1982, 264). The spokesperson of the Defense Ministry has a staff that is much larger than the staff of any other information department. He handles both the local and foreign press, providing on-the-record and off-the-record briefings. He also issues military communiqués on war events.

Commenting on the spokesperson system in Israel, Schleifer (1987) said the Israelis are "masters" of modern public relations. "Israel maintained one of the most accessible and imminently quotable round-the-clock ministerial spokesman systems to be found in the world" (348). According to Schleifer, the Israeli spokesman system was reinforced by a pool of skilled Western journalists who immigrated from Central and Western Europe, spoke and wrote in professionally competitive English, and were available to staff the official Israeli information bodies dealing with the foreign press.

Israeli spokespeople provide primarily formal services. They supply data and arrange interviews with the minister or the director general (the chief administrator) of their ministries. Spokespeople also notify journalists of pending developments. Reporters make use of these services, but do not rely only on official spokespeople for information. "Notwithstanding the legal prohibitions, most reporters develop and cultivate their own network of sources within the ministries" (Goren & Rothman, 1982, 263).

Israel has a news agency, ITIM (Hebrew acronym for the Associated Israeli Press Service). This agency includes representatives and stringers from all the major newspapers. It distributes material on domestic and international levels. Moreover, it translates material issued by foreign agencies, especially the Associated Press, Reuters, and Agence France Press.

CONCLUSION

It can be concluded from this chapter that the public relations asymmetric model is the best public relations model that can be used to describe the government-press relationship in Israel and Egypt. According to this model, government officials use various public relations tactics, such as press conferences, backgrounders, and press releases to disseminate information to the news media.

In the next chapter, I assess both the news making and the asymmetric models in the context of the government-press relationship in Israel and Egypt.

13

A Personal Assessment of Newsmaking and Public Relations Asymmetric Models in the Context of Government-Press Relationships in Israel and Egypt

Both the newsmaking and the two-way asymmetric models are similar in that they shed some light on the nature of the relationship between the government and the press. They both help make sense of this relationship by providing some explanations on how public officials deal with reporters and how the information is exchanged between the two sides. However, both models differ in the way they approach and explain the government-press relationship. The two-way asymmetric model is an administrative rather than a critical model. That is, this model is designed to help the government organization further its ends rather than to critique the performance of that organization.

Unlike the newsmaking model, which assumes that the government and the press can make some compromises to reach a point of agreement, the asymmetric model suggests that public relations is a way of getting what a government organization wants by changing the public's behavior without having to change its own behavior or without compromising. Through the asymmetric model, the desired change in behavior benefits the government, not the public.

One major shortcoming of the asymmetric model is that it rests on the passive reception paradigm, in which the government, acting as the persuader or the primary symbolizing agent, encodes and transmits a message to a relatively passive audience. Even when the opportunity for audience feedback exists, persuadees are relegated to a relatively inactive role. Therefore, persuasion in the asymmetric model is conceptualized as a unidirectional process in which the persuader acts and the persuadees are acted upon.

The asymmetric model assumes that the government can successfully persuade the journalists and the public to follow its policies if it can adequately and efficiently communicate the right message to the right people in the right way at the right time. Under this assumption, the asymmetric model attributes all the power to the government. Moreover, it underestimates the "watchdog" role that the journalists can play in searching for the truth and uncovering the pitfalls of the government. The asymmetric model also tends to ignore the fact that journalists can conduct investigative reporting in which they can inspect government activities and prove the government's falsities, if there are any.

This is in contrast to the newsmaking model, which assumes that there is a symbiotic or a cooperative relationship existing between the government and the journalists through which the norms of giving and receiving are continually negotiated. Sometimes, the government might depart from these norms by trying to enhance a message's credibility by hiding its origins from reporters. However, reporters have their own ways of revealing the hidden truth.

In this symbiotic relationship, proponents of the newsmaking model argue that power is not necessarily in the government's hands. Reporters might have the upper hand at some point, and government officials might have the upper hand at another point depending on the social and political situation at a given time. Therefore, the newsmaking model regards journalists as active participants in the political process. They can even help shape political decisions by acting as consultants for government officials. Through their investigative reporting and journalistic crusading, they undertake a significant symbolizing role on the political scene.

In the Middle East, governments might have the upper hand most of the time in their relationship with journalists, and the press might play the role of a "lapdog" rather than a "watchdog" of the government. However, there is still some room for negotiations and compromise between officials and reporters. On occasion, the government might consult journalists on sensitive political issues, especially if those journalists hold prestigious positions at their news organizations.

Another major shortcoming of the asymmetric model is that it tends to focus on the way the government formulates its relationship with the press, and it ignores all the other multiple influences that might come into play in this relationship. Unlike the newsmaking model, which studies the personal and craft values of journalists, as well as the organizational time and space constraints of news gathering, the asymmetric model ignores these factors completely.

One of the basic aspects of the asymmetric model is that the government uses scientific research and public opinion polls to identify the messages most likely to produce public support. This makes it hard for the asymmetric model to be applied to many Arab countries simply because it is very rare and unusual for Arab governments to carry out such research to study public opinion.

According to Boyd (1993), a major characteristic of the Arab and Middle Eastern governments is that they do not support media and public opinion research efforts. "A possible explanation of this is the reluctance of a traditional people to respond to official questioning, and the fear among officials of negative questioning" (54). Israel might be an exception to this argument because it is known as a world leader in public opinion research studies. In this context, Katz (1971) pointed out that the advent of television in Israel in the late 1960s was preceded and followed by national survey research to study the state of "civilian morale" and public opinion preparedness for this medium. A large sum of money was allocated for the national survey, which was conducted by the Israel Broadcasting Authority and the Israel Institute of Applied Social Research. This research dealt with issues such as time-budgeting of evening hours, the uses of leisure by the population of Israel, and the gratification people get, or expect to get, from viewing television. In his comment on this research, Katz said that "no other country has managed to get good 'before' and 'after' data on the introduction of television as Israel did" (268).

CONCLUSION

Although not completely developed, the newsmaking model and the asymmetric model can be applied to studying foreign correspondents' access to information and the government-press relationships in Israel and Egypt. The asymmetric model distinguishes the relationship between Middle Eastern governments and foreign correspondents. It reflects a government's official position in the business of persuasion. Meanwhile, the newsmaking model comes into play after the information is disseminated to the correspondents. It reflects the nonofficial making of news on the part of the correspondents.

Regardless of which position to take or which theory to apply, the local journalists and the foreign correspondents operating in Israel and Egypt need to improve their news-gathering techniques and their means of accessing information about government activities. In doing this, they have two alternatives: to obtain exclusives the hard way through their own investigative work and research or to take the easy way of relying on inside tips, interviews, press conferences, news releases, and leaks handed to them by officials. If the journalists rely totally on government information, they will be forced into a bargain that requires them to accept the far more common news delivered through routine channels.

The news media need the help of social science, and journalists would be less dependent on governments' public relations if they had more knowledge of social science evidence and how to find it. According to Tunstall (1971), "surveys, studies reports, and investigations by various sorts of social scientists play a larger and larger part in political and semi-political journalism; yet, the journalists who produce the stories sometimes show a startling ignorance of the simplest conventions of such work, and a failure to search for the most easily available published sources. Many journalists—despite their professed hostility to government organizations—when faced with government publications and statistics often accept them with complete credulity" (278). This is why journalism needs to be integrated with social sciences, and journalists should place more emphasis on scientific ways of observing the world and systematically recording and analyzing such observations.

Wise (1973) argued against journalists' taking government information for granted by saying:

There is, of course, only one side that a constitutionally free press can be on, and that is the side of truth. But to fulfill that role requires a singular tough-mindedness. The press, despite criticism from political leaders, needs to question, probe, analyze, and interpret more, not less. It should resist government pressures and self-generated pressures. It must not succumb to the seduction of power, nor automatically accept government handouts and leaks as fact. If the press acts as a mere transmission belt for government pronouncements, then it contributes to the credibility gap, and to the erosion of trust that has already divided the people from the government. (311)

In the next chapter, I apply the newsmaking and the asymmetric models to the reporting of the Western journalists I interviewed in Israel and Egypt. This will help readers understand the intricacies of the two models as perceived by Western correspondents.

14

AN ANALYSIS OF NEWSMAKING AND ASYMMETRIC MODELS IN THE RECENT REPORTING OF WESTERN JOURNALISTS ON THE ISRAELI-EGYPTIAN PEACE PROCESS

In this chapter, I present the results of the data analysis of the survey I conducted among Western journalists in Israel and Egypt that addresses the hypotheses and research questions mentioned in Chapter 8. I also present selective quotations from the correspondents' answers to the open-ended questions. These results and quotations identify how the governments of Israel and Egypt deal with Western correspondents, what kinds of governmental constraints correspondents are subject to, how they perceive the news-making roles, and how Israeli and Egyptian public relations officials release information to them.

NEWS-MAKING ROLES

Results showed that three journalistic roles were rated as extremely important by a majority of Western correspondents interviewed in Israel and Egypt combined: providing analysis of complex problems (67.3 percent of correspondents said this is their role); investigating government claims (55.4 percent of correspondents said this is their role); and getting information to the public quickly (54.8 percent of correspondents said this is their role).

The majority of correspondents in Israel agreed that it is extremely important that the news media undertake these three roles: providing analysis of complex problems (70.2 percent); investigating government claims (59.6 percent); and getting information to the public quickly (55.3 percent). The correspondents in Egypt ranked these same roles as the most important roles, but in a different order. Providing analysis of complex problems came first (63.5 percent), followed by getting information to the public quickly (54.1 percent) and investigating government claims (50 percent).

These results show that the news-making roles with the highest rankings among correspondents in Israel and Egypt are the investigative and the disseminator roles. Although the rankings of these roles by correspondents in Egypt are almost the same as the ones in Israel, there are slight differences in the percentages of correspondents who ranked these roles as extremely important.

These differences show that more correspondents in Israel think it is extremely important to provide analysis of complex problems and investigate government claims. However, these differences (less than 10 percent) are not large enough to suggest that the correspondents in Israel undertake a different news-making role from their counterparts in Egypt. More important, because the numbers involved in this study are small, a 10 percent difference cannot be relied on to say that correspondents in Israel are different from their counterparts in Egypt in their news-making roles. Based on these results, research question one can be answered by saying that correspondents in Egypt undertake similar news-making roles as their counterparts in Israel.

JOURNALISTS' EDUCATIONAL LEVELS AND THEIR INVESTIGATIVE ROLES

Before undertaking this study, I hypothesized that the higher the correspondents' educational level, the more supportive they are of the investigative role of reporting.

Answers to the question on educational levels were converted to years of education ranging from 12 years (high school) to 22 years (doctorate degree). The frequency of undertaking the investigative role of reporters was measured by a statement asking correspondents to rate the likelihood of their conducting further investigation of government information on the Arab-Israeli conflict.

Results showed that there is no relationship between the journalists' educational levels and their investigative roles. Failure to support this hypothesis may be because there is little variation in the years of schooling of the correspondents who participated in this study. Almost 90 percent of the correspondents in Israel and Egypt had either a bachelor's degree (16 years of education) or a master's degree (18 years of education) (see Table 2).

HOW CREDIBLE ARE ISRAELI AND EGYPTIAN OFFICIALS IN WESTERN JOURNALISTS' EYES?

The majority of journalists interviewed in Israel and Egypt perceived the Israeli official public relations machinery (press conferences, news releases, pub-

Table 2
Correspondents' Educational Levels in Egypt and Israel

Educational Degree	Israel	Egypt	Total	Percentage %
High school	3		3	1.9%
Some college	3	3	6	3.8%
Bachelor's	48	31	79	49.4%
Master's	33	33	66	41.3%
Doctorate	4	2	6	3.8%

lic information offices, and government spokespersons) to have a higher level of credibility with Western correspondents than the Egyptian government information establishment has with Western correspondents.

To better understand these differences, answers to the open-ended question about the government's public relations apparatus were examined. Overall, Western correspondents in Israel said that despite the unreliability of many of the official announcements delivered to them by the Israeli government they still trust these announcements more than their counterparts in Egypt trust the Egyptian announcements.

Tom Aspell, NBC bureau chief in Jerusalem, said: "The Israeli government provides as much information as possible by all possible means, and this information is reliable most of the time" (1998).

A Jerusalem-based Australian correspondent said the Israeli government supplies journalists with a lot of background information, which can be very useful, but it needs to be checked on a case-by-case basis.

However, not all correspondents trusted the Israeli government. Despite the high accessibility levels of Israeli government officials, many correspondents dealing with Israeli officials questioned the reliability of the information they received. Among those correspondents was Gisela Dachs, a Jerusalem-based bureau chief of *Die Zeit* (a German newspaper). According to Dachs, "journalists should not fall in the public relations trap set by the Israeli government. I do not use all of the information I get from the Israelis because I am not a public relations agency" (1998).

A Tel Aviv–based Canadian correspondent said: "I do not trust them [Israeli officials] all the time. Sometimes, the government information is true and reliable, but at other times it is lacking and insufficient."

Steffen Jensen, a Jerusalem-based correspondent for Danish television, said information from Israeli official sources is always readily available, but the quality of this information is not always very high. According to Jensen, "It is often better to find information on our own or to have our own sources in the ministries than to rely on official spokespersons. The Israeli Government Press

Office (GPO) is used as a propaganda machine, and most of the information it releases is useless for any critical reporters" (1998).

Jurgen Hogrefe, a Jerusalem-based bureau chief of *Der Spiegel* (German magazine), said the Israeli government is very accessible, but it is almost impossible to get valid information from it. "We get more rumors than accurate information" (1998).

"There are lots of rumors here, but we try to verify the information we get, and we do not rely on government information per se, but we check by calling our contacts or getting in touch with local journalists," said Remi Cadoret-Manier (1998), a Jerusalem-based correspondent for French TV (TF1).

Lisa Beyer, Jerusalem-based bureau chief of *Time* said: "The current government [Netanyahu government] is very open, but it deliberately gives false information" (1998). Similarly, Petra Yaacobi, a producer for German television in Jerusalem, said: "We get the information that they want us to get. We have to dig for the rest by ourselves" (1998).

Heinz-Rudolf Othmerding, bureau chief of the German News Agency (dpa) in Israel, said: "The Israeli officials are very professional in presenting the facts in a way that we swallow, and therefore, we have to carefully check what they tell us and compare it to what they said the day before" (1998).

In their assessment of the credibility of the Egyptian public relations apparatus, Western correspondents in Egypt have different opinions about the government than their counterparts in Israel. "Egyptian officials have a tendency towards exaggeration and hyperbole in the excitement of the event, and this undermines their credibility," said Patrick Werr (1998), an American correspondent in Cairo.

Anthony Shadid, a correspondent for the Associated Press in Cairo, said: "The Egyptian government makes efforts, but the information here is nowhere near the capabilities of Israel. There is an incredible misunderstanding here between the government and the correspondents. They [the government officials] always want to know the goals of distributing information among correspondents. They think we always have a hidden agenda" (1998).

"Checking information is often perceived here as a lack of confidence in official speeches. The Egyptian administration reacts very angrily to this basic task of reporting and thinks we [correspondents] accuse them of lying when we check, which is not always the case," said Christophe Ayad (1998), a Cairo-based French correspondent for *Liberation*.

In this context, Christine Hauser, a correspondent for Reuters in Egypt, said: "The PR machinery here is pretty bad and there is much to be desired when it comes to the Foreign Ministry spokespersons. There is a State Information Service whose director does not tell us something of use. Egypt presents itself as a major regional mediator, and therefore, one would expect that it would have something to say at crucial moments of the conflict, but this is not always the case" (1998).

Based on the correspondents' answers to the close-ended and the open-ended questions, it is clear that neither government gets high marks. However the correspondents think the Israeli government is more successful in presenting itself as having a more credible public relations apparatus than the Egyptian government is.

JOURNALISTS' PERCEPTIONS OF THE ACCESSIBILITY OF ISRAELI AND EGYPTIAN OFFICIALS

An overwhelming majority of the Western correspondents interviewed agreed that Israeli government officials are more accessible and easier to reach than Egyptian officials.

A Jerusalem-based U.S. correspondent said the Israeli government sought to put its face forward and to give its perspective exclusively, and this allows for much accessibility and openness in Israel. An Australian correspondent in Jerusalem said Israeli government officials always made a wealth of information about the Arab-Israeli conflict available, but it often took the correspondents a lot of work to find and link the pertinent pieces of information together.

An Associated Press correspondent in Israel said Israeli officials were very interested in expressing their views and availing themselves to the news media. They bombarded the correspondents with e-mail messages, phone calls, and press releases. According to that correspondent, "Israel is informal in that you can call an important official at home at 10 o'clock on a Friday night [Jewish Shabbath holiday] to inquire about anything. It is not a business-hours mentality in Israel. You can call officials anytime and anywhere, and they will be available. This is not the case even in the United States."

Another U.S. correspondent in Jerusalem said: "The Israeli government floods correspondents with information through beepers, e-mail messages, and phone calls. Every day, I get flooded by e-mail messages from government officials. It is lots of information but only what they need to tell us, and they put their own 'spin' on it."

Jim Hollander, chief photographer for Reuters in Israel, said the Israelis were very savvy about delivering their side of the story to the foreign news media. According to Hollander, "The Israeli officials are very literate and very professional in presenting their points of view and availing themselves to the media" (1998).

A prominent U.S. correspondent in Israel said: "The Israelis are professional 'spinners' in that they are media conscious and media 'savvy' and they know how to get their views through."

In this same context, Nicolas Tatro, the bureau chief of the Associated Press in Israel, said: "Each Israeli government is different; they all flood us with information, but this current government has been more aggressive in presenting its points of view. It very much has an edge to it. The rhetorical factor is much higher than it has been since the early days of the Begin government" (1998).

In commenting on the accessibility of the Israeli public relations system, Lyse Doucet, a Canadian reporter for the BBC, said Israel has a very well-established public relations body that is unparalleled in the Middle East because the Israelis love to talk to the media and they are good at it. According to Doucet, Benjamin Netanyahu (the then Israeli Prime Minister) is the "ultimate spin-doctor" when it comes to public relations (1998).

A German correspondent in Israel said: "BB [Benjamin Netanyahu] is the master of the sound bite, and he does it the American way. He believes that what is important is not what you say but the way you say it. He is regarded as a superficial politician who prefers style over substance."

Paul Holmes, Reuters bureau chief in Jerusalem, said the Israeli government was very active in setting the news agenda, and very professional in its public relations techniques. According to Holmes: "In other countries, one has to go and seek information or run after it, but here we get information on a more systematic and professional basis that reflects a more American approach to news" (1998).

An Australian correspondent in Jerusalem said: "While it is very easy to be critical of the Israeli government, their information channels are much better than other governments in the area. I have reported from many countries in Africa, Asia, and the Middle East, and in many ways, getting information here is much easier than most of the countries I have worked. However, making sense of this information is not easy. I do not think correspondents can, in any way, 'blame' Israel for the manipulation of data or material. It is the responsibility of correspondents to ensure they cross-check information with other sources."

The majority of foreign correspondents interviewed in Egypt said the Egyptian government was not always accessible and did not release sufficient information on the conflict. Claude Guibal, a Cairo-based French correspondent, said: "The Egyptian government gives us the minimum, and often no information. The Press Office of the Ministry of Information never called me to say if there is going to be a press conference or a visit. I know of press conferences from my colleagues, not from the government officials" (1998).

Michel Rauch, a German correspondent in Cairo, said the Foreign Ministry was the only place to find accessible sources in the Egyptian government. According to Rauch, "The strange thing is there may be bilateral talks going on in Cairo on the Arab-Israeli conflict, but the hot place to get faster access to reliable information about these talks is Jerusalem, or the sources closer to the Israeli side" (1998).

Cairo-based Associated Press chief correspondent Gerald La Belle said the Arab governments, like all governments, wanted to get their point of view across. However, in most cases, they were not attuned to the needs of the news media. Thus, Arab governments were willing to disseminate plenty of information about the conflict, but it was largely repetitive and often did not speak to the issue immediately at hand. (1998).

Alexander Buccianti, a Cairo-based correspondent for *Le Monde* (the French newspaper), said there was a general secrecy trend in the Egyptian government, and this trend was inherited from late Egyptian President Nasser's era. According to Buccianti, the general problem in Egypt was that only the "boss" can release the important information, and usually this "boss" was not accessible. "The PR machinery in Egypt is anti-productive, and it works against the policies of the government because of the inaccessibility of government sources." The lack of government announcements on the Arab-Israeli conflict creates misunderstanding and contributes to the misconceptions that make the public encourage war against Israel (1998).

In this context, Gerald La Belle, Associated Press chief correspondent in Cairo, said Arab officials were often late in commenting on developments, and lower officials refused to comment until ones higher up had indicated the political direction. Therefore, an Israeli comment or accusation could go unanswered until the Arab answer was no longer news. When the comment finally did come, it was often in the form of an editorial in the state-run press or from an unidentified official, which did not carry the same weight as a government leader or official spokesman (1998).

According to John Daniszewski, Cairo-based bureau chief of the *Los Angeles Times*, the Egyptian government was not very forthcoming with information of any kind, and it tended to use the Arab-Israeli conflict as an issue to build up its own popularity and legitimacy with the people by sympathizing with the Palestinian side (1998).

Patrick Angevin, a Cairo-based French correspondent, said: "The Egyptian government is totally inefficient in its dealings with the news media. In six years, I have not received one single press release." According to Angevin, speaking with foreign correspondents is regarded by officials in Egypt as something "dangerous" (1998).

Siona Jenkins, a Cairo-based correspondent for the *Irish Times*, said: "The PR machinery in Egypt is clumsy and ineffectual; we do not get much information, but we extrapolate it. There is only one official spokesperson (the director of the State Information Service) who talks on behalf of all the Egyptian ministries." According to Jenkins, the Egyptian officials are not aware of how important information is to the foreign media. "They should be more articulate in projecting Egypt's points of view" (1998).

A Cairo-based U.S. correspondent reporting for a major American broadcast news organization said that although the Egyptian officials were more open on the Arab-Israeli conflict than on other matters, it was always difficult to get them to talk on camera. "Overall, the information we get on the conflict is sufficient, but access is not always easy, especially with top officials. There are so many levels of hierarchy in the Egyptian government, and the messages often get lost between these levels. Here, we have to call and beg and we have to go to the officials only when they feel like it. Either they do not want to talk to us or we cannot find them."

Gerald La Belle, a chief Middle East correspondent for the Associated Press in Cairo, said: "Many Arabs view the United States, and by extension American newspapers and reporters, as pro-Israel; that means they doubt that reporters are truly interested in their views or that newspapers will print them. That affects their willingness to speak openly" (1998).

Jacqueline Burrell, a Cairo-based British freelance journalist, said Egyptian officials have a desire to prevent foreigners from accessing information because they fear that foreigners will have a bad impression of their country, and they think foreigners will misunderstand the information released to them. According to Burrell, "the information released by the Egyptian officials is confusing, and we do not know the bottom line of it" (1998).

Volkhard Windfur, the correspondent for Germany's *Der Spiegel* (German magazine) in Cairo and chairman of the Cairo Foreign Press Association, said the Israeli government was more successful in presenting its point of view to the foreign news media than the Arab governments because the Israelis have a better public relations apparatus. According to Windfur, the Egyptian Ministry of Foreign Affairs has spokespersons, but they were disorganized and inaccessible to the foreign press. "The Egyptian Foreign Minister attended a press conference organized by the FPA only once in five years. We are dismayed and astonished by that" (1998).

In her assessment of the accessibility of Egypt's public relations apparatus, Eileen Alt Powell, a correspondent for the Associated Press in Cairo, said: "Egypt has nothing like the public relations machinery that has been developed in Israel. There [in Israel], you are overwhelmed with interviews, facts, figures, and translations of pro-government editorials and the like. Here, translation services are weak. Government statistics are getting better, but they are still released with considerable delay. And sometimes briefings are done only for the Egyptian reporters assigned to a particular ministry. Other reporters, whether Western or local, are excluded" (1998).

A Cairo-based U.S. correspondent said: "The government officials are hard-to-reach, and they do not call us back. They are very disorganized and totally unsavvy when it comes to dealing with the foreign media."

Drusilla Menaker, a Cairo-based U.S. correspondent, said: "To make an appointment here is very hard—it is a very bureaucratic approach. It takes weeks to schedule an appointment with an official. They hurt themselves this way as opposed to the Israeli officials who avail themselves all the time to the news media. The PR machinery here is stagnant, hostile, bureaucratic, and not quick" (1998).

These quotes taken from Western correspondents' answers to the open-ended questions provide additional support to the hypothesis that government accessibility levels in Israel were higher than in Egypt.

JOURNALISTS' PERCEPTIONS OF THE AMOUNT OF LEAKS RELEASED BY ISRAELI AND EGYPTIAN GOVERNMENTS

Results of the survey showed that an overwhelming majority of the correspondents interviewed in Israel received leaks on a frequent basis, whereas in Egypt very few correspondents ever received leaks. The Israeli public relations apparatus delivered more leaks to the foreign news media than did the Egyptian government officials. To get a full grasp of the difference between the two countries with regard to the release of leaks, answers to the open-ended questions were examined.

According to Jeff Abramowitz, a German correspondent based in Tel Aviv, "leaks are unbelievably frequent, and Israeli officials leak even before the cabinet meetings, not only afterwards." There are "controlled leaks" through which the government officials plant a question or urge the reporters to ask a question based on some leaked information during a press conference so that they can respond to it (1998).

Hanne Foighel, a Danish correspondent in Tel Aviv, said Israel had a strong tradition of leaking information, and no information could remain secret for long. According to Foighel, most leaks in Israel were for "trial balloons," as they were meant for local consumption to test a certain political issue. That is why most leaks are released to the local press, which provided the foreign press with many of the released leaks (1998).

Lisa Beyer, *Time* bureau chief in Jerusalem, said: "Although this Israeli government is particularly deceptive and untrustworthy, Israel is a society where you can easily check things; often you can find someone who is in the loop, who will tell you the real story or give you reason to doubt the official story; you can always find 'another' source who will leak information to you; this is not a society where people are afraid to speak" (1998).

A prominent U.S. correspondent in Jerusalem said the Israeli officials were selective in delivering leaks to correspondents depending on two criteria: distribution [whether it is the audience they cared about], and trustworthiness [whether it is someone they trusted]. According to this correspondent, the Israeli intelligence body [Mossad] had a long history of leaking to the American correspondents, and the Israelis cared more about American opinion than about any other country's opinion because of the financial and military aid that Israel receives from the United States.

Many American correspondents stationed in Jerusalem reported that they usually receive more leaks than their counterparts from other Western countries. "Being an American correspondent, I receive more attention and I am more overwhelmed by government information and leaks because of the knowledge that there is a very effective Jewish lobby in the United States that has a heavy weight in the Congress and the executive branch," said Joseph Contreras, Jerusalem bureau chief for *Newsweek*. According to Contreras, the Israelis know that one effective way to advance their interests in Washington is through the American news media stationed in Israel, and that is why they leaked a lot of information to the U.S. correspondents (1998).

In his comment on leaks, Lee Hockstader, Jerusalem bureau chief of the *Washington Post*, said: "This place leaks like crazy. Israel is like Washington in that the government officials are very bad in keeping secrets. Washington is an 'information supermarket' and so is Israel." According to Hockstader, the reason for the prevalence of leaks in Israel was that it is a small, tightly-knit society, where people talk to each other a lot and this makes information circulate very quickly. The U.S. broadcast networks, especially CNN, were the major recipients of leaks from the Israeli government because these networks are believed by the Israeli officials to have the greatest influence on the American public opinion (1998).

Jim Lederman, a Jerusalem-based Canadian analyst for *Oxford Analytica* (a British publication) said most of the leaks were directed to the daily newspapers because they were self-serving leaks aimed at enhancing the politicians' interests. If one was writing an in-depth analysis, he received almost no leaks (1998).

Unlike their counterparts in Israel, the Western correspondents in Egypt reported that they rarely received leaks from government officials. Very few correspondents in Cairo (less than five) said they benefited from leaked material. Those correspondents said the major American news organizations are the main targets of these few leaks.

Volkhard Windfur, a Cairo-based German correspondent and chairman of the Foreign Press Association, said: "I get occasional leaks because I have been living here for a long time and I know almost all the officials personally" (1998).

Most other correspondents based in Cairo said they had never received even a single leak from the government during their time in Egypt. These remarks lend considerable additional support to the hypothesis that the Israeli government releases more leaks about the Arab-Israeli conflict to Western correspondents than the Egyptian government.

JOURNALISTS' PERCEPTIONS OF THE LEGITIMACY OF USING SECURITY BY ISRAEL AND EGYPT TO WITHHOLD INFORMATION

Several studies have suggested that governments use security concerns as a public relations tool, and that this tool is certainly a major component of the Middle East's political scene. Most of these studies highlighted the differences between the use of security in Israel and Egypt.

Before undertaking this study, I hypothesized that Western correspondents operating in Israel would cite security as a legitimate reason for government's withholding of information on the Middle East conflict more than their counterparts in Egypt. However, my hypothesis was not supported by the results of this study, which showed no difference between the correspondents stationed in Israel and Egypt with regard to their perceptions of the legitimacy of the governments' use of security to withhold information on the Arab-Israeli conflict.

The correspondents' answers to the open-ended questions showed that the security issue was not seen by the majority of correspondents in either Egypt or Israel as a legitimate reason for withholding information, not only on the Arab-Israeli conflict, but on any other issue.

However, some correspondents in Israel who cited the government's use of security to withhold information on the Arab-Israeli conflict argued that Israel was justified in doing so. Among those correspondents was Ron Grossman, acting bureau chief of the *Chicago Tribune* in Jerusalem, who said: "The Israeli government has the right to raise the security issue because security is a very real issue in this country. I can write anything I want, but if I feel, in my judgment, that it fringes on the security issue, I can contact the concerned officials. But eventually, the decision is mine. There are not many societies where that is the case" (1998).

Nicolas Tatro, bureau chief of the Associated Press in Jerusalem and chairman of the Foreign Press Association in Israel, said a sense of personal security was what the Israelis want out of the peace process. "This is an emotional issue deeply felt by everyone and not a trick by the government. It is a really day-to-day tension among the common people in Israel" (1998).

Although a few correspondents in Israel said that the national security concerns raised by the Israeli government could sometimes be legitimate concerns, most of them did not fully justify the Israeli government's use of these security concerns to withhold information. "In many cases, there is no logic at all to the use of security in this country. Officials here use it as an easy way to avoid releasing information. This is not always acceptable to us," said Jorgen Hogrefe, Jerusalem-based bureau chief of *Der Spiegel* (German magazine) (1998).

Enrico Franceschini, Jerusalem-based bureau chief of *La Republica* (the Italian newspaper), said: "Israelis use the security issue as an alibi to look more scared than they really are. This is especially the case with the current Likud government, which uses the security issue to slow down the peace process" (1998).

As for correspondents in Egypt, the security issue was not a major concern for them because they said the Egyptian government does not use it very frequently as a justification for withholding information on the Arab-Israeli conflict.

JOURNALISTS' PERCEPTIONS OF THE FREQUENCY OF USING SECURITY TO JUSTIFY WITHHOLDING INFORMATION IN ISRAEL AND EGYPT

The majority of correspondents I interviewed in this study reported that the security issue is used more by the Israeli government than by the Egyptian government as a justification for withholding information on the Arab-Israeli conflict. To better understand this difference, the correspondents' answers to the open-ended questions were examined. Overall, correspondents reported that the Israeli government used security to withhold information on a more frequent basis than did the Egyptian government. In fact, the majority of the correspondents interviewed said the Egyptian government did not use the security issue to withhold information on the Arab-Israeli conflict. But correspondents said security was used frequently in Egypt to withhold information about domestic issues. Most correspondents in Israel said the Israeli government used security very frequently to justify the withholding of information on the Arab-Israeli conflict.

A prominent U.S. correspondent in Israel said the Israeli officials misused security in the political and religious arena. This correspondent said: "Speak to any Israeli military general who is not a member of the Likud camp [Likud is a major Israeli political party], and he will laugh at what the Likud considers to be security issues concerning the West Bank."

An American correspondent for the Associated Press in Jerusalem said: "Security is a kind of God in this country. It is the first priority, even if it does not exist. The army routinely abuses the concept of 'closed military zones' to keep us away from those areas. This is the most widespread and constant abuse of the concept of security."

Willy Werkman, a Dutch correspondent in Tel Aviv, said the history of the Jewish people is a "trauma," and therefore, many Israelis are "paranoid" when it comes to security. According to Werkman, the Holocaust affected the way Israelis view security, and the memory of it is still strong decades later (1998).

Jay Bushinsky, a U.S. correspondent in Tel Aviv, said the security issue was used by Israeli officials to withhold information on military and nuclear weapons, but this information was obtained eventually one way or the other (1998).

Nicholas Goldberg, Jerusalem-based bureau chief of *Newsday* (U.S. publication), said the Israeli government often hid behind the claim of security to avoid having to talk about certain things. However, Goldberg said using the security claim as an excuse was not unusual, even in the United States (1998).

Most correspondents in Israel said military censorship was a tool used by the Israeli government to censor materials for security reasons. All accredited foreign correspondents in Israel said they have to sign a statement that they are aware of censorship restrictions, especially when it comes to nuclear and military matters. However, almost all the correspondents in Israel said the military censor was not at all effective and did not have any impact on the way they accessed information or covered stories. The reason for the military censor's ineffectiveness, according to correspondents, was that Israel is a very small country where correspondents have lots of contacts and where everybody likes to talk. This makes it hard to hide information. Moreover, some correspondents mentioned that the changing communication technology, which allows them to send their stories via their cellular phones or the Internet in a matter of seconds, has made effective censorship more or less impossible.

Despite the ineffectiveness of the military censorship body in Israel, several correspondents expressed their disapproval of the very existence of such censorship. Among those correspondents was Adrian Wells, Jerusalem-based bureau chief for the BBC, who said: "I do not like the idea of having to deal with the military censor. It is not particularly good in principle, but in practice it has never made us compromise our editorial integrity" (1998).

Philippe Gelie, Jerusalem-based bureau chief of *Le Figaro* (a French newspaper), said the Israeli local media were subject to direct military censorship, but when it came to the foreign press, the military censor was almost ineffective. According to Gelie, the local Israeli journalists, unlike the foreign journalists, have to submit their stories to the military censor prior to publication (1998).

Some correspondents in Israel said they did occasionally practice self-censorship in reporting nuclear and military matters, especially when they knew that the information they had might endanger the national security of the state. This was because Israeli officials always referred to the security issue and the threats that Israel was subject to.

A Jerusalem-based Australian correspondent said the free information flow in Israel meant that even when the Israeli government withheld information for military or security reasons, this information found its way to the press. "In all but the most rare cases, we know what is going on."

Joseph Contreras, Jerusalem-based bureau chief for *Newsweek*, said: "I think security is misused by the Israeli government to the extent that it is employed as a pretext for delaying the peace process and for carrying out collective punishments in the Palestinian territories" (1998). A Jerusalem-based American correspondent said: "Security is used here as an excuse for not releasing information about everything from bombs to air pollution."

Correspondents in Egypt said that unlike the Israeli government, the Egyptian government did not use security issues as a justification for withholding information on the Arab-Israeli conflict. Most correspondents in Egypt said the Egyptian officials used security only in domestic issues. In this context, Volkhard Windfur, a German correspondent in Cairo and chairman of the Foreign Press Association, said: "I do not recall a case where the Egyptian government withheld information on the Arab-Israeli conflict for security reasons." According to Windfur, the Egyptian officials misused security when it came to domestic issues, such as Islamic fundamentalism, terrorism, or the tension between Moslems and Coptics (1998).

In this same context, Scott MacLeod, *Time* bureau chief in Cairo, said there was no longer a state of war between Egypt and Israel, and so Egypt was no longer a primary actor or participant in the clashes. It did play the role of a mediator in the peace negotiations. This means that the conflict does not have a direct impact on Egyptians' lives. According to MacLeod, this was the main reason why the Egyptian government did not use security to hide information on the conflict (1998).

Max Rodenbeck, Cairo-based bureau chief for the *Economist* (Great Britain), said: "The security issue is massively misused in general, but not regarding the Arab-Israeli affairs. In fact, this aspect of Egypt's information policy is less restrained by security concerns than others. In general, Egypt's approach to the Arab-Israeli conflict is limited to diplomacy and diplomatic channels, and so a limited degree of secrecy is understandable, particularly since Egypt likes to present itself as a reliable facilitator" (1998).

Based on the correspondents' quotes, it is clear that in Israel, the Arab-Israeli conflict is a domestic issue, but in Egypt it has become a nondomestic issue because there is no longer a state of war between Egypt and Israel. Egypt is no longer a primary actor or participant in the clashes, but it does play the role of a mediator in peace negotiations. This means that the conflict does not have a direct impact on Egyptians' lives, and therefore the Egyptian government does not use security to hide information about the conflict.

WESTERN JOURNALISTS AND INFORMAL SOURCES IN ISRAEL AND EGYPT

Western correspondents, in their day-to-day activities as reporters, rely not only on government officials but also on nonofficial and informal sources to verify information they get from the government.

Results of this study showed some differences between correspondents in Israel and their counterparts in Egypt with regard to the number of friends and acquaintances they have and the sufficiency of these sources to verify government claims on the Arab-Israeli conflict. My hypothesis that Western correspondents in Israel would perceive themselves as having a better network of informal social and professional sources than would their counterparts in Egypt was supported by the results.

Western correspondents in Israel perceived themselves as having more friends and acquaintances than did their counterparts in Egypt. Many correspondents in Egypt admitted that they found it hard to make friends, establish informal networks, and find unofficial sources. Among those correspondents was Sarah Gauch, a Cairo-based correspondent for the Christian Science Monitor. Gauch said: "I do not find it easy to make Egyptian friends; maybe it is a cultural gap. Egyptians seem to be family-oriented and they do not have the time to reach out to foreigners. I always feel that I am an 'outsider' here. Egyptians might not be very Westernized" (1998).

Moreover, Western correspondents in Israel perceived themselves as having more informal sources for verifying government claims on controversial issues with regard to the Arab-Israeli conflict than did their counterparts in Egypt.

IMPLICATIONS OF CORRESPONDENTS' RESPONSES
IN THE CONTEXT OF NEWSMAKING AND
ASYMMETRIC MODELS

Correspondents in Israel and Egypt said they do not take the governments' announcements at face value—they conduct further investigation on their own to double-check the validity and reliability of the official information released by the government. Many correspondents in both countries said they always conduct their own research and try to find other sources besides government sources to cite in their stories. This supports the hypothesis that correspondents work under the newsmaking model, where the news is seen as a product of the interplay between government sources and newsmen, and where the reporter and the official use each other to advantage their own organization.

There are no major differences between correspondents in Israel and their counterparts in Egypt with regard to their ranking of the extremely important news-making roles. However, I cannot totally overlook a real, but small difference between correspondents in Israel and their counterparts in Egypt with regard to their perceptions of the news-making roles.

As was previously mentioned, more correspondents in Israel thought it is extremely important to provide analysis of complex problems and investigate government claims than did their counterparts in Egypt. This difference can be attributed to the fact that the Israeli government releases much more information on the Arab-Israeli conflict and has more officials with whom to double-check facts than does the Egyptian government. Correspondents in Israel conduct more analysis and investigation because there is so much more official information distributed to them.

Several correspondents in Israel commented that it was not so much a question of having access to information; the flow was so intense, varied, insistent, and organized that it was rather a matter of sifting through it, filtering it, and deciding how to handle it. For the correspondents stationed in Egypt, the question was one of getting the information in the first place. Most correspondents in Egypt said officials release a minimum information, and, therefore, there is nothing much to check or investigate. Moreover, some correspondents said the tradition of checking information is not always acceptable to the Egyptian officials.

As an analogy, it is as if correspondents in Israel are given daily a large basket of apples by the Israeli government. Many apples are firm and ripe, but many others are soft and suspect. In Egypt, correspondents find only a couple of apples in their basket every few days. Because the basket is delivered to the market in the village, they are all that is available. In Israel, however, the basket sits beneath an apple tree filled with still more apples.

Another reason it is difficult for correspondents in Egypt to conduct investigations is that most of them cover not only Egypt but the rest of the Middle East as well, except for Israel. Often, this does not allow them the time or the resources to investigate the government's announcements. "I cover from Iran to Libya. Having few resources and less time, I spend most of my time providing the reader with general interpretation, perspectives, and scenarios, rather than doing much fact-checking or 'news-hunting' myself," said Joris Luijendijk, a Cairo-based correspondent for Dutch radio (1998).

But the newsmaking model has more to it than just the professional roles of reporters and the techniques they follow in covering their stories. One major aspect of the newsmaking model is that when a story is controversial, reporters are expected to gather proof from several separate and independent sources. In covering a story as complex and controversial as the Arab-Israeli conflict, most correspondents in Israel and Egypt said they always obtain several sources to verify their stories. In Israel, where official sources avail themselves to the news media, correspondents have no problem locating several sources. However, in Egypt, where there is a problem of accessibility, correspondents said they are forced to rely on only a few sources, such as the Egyptian Foreign Minister, whom they said is one of the most accessible government figures.

According to the newsmaking model, government officials also have their own criteria for selecting the news reporters to whom they release information. Among these criteria are the status of the reporters and the prestige of their news media organizations. This aspect is very clear in the governments' release of leaks to a select group of correspondents. In Israel, where leaks play a major role in the news flow between government and correspondents, many correspondents said the Israeli officials are very selective in leaking information. They said information is always leaked to American correspondents working for major U.S. news media, such as *Time* and CNN. Even in Egypt, where leaks are far less prevalent, only very few correspondents (mainly those working for major news organizations and those who have been in Egypt for a long time) reported that they receive occasional leaks from government officials.

The reason many correspondents said leaks are more prevalent in Israel than they are in Egypt is because Israel is a very small society where people know one another and where it is very hard to keep a secret. In this context, it can be speculated that the Israelis are not afraid to talk because they have been brought up in a tradition of democracy and free speech. Egyptians, however, are generally reluctant to say what they know, especially on sensitive political matters, because of real or imaginary fear that they are going to be penalized. This fear has been inherited from past eras of opinion suppression and the absence of a democratic atmosphere.

The data supported my argument that government officials work under the public relations asymmetric model, where the government tries to maintain the upper hand in its relationship with the news media and tries to gain compliance to its policies from the media. However, the correspondents' responses show that there are major differences between the public relations apparatuses in Israel and Egypt. According to most correspondents, the Israeli public relations system is much more professional and sophisticated in presenting its points of view than is the Egyptian public relations system. But despite differences in sophistication, correspondents said that both the Egyptian and the Israeli governments try to manipulate the foreign news media and use them for their advantage in a way that would advance the officials' own interests and present their country in the best way possible.

The difference between the two governments in applying the asymmetric model is that the Israeli government does it in a more subtle and professional way, using a Western style and manner that seems natural and spontaneous. In contrast, the Egyptian government is more blunt and less professional in applying the asymmetric model. This is reflected in the unavailability of Egyptian officials to correspondents and their reluctance to give interviews to the foreign news media.

Because the Israeli officials know how to present their case in a more convincing manner than their Egyptian counterparts, their announcements are more credible for many of the Western correspondents, despite the fact that many of these announcements are deceptive according to Western correspondents' answers. Israeli officials know how to play the public relations game. They try to co-opt correspondents by bombarding them with leaks and invitations to press conferences and news briefings and by being extremely friendly with them. In contrast, Egyptian officials have not yet mastered the public relations game. They rarely hold press conferences or news briefings for members of the foreign news media, and they do not contact correspondents on a regular basis.

As was mentioned before, the regular contact between reporters and sources might eventually lead to assimilation, personal identification, and friendship, which might result in a hesitancy on the reporters' part to reveal negative information about their sources. Whether this is the case with Western correspondents in Israel cannot be speculated, but perhaps the professionalism of the Israeli public relations machinery might be successful, to some extent, in its attempts to co-opt correspondents.

Unlike the Egyptian officials who are not always successful in making the outside world relate to their problems, the Israelis are very capable of generating sympathy for their causes. It would be very hard, for example, not to identify with the image of the "innocent" Israeli citizen trying to survive the threats of his more numerous Arab neighbors as projected by the Israeli public relations apparatus.

The terms "spin" and "media savvy" were used repeatedly by several correspondents in Israel to describe the public relations body of the Israeli government. This is an indication that the Israelis appreciate the news media role in projecting their image to the West and they do whatever they can to present themselves in the best manner possible. But, in doing that, the Israelis also try to devalue the image of their enemies. The is the ultimate use of the "spin" policy in dealing with the news media.

The terms "spinners" and "media savvy" were never used by the correspondents in Egypt, who said the Egyptian government is not always successful in getting its points of view across to the news media.

A major difference between the Israeli and Egyptian public relations systems (as they seemed to correspondents) is that in Israel, all government officials are capable of releasing information to the news media. In Egypt, however, only the bosses or the superiors (e.g., ministers, the prime minister, or the president) can give answers to the correspondents' questions. This situation stems from the hierarchical nature of the Arab governments. Superiors know everything and subordinates do not know as much, and even if they do know something, they cannot release information without their superiors' permission.

One of the major functions called for by the public relations asymmetric model is that government officials serve a proactive function by originating information and providing it to the news media through press conferences, press releases, or official documents and reports. Officials also serve a reactive function, responding to requests for information and clarification from news personnel. This includes activities such as making and returning telephone calls to answer journalists' questions or arranging for reporters to interview certain officials for the information they seek. These proactive and reactive public relations routines require a high level of accessibility on the part of the government officials. The findings of this study strongly show that the Israeli government officials are much more accessible than the Egyptian officials as perceived by the correspondents.

Most of the correspondents interviewed in Israel said Israeli officials are actually "overaccessible," and they avail themselves to the news media at all times. They also said the Israeli government is impressive and aggressive in presenting its views to the news media. It has a complex system of delivering information through regular briefings, press releases, or press conferences. However, the correspondents in Egypt said the Egyptian officials are hard to reach and are reluctant to schedule appointments with the correspondents.

The correspondents' comments make it clear that the governmental public relations system in Egypt is not as sophisticated or professional as the public relations apparatus developed by the Israeli government. But the professionalism and sophistication of the Israeli public relations apparatus are not necessarily indications of the success of Israeli officials in influencing the correspondents. As the results suggest, the correspondents in Israel are very critical of Israeli officials whom they accuse of presenting distorted versions of information and of disinforming the news media.

The correspondents in Israel said they do not "swallow" what they get from the Israeli officials, and they double-check every piece of information carefully. In fact, the findings indicate that correspondents in Israel are more fault-finding and more critical of the Israeli government than their counterparts in Egypt are of the Egyptian government. This is an indication that the correspondents do not buy into the Israeli public relations system despite its professionalism.

CONCLUSION

Based on the findings presented in this chapter, it can be speculated that a public relations system that is as slick and as sophisticated as the one developed by the Israelis might actually have some counterproductive results. Such a system can lead to more scrutiny, more fact-checking, and more critical attitudes on the correspondents' part. The fact that correspondents in Israel are being regularly spoon-fed with information by Israeli officials makes them more suspicious of the reliability of the official information they get and makes them question everything they obtain from the government.

In a nutshell, both the newsmaking model and the public relations asymmetric model seem to operate in Israel and Egypt, but they are colored by the levels of professionalism, political skills, and expertise of the public officials and the news reporters.

In the next chapter, I provide an analysis of the impact of culture on the reporting of Western journalists stationed in Israel and Egypt.

15

AN ANALYSIS OF THE CULTURAL IMPACT ON THE REPORTING OF WESTERN JOURNALISTS IN ISRAEL AND EGYPT

Within the cultural context, this study has sought to show how access to information about the Arab-Israeli conflict by Western correspondents in Israel and Egypt is affected by the correspondents' level of familiarity with the culture, specifically language and religion of both countries.

Before undertaking this study, I hypothesized that Western correspondents in Israel would be more familiar with the Israeli culture than their counterparts in Egypt would be with the Egyptian culture. This hypothesis was based on the assumption that the Israeli society is more Westernized than the Egyptian society. However, results of the study showed no major difference between correspondents in the two countries when it comes to their familiarity with the domestic cultures.

WESTERN JOURNALISTS AND LANGUAGE

Most correspondents in Israel said their ability to speak and or read Hebrew (Israel's official language) was not an important factor in their access to information about the conflict because all Israeli officials speak English. As for correspondents in Egypt, they also said that their ability to speak and or read Arabic (Egypt's official language) was not an essential factor in their work because most Egyptian officials can speak English. In cases in which officials cannot speak English, correspondents said they rely on translators. So language was not a barrier in either country, according to correspondents.

But a few correspondents in both countries said there is no substitute for being able to talk to people directly in their own language. According to those correspondents, speaking the native language of the country where they were stationed allowed them to gain greater insight into how local people think and it enabled them to gain people's trust more easily. Moreover, those correspondents said translators, in many cases, may not be very reliable in translating every word.

WESTERN JOURNALISTS AND RELIGION

Along with language, religion is another essential component of any cultural framework. My hypothesis that religion would be perceived by Western correspondents in Egypt as more of a barrier to their access to information than it is to their counterparts in Israel was not supported by the results. The findings showed no major difference among correspondents in both countries when it comes to their familiarity with Judaism (Israel's official religion) and Islam (Egypt's official religion).

The majority of the correspondents interviewed in Israel and Egypt said neither their own religion nor the religions practiced in Egypt and Israel (Islam and Judaism) affected their coverage of the conflict. An overwhelming majority of the correspondents said they practiced no religion.

Max Rodenbeck, Cairo bureau chief of the *Economist* (Great Britain), said, "Religion may change people's attitudes, but not necessarily what they say; it has not been a problem in my experience" (1998).

Similarly, Christophe Ayad, a Cairo-based correspondent for *Liberation* (the daily French newspaper), said: "I do not think my religion affects my coverage of the conflict because I do not practice it. Of course my religious background as a Christian is supposed to make me close to Christian/Jewish culture. But I feel I made an effort to understand Islam as a religion and a culture" (1998).

A U.S. correspondent in Cairo said, "People here assume that almost any Westerner is Christian, but this does not affect the way they deal with us. Because we are Americans, people here think we are pro-Israel and we are Zionist supporters."

Barbara Plett, a Cairo-based correspondent for the BBC, said, "Egyptians generally prefer believers over nonbelievers, but this does not prohibit access to information" (1998).

In Israel, as in Egypt, most correspondents thought religion was not a major factor in accessing information. In this context, Lisa Beyer, the Jerusalem-based bureau chief for *Time*, said: "There is a curiosity in Israel about one's religious affiliation. Many people here ask me about my religion, which is a 'taboo' question in the United States But I do not think it has a bearing on my job here" (1998).

Another U.S. correspondent in Israel said, "I am a secular Jew and I basically go out of my way to not allow religion to play a role in my coverage, which I feel is my professional duty and obligation."

But a few correspondents said religion did play a role in covering the Arab-Israeli conflict. Among those correspondents was Jeff Abramowitz, a Tel Aviv correspondent for the German News Agency, who said: "Religion is definitely important in dealing with the current Israeli government, which is a conservative, right-wing, religious government. This government regards me as not really part of the 'Jewish family' because I am working for the foreign press. Although I am Jewish, this government considers me an outsider, and some people told me outright that I am betraying Israel because I work for the foreign press" (1998).

Another German correspondent in Israel, Astrid Frohloff, bureau chief of SAT.1, German TV, said: "Everything in Israel is based on religion, and this is hard for us to understand because we come from different cultural and religious backgrounds. As a woman, I always have a great difficulty in approaching the ultra-orthodox Jews in Israel, who refuse to talk to women as part of their religious beliefs" (1998).

Renee-Anne Gutter, a Belgian correspondent in Jerusalem, said Israeli officials have more trust for Jewish correspondents, and therefore, they might release more information to Jews than to non-Jews. "It does not, however, affect the quantity of information as much as it affects the attitudes. Israelis are more friendly to Jewish correspondents than they are to non-Jewish ones" (1998).

"If you share the religion with a party or a politician in Israel," said Inge Gunther, a Jerusalem-based German correspondent, "your job becomes easier. Sometimes there is the impression that you, as a non-Jewish person, will be treated as an 'outsider' and will get only part of the official side of the story" (1998).

Some correspondents in Israel even said that religion had a direct effect on their lives and on how the Israelis regarded them. "I do not feel accepted by the Israeli society because I am not Jewish; after all, this is a Jewish state," said Maureen Meehan, a U.S. correspondent in Israel (1998).

A few correspondents in Egypt also believed that religion played a role in their access to information. Among those correspondents was Jacqueline Burrell, a British freelance journalist in Cairo, who said people in the Islamic World assume that Western correspondents have not learned enough about Islam, and therefore, they mistrusted those correspondents (1998).

Some correspondents stationed in Egypt said Jewish journalists might have a problem in dealing with the people. "Religion here is not really important except when I am asked if I am a Jew," said a Cairo-based U.S. correspondent. " I usually reply that I am Catholic, and this makes people feel more at ease. If I were Jewish, people would be more reserved with me."

Most correspondents in both countries agreed that regardless of one's own religious affiliation, a good understanding of the official religion of the country where a correspondent is stationed helps a lot in getting a better idea of what is going on in that country. Steffen Jensen, a Danish correspondent in Israel, said: "The fact that I am Jewish, though not orthodox, and that I do take religion seriously makes it easier for me to understand how religion can play such a strong role in shaping the policies of the day in Israel. In a region like the Middle East, even secular people often react in ways that are based on religious traditions. This requires a good understanding of the local official religions" (1998).

NATIONALITY RATHER THAN RELIGION

Many correspondents said nationality was more important than religion in their coverage of the conflict in the sense that a correspondent's country of origin may partly determine how he or she was viewed by officials, and this consequently determined his or her access to information. For example, several U.S. correspondents said they have more access to official sources in both countries than the other correspondents. This was especially true in Israel, where U.S. correspondents are held in high regard by Israeli officials.

ISRAEL: A HEAVEN FOR WESTERN JOURNALISTS

Although the responses to the close-ended questions showed no major differences between correspondents in Israel and their counterparts in Egypt with regard to their familiarity with the Israeli and the Egyptian languages and religions, journalists' answers to the open-ended questions showed that correspondents in Israel related more to the Israeli culture than the ones in Egypt did to the Egyptian culture.

In this context, a Jerusalem-based U.S. correspondent said Israel is a very Westernized society that is very approachable to Western journalists. Echoing this argument, Lisa Beyer, Jerusalem bureau chief of *Time*, said: "Israel is an open democratic society politically and culturally, and the Israelis feel very comfortable in releasing information. It is easy for us to work here because it is a Westernized society where you can always get all the opinions you are after. There is a pretty natural fit between foreign correspondents and Israeli official and nonofficial sources. Being an American reporter and working for a major American magazine makes Israelis friendly to me because they are familiar with the U.S. culture and because there is no huge cultural gap between Israel and the U.S." (1998).

Nicholas Goldberg, Jerusalem-based bureau chief of *Newsday*, said Israel is a very open and democratic society that has a tradition of providing a lot of information in a very sophisticated manner. "Israelis know that if they provide information and become friends with journalists, it will be easier for them to make their point and to have their side of the story told in the foreign press; however, in many Arab countries, people do not understand that, and they think that the easiest thing to do is to block information" (1998).

Hanson Hosein, a chief producer for NBC in Tel Aviv, said: "When you are working in Israel, you know you have certain rights and that there is a certain amount of openness. You certainly feel like you are in the U.S. and like you have the right to interview any government member about any issue and that you are guaranteed that right and access." According to Hosein, Israel is the most overcovered part of the world, and Israeli officials are aware that Israel is a high-profile country (1998).

Dan Mogulof, CBS bureau chief in Tel Aviv, said: "Israelis have been used to the idea of a free press for over 50 years, and the local Israeli press establishes and protects the tradition of a free flow of information by having a critical view of the government" (1998).

EGYPT: SOME SUSPICION OF WESTERN JOURNALISTS

The level of comfort and closeness to Israeli society by the Western correspondents in Israel was not felt by their counterparts in Egypt. A Cairo-based German correspondent, Birgit Tofall, said there were many prejudices, especially among officials, against Western journalists, who the officials think do bad reporting. In general, officials were against the idea of a free press as adopted by the West.

Christine Hauser, a Cairo-based Reuters correspondent, said: "As an American, I am viewed by many people here with a lot of suspicion; they think I am working for the CIA or the American Embassy" (1998). Similarly, Drusilla Menaker, Cairo-based correspondent for the *Dallas Morning News*, said: "There is a general distrust of Westerners, non-Arabs, and non-Moslems by opinion makers and a sense that the foreign media are conspiring against the Arab world. People here have no understanding of what a free press is like, and they expect us to write in their favor. They do not facilitate interaction" (1998).

A Cairo-based Swedish journalist said: "We do try to understand the Egyptian society, but people here are very suspicious of Western correspondents and feel we want to destroy the image of the country. They feel we are part of a big Zionist conspiracy against Egypt. Even very high up in the official hierarchy, there is a lack of understanding of how the Western media operate."

Christophe Ayad, a Cairo-based French correspondent, said: "There is a general feeling of defiance towards everybody who is a foreigner here. Among officials, there is still a very high degree of anticolonialist feelings which prevent relaxed relationships and discussions with foreign, and specifically Western, correspondents" (1998).

DOES CULTURAL FAMILIARITY AFFECT JOURNALISTIC ROLES?

For some correspondents, the lack of familiarity with the domestic cultures did not impede their professional jobs as correspondents. "While it is completely fair to criticize journalists who lack cultural familiarity, it would be equally unfair to assume that this unfamiliarity would make their work less valid. It depends almost exclusively on the correspondents' skills as reporters," an ABC correspondent in Jerusalem said.

According to that correspondent, "Although the inability to speak the language[s] and the lack of familiarity with both Islamic and Israeli cultures might be a problem or hindrance, being 'an outsider' can sometimes help in reporting here, as one sometimes sees events more clearly than when viewed through a prism of cultural bias. One's lack of intimate knowledge of a culture does not preclude good coverage. A good reporter admits what he or she does not know and then exerts an effort to find out. It just means, perhaps, that you have to work harder, especially in this part of the world where cultural bias is a problem and where people are not able to see or admit the valid points of the 'other' side."

JOURNALISTS' LENGTH OF STAY AND CULTURAL FAMILIARITY

Several studies have shown a direct relationship between the correspondents' length of stay in a certain country and their familiarity with the local culture of that country. Results of this study supported my hypothesis that the longer correspondents have lived in either Egypt or Israel, the more familiar they are with that country's culture.

AMERICAN AND EUROPEAN CORRESPONDENTS: ARE THEY DIFFERENT IN THEIR REPORTING ON ISRAEL?

During my stay in Israel, I was told by several U.S. correspondents, and in particular those working for American news organizations understood to be the most politically influential, (such as the *New York Times* and CNN), that they sometimes get special treatment from Israeli officials. For example, a few U.S. correspondents told me that they are always invited to news briefings and other special occasions organized by Israeli officials.

The United States has a great cultural impact on the Israeli community. Because the Jewish diaspora community in the United States is so large, and American-Israeli relationships are generally so close, the feedback to U.S. correspondents both from home audiences and in Jerusalem tends to be particularly intense.

Does this special treatment given to U.S. correspondents make their reporting on Israel different from their counterparts from other Western countries? Well, I am not in a position to answer that question because I have not analyzed their reporting and compared it to that of other Western correspondents. However, according to Robert Fisk, a BBC correspondent in Lebanon,

"U.S. journalists are not very courageous . . . They go for safe stories . . . Because there is a very powerful lobby in the United States, . . . American journalists are very frightened of writing a report which is going to make Israel—or, more important, Israel's supporters in the United States—unhappy" (cited in Rothschild, 1998, 39).

IMPLICATIONS OF THE CORRESPONDENTS' RESPONSES IN THE CONTEXT OF CULTURAL FAMILIARITY

The data did not support my hypothesis that Western correspondents in Israel were more familiar with the culture (language and religion) than their counterparts in Egypt. But this does not mean cultural differences between Israel and Egypt do not have an impact on Western correspondents' coverage of the two countries. As was shown in the findings, correspondents' answers to the open-ended question on culture strongly suggest that there are major differences in the way they view the domestic cultures of Israel and Egypt.

These differences are more subtle than simple familiarity with language and religion. Many correspondents in Israel said they are familiar with Judaism (the official religion of Israel) and Hebrew (Israel's official language), and many correspondents in Egypt said they are familiar with Islam (Egypt's official religion) and Arabic (Egypt's official language). But, it seems that familiarity with language and religion does not fully capture how the correspondents cope with a specific culture.

Correspondents' answers to the open-ended question on culture showed that there is more to culture than just language and religion. Correspondents in Israel said they felt comfortable operating in the Israeli society, which they said is Westernized and politically and culturally open in a way that allows for a continuous flow of information in a free and unrestricted manner. Correspondents in Israel also said Israeli society cherishes Western news values of democracy, openness, and freedom of speech in a way that increases its cultural affinity to the West. They also said Israeli government officials are able to understand Western correspondents' mentality, and those officials know how to address Western sensibilities in a very effective manner.

Western correspondents in Egypt said Egyptian officials do not support the idea of a free press, and they are always suspicious of Western correspondents' motives. Moreover, correspondents in Egypt said Egyptian officials are not tolerant of any criticism on the correspondents' part, and they expect those correspondents to write in their favor all the time.

Therefore, correspondents' comments show that Israel adopts the Western news values of democracy, openness, and freedom of speech in a way that is not as clearly expressed in Egyptian society.

The comments by Western correspondents in Israel and Egypt suggest they perceive major differences between Israeli culture and Egyptian culture. Correspondents in Israel identify with the Israeli culture, which is Western in nature. However, in Egypt, there is a mutual cultural mistrust between officials and correspondents. The suspicion many Egyptians (officials and nonofficials) have of foreigners, especially Westerners, results from the fact that the West is associated in their minds with colonialism and foreign conspiracies to destroy the country's image. This widens the gap between the two sides.

The cultural differences between Egypt and Israel are best expressed in the words of Walter Rodgers (1998), former CNN bureau chief in Jerusalem, who said: "For a journalist, Israel is the best country in the world to work in because it is far more open than what you would find in many Third World countries. On the Palestinian side, as is the case in the rest of the Arab world, there is always that deep divide between Islam and the West."

Based on the correspondents' answers to the close-ended and open-ended questions on culture, it becomes clear that the cultural aspects as defined in the literature (language and religion) are not significant factors, and they have little bearing on the correspondents' work in Israel and Egypt.

The freshness of the approach used in this study (the very intense research in two countries) and the newness of doing quantitative research on international correspondents has revealed some cultural differences between Israel and Egypt from the Western correspondents' perspectives. Hardly any studies go beyond correspondents' personal impressions, memoirs, recollections, and autobiographies. So, this project, which is the first to study correspondents in Israel and Egypt on a systematic basis, can serve as a guidance for future researchers.

It is worth mentioning here that there are more Jews among Western correspondents in Israel than there are Moslems among Western correspondents in Egypt. This possibly increases the cultural affinity between Western correspondents and Israelis, but it does not reduce the cultural gap between the Western correspondents and Egyptian society.

What are the major implications of these cultural differences between Israel and Egypt and how do they affect Western correspondents' professional roles? Although diplomatic efforts led to the signing of a peace treaty by the two countries more than two decades ago, there is still a sea of cultural incompatibility separating Israelis and Egyptians. This has resulted not only from religious and language differences but more importantly from drastically different social and historical circumstances. As mentioned earlier, the Egyptian culture is a product of the village community in which individual autonomy is subordinated to the group's needs. However, the Israeli society was founded by immigrants from many cultural and ethnic backgrounds, and it cherishes individuality.

I speculate that these cultural differences have an impact on the way Western correspondents report about the two countries. Because Western correspondents feel closer to Israeli society, they can relate directly to it, and they have a more insightful understanding of the intricacies of that society. This consequently leads to better reporting. This is not the case with Egypt, where the barrier of cultural incomprehension on the correspondents' part might lead to an incomplete or, under worst circumstances, inaccurate reporting of Egyptian society.

Having said that, I do not want this speculation to be understood as an indication that Western correspondents in Egypt do a less effective job than their counterparts in Israel. In fact, during my interviews with correspondents in Cairo, I got the impression that they do their best in trying to overcome the cultural barrier and understand Egyptian society in a way that allows them to report objectively and accurately about that society. In support of that argument, a Cairo-based Swedish journalist said: "We do try to understand Egyptian society, but people here are very suspicious of Western correspondents and feel we want to destroy the image of their country."

Nevertheless, the discrepancy between correspondents in Israel and their counterparts in Egypt with regard to their understanding and comfort with the two cultures might lead correspondents in Israel to unconsciously present a better and more comprehensive picture of Israeli society than that presented by their counterparts in Egypt in their coverage of Egyptian society.

A WEALTH OF INFORMATION

Most correspondents in Israel and Egypt were forthcoming in their answers to me, even on such sensitive issues as their religious affiliations, security, the prevalence of leaks, and the credibility of government officials. This was unexpected, especially in Israel, where I thought I might be regarded with suspicion as an "Arab."

The question is: Why were those correspondents very open and forthcoming in their answers to me? Were they pleased that an Arab scholar with credentials and a Western liberal education at a U.S. university is willing to address some of the problems those correspondents face in their dealings with the Israeli and the Egyptian governments? Did they want to pass a message to these governments through me?

There are no definite answers to these questions except that correspondents were very interested in discussing the problems and concerns that they face in their dealings with Israeli and Egyptian government officials on a daily basis.

Although the majority of correspondents interviewed were open in their answers, some were more open and more willing to talk than others. Generally, correspondents from smaller countries working for lesser-known news organizations were less reluctant to talk than their counterparts from bigger countries who worked for major news organizations. Perhaps this was because correspondents with big names who work for major news organizations feel they are always in the spotlight, and this makes them very careful in what they say.

The fact that I had the opportunity to interview personally an overwhelming majority of the correspondents who participated in this study made the correspondents relate more to me on both a personal and a professional level. I got to know the correspondents as human beings after my long conversations with them. This enabled me to reach deep down in those correspondents' thinking and discuss with them highly sensitive issues in an open, genuine, and friendly atmosphere. This could not have been achieved had I mailed or e-mailed them the questionnaire.

Moreover, the correspondents trusted me more after knowing that I am a journalist, and they found a common ground between them and myself in a way that allowed for more accurate, thoughtful, and reliable responses within the context of the interpersonal communication. In fact, many correspondents were curious to know about my journalistic background, and they expressed their interest in sharing the problems they faced in their day-to-day professional lives with me, even if these problems were not addressed in the questionnaire. This indicates that I gained those correspondents' trust during my conversations with them and that they were willing to share their thoughts with me as a colleague, not just as a scholar.

My direct interaction with the correspondents also increased the response rate for the close-ended questions. This is because many correspondents were reluctant to answer some of these questions, especially the ones dealing with security and leaks, before actually discussing them with me. This discussion led to more understanding on the correspondents' part and increased their willingness to answer these sensitive questions.

Furthermore, the interpersonal context helped me build a good reputation among those correspondents in a way that increased my network of contacts. Many correspondents volunteered to contact their colleagues and ask them to help me with my project. My interpersonal communication with the correspondents made this study an insightful one, not just an adequate one.

CONCLUSION

It can be concluded from this chapter that culture plays a vital role in facilitating or hindering the correspondents' access to information. It is clear from the Western correspondents' comments that the Israeli culture is closer to their backgrounds than the Egyptian culture. Most correspondents said that the openness and transparency of Israeli society makes it easier for them to operate than the Egyptian society does, which they said is very suspicious of what they do.

EPILOGUE: LESSONS LEARNED

After discussing the findings of this project and explaining the nature of the government-press relationship in Israel and Egypt within the context of the correspondents' answers, the question that poses itself is: How does this study contribute to our understanding of the role played by the news media in solving the Arab-Israeli conflict and what lessons can be learned about the nature of the government-press relationship in Israel and Egypt?

One of the basic premises made earlier in the study is that decision makers rely on the information made available to them by the news media to make political decisions in periods of conflict. Consequently, the decision-making process in Israel and Egypt is affected by the information exchanged between government and news media in both countries.

In a region such as the Middle East, there is a general lack of understanding and a lot of misconceptions among governments that frequently result in conflicts. Western correspondents have been accused, especially by the Arabs, of contributing to this misunderstanding by not being objective in their reporting, by taking a pro-Israeli stand, and by presenting half-truths about the conflict. These accusations are, to a great extent, true. The Arab-Israeli conflict has been presented in the Western news media primarily from the Israeli side. The Arab side has been largely absent. But Western correspondents are not solely to blame for this situation. In fact, this study showed that the majority of Western correspondents stationed in Israel and Egypt exert great effort to understand both the Israeli and the Egyptian cultures in order to be objective and balanced in their reporting.

In this context, an ABC correspondent in Jerusalem said: "One's lack of intimate knowledge of a culture does not preclude good coverage. A good reporter admits what he or she does not know and then exerts an effort to find out. It just means, perhaps, that you have to work harder, especially in this part of the world where cultural bias is a problem and where people are not able to see or admit the valid points of the 'other' side."

So, correspondents try hard to comprehend the intricacies and cultural subtleties involved in such a complicated and confusing region as the Middle East. Israelis play to and support these efforts; Egyptians resist and confound them.

The unpreparedness and unwillingness of Arab officials to project their ideas in an open and robust manner and to make themselves available to the foreign press harms the Arab cause by making it practically impossible for correspondents to have access to information that might benefit the Arabs if it is reported in the international news media. Therefore, it can be said that the Arabs are at least partly responsible for misconceptions about themselves and for increasing the discrepancy between themselves and the Israelis, who are more accessible and open in dealing with the foreign news media.

The majority of correspondents interviewed in the Middle East said Egyptian officials hurt the Egyptian cause by not holding press conferences or news briefings, by too infrequently distributing press releases, by failing to respond to requests for information and clarification, and by rarely returning Western correspondents' telephone calls. Israelis do all these things and more, and they get their position into the Western news media with clarity and considerable precision.

Although Egypt is no longer directly involved in the Arab-Israeli conflict, it has an impact on the political matters in the region, and it plays a major role in the negotiation and mediation process between the Israelis and the Palestinians. Therefore, Egyptian officials should deal with Western correspondents, not as opponents but as persons who will help project Egyptian ideas and policies to the Israelis and to the rest of the world. This would be the first step toward clarifying the current misconceptions in the Middle East and balancing the flow of information, which is currently dominated by the Israeli side.

The public relations asymmetric model is practiced in both Israel and Egypt but in two different styles. On the one hand, the Israeli government tries to manipulate the foreign news media by co-opting correspondents, by increasing officials' accessibility to correspondents, and by aggressively projecting the Israeli image abroad. On the other hand, the Egyptian government manipulates the foreign news media by withholding information at times and by denying access to official sources. Either way, the Western correspondents in the Middle East are experienced enough to escape co-optation by Israeli officials and get access to the information denied to them by Egyptian officials by contacting other nonofficial sources.

RECOMMENDATIONS FOR FUTURE RESEARCH

This is the first study to take a census of foreign correspondents in one region of the world. It investigated the nature of their relationship with the governments, the kinds of news-making roles they undertake, and how well they cope with the cultures of two countries in that region: Israel and Egypt. Future researchers can study foreign correspondents in other regions of the world and compare their findings to those of this study to highlight the differences, if any, among the professional roles of correspondents in various parts of the world.

I did not investigate the impact of organizational factors on foreign correspondents' work because this is not the main focus of this study. However, future researchers might investigate the correspondents' job satisfaction, their relationships with superiors in the home offices, their job stability, and other organizational factors that are of importance to the correspondents inside their news organizations. These organizational aspects might have an impact on the correspondents' familiarity with the local cultures in which they operate. For example, many Western news organizations in Israel employ Israeli local stringers, who might be more familiar with the Israeli culture than the Western correspondents.

CONCLUSION

One final word. Because few Israelis get the chance to visit Egypt and apparently very few Egyptians visit Israel, each one of these cultures is virtually a closed book to the other. It can be concluded that foreign correspondents might be the only link to bridge the gap between the two cultures by contributing to the information exchange between Israel and Egypt. Israeli officials seem to understand and encourage the vital role played by correspondents in this respect. However, this role is still not apparent to Egyptian officials.

APPENDICES

APPENDIX A: WESTERN CORRESPONDENTS' DEMOGRAPHIC BACKGROUNDS IN ISRAEL AND EGYPT

Characteristic	Israel N.	Israel %	Egypt N.	Egypt %	Total N.	Total %
Gender						
Males	65	69.1	49	66.2	114	67.9
Females	29	30.9	25	33.8	54	32.1
Total cases	94	100	74	100	168	100
Age in years						
Under 25	0	0.0	0	0.0	0	0.0
25–34	18	19.1	15	20.3	33	19.6
35–44	39	41.5	32	43.2	71	42.3
45–54	25	26.6	14	18.9	39	23.2
55–64	9	9.6	7	9.5	16	9.5
65 and older	3	3.2	2	2.7	5	3.0
Missing cases	0	0.0	4	5.4	4	2.4
Total cases	94	100	74	100	168	100
Professional Title						
Bureau Chief	42	44.7	15	20.3	57	33.9
Correspondent	34	36.2	44	59.5	78	46.4
Photographer	3	3.2	6	8.1	9	5.4
Cameraman	2	2.1	1	1.4	3	1.8
Editor	3	3.2	1	1.4	4	2.4
Other	10	10.6	7	9.5	17	10.1
Total cases	94	100	74	100	168	100
Religion Raised						
Christian	48	51.1	56	75.7	104	61.9
Moslem	1	1.1	1	1.4	2	1.2
Jewish	28	29.8	1	1.4	29	17.3

Characteristic	Israel N.	Israel %	Egypt N.	Egypt %	Total N.	Total %
None	17	18.1	9	12.2	26	15.5
Other	0	0.0	1	1.4	1	.6
Missing cases	0	0.0	6	8.1	6	3.6
Total cases	94	100	74	100	168	100
Religion Practiced						
Christian	12	12.8	24	32.4	36	21.4
Moslem	1	1.1	4	5.4	5	3.0
Jewish	17	18.1	1	1.4		
None	62	66.0	33	44.6	95	56.5
Other	2	2.1	3	4.1	5	3.0
Missing cases	0	0.0	9	12.2	9	5.4
Total cases	94	100	74	100	168	100
Nationality						
Dutch	5	5.3	3	4.1	8	4.8
French	7	7.4	9	12.2	16	9.5
American	30	31.9	27	36.5	57	33.9
Spanish	2	2.1	5	6.8	7	4.2
Austrian	2	2.1	1	1.4	3	1.8
German	13	13.8	12	16.2	25	14.9
British	7	7.4	7	9.5	14	8.3
Canadian	8	8.5	2	2.7	10	6.0
Swedish	1	1.1	2	2.7	3	1.8
Swiss	1	1.1	3	4.1	4	2.4
Greek	0	0.0	1	1.4	1	.6
Italian	4	4.3	1	1.4	5	3.0
Belgian	2	2.1	1	1.4	3	1.8
Danish	3	3.2	0	0.0	3	1.8
Irish	2	2.1	0	0.0	2	1.2
Australian	5	5.3	0	0.0	5	3.0
Portuguese	1	1.1	0	0.0	1	.6
New Zealand	1	1.1	0	0.0	1	.6

Characteristic	Israel N.	Israel %	Egypt N.	Egypt %	Total N.	Total %
Languages						
Spoken Arabic						
Correspondents speaking Arabic	24	25.5	53	71.6	77	45.8
Correspondents not speaking Arabic	70	74.5	19	25.7	89	53.0
Missing cases	0	0.0	2	2.7	2	1.2
Total cases	94	100	74	100	168	100
Spoken Hebrew						
Correspondents speaking Hebrew	46	48.9	2	2.7	48	28.6
Correspondents not Speaking Hebrew	48	51.1	70	94.6	118	70.2
Missing cases	0	0.0	2	2.7	2	1.2
Total cases	94	100	74	100	168	100
Years spent in Middle East						
0–3	35	37.2	22	29.7	57	33.9
4–10	23	24.5	25	33.8	48	28.6
More than 10	36	38.3	27	36.5	63	37,5
Total cases	94	100	74	100	168	100
Years spent as correspondent						
0–3	16	17.0	15	20.3	31	18.5
4–10	32	34.0	29	39.2	61	36.3
More than 10	46	48,9	28	37.8	74	44.1
Missing cases	0	0.0	2	2.7	2	1.2
Total cases	94	100	74	100	168	100
Educational Degrees						
High School	3	3.2	0	0.0	3	1.8
Some College	3	3.2	3	4.1	6	3.6
B.A.	48	51.1	31	41.9	79	47.0
M.A.	33	35.1	33	44.6	66	39.3
Ph.D.	4	4.3	2	2.7	6	3.6
Missing cases	3	3.2	5	6.8	8	4.8
Total cases	94	100	74	100	168	100

Appendix B: A Questionnaire

Dear Correspondent:

My name is Mohammed el-Nawawy. I am a doctoral candidate in the School of Journalism at Southern Illinois University at Carbondale. Attached is a questionnaire for my dissertation study. Its purpose is to investigate how Western media correspondents' access to information about the Arab-Israeli conflict in both Egypt and Israel is affected by cultural environments (e.g. language and religion); the correspondents' educational backgrounds and professional roles, and the organization of the information delivery system of governments in both countries.

This questionnaire has been reviewed and approved by the Committee for Research Involving Human Subjects at Southern Illinois University and by the graduate committee in the School of Journalism.

The questionnaire will take about twenty minutes to answer. Your participation is voluntary and you can quit at any time you like; however, **I would appreciate getting the questionnaire back, whether it is complete or not.**

I would like to attribute your comments to you by name. However, if you do not want your answers to this questionnaire to be attributed to you, your responses will be kept confidential. By supplying answers to this questionnaire, you express your informed consent to participate in this study.

If you have any questions on your participation in this study, you can contact my dissertation advisor, Dr. James Kelly; phone: (618) 453–3278; email: jkelly@siu.edu. You can also contact the Committee for Research Involving Human Subjects; Office of Research Development and Administration, Woody Hall C217, SIUC, Carbondale IL 62901–4709; phone (618) 453–4533.

Thanks in advance for your cooperation.

Cordially,
Mohammed el-Nawawy
Doctoral candidate
School of Journalism
Southern Illinois University at Carbondale

Questionnaire

Would you mind if your responses are attributed to you by name in the dissertation? If you mind, your responses will remain confidential.

a) You may quote me   b) I want my responses kept confidential

Personal Data:
1) What is your name?
2) What news organization are you corresponding for?
3) In what year were you born?
4) What is your current nationality?
5) What is your professional title?

6) In what religion were you raised?

7) What religion do you practice now?

8) What languages do you speak?

9) What is the highest educational degree you hold?

10) How long have you been a foreign correspondent?

11) How long have you been stationed in the Middle East?

12) How long have you been stationed in this country (Egypt/Israel)?

Newsmaking & Asymmetric Models:

13) How important do you think the following roles are that the news media do or try to do today:

a) Get information to the public quickly

Extremely Important	Quite Important	Somewhat Important	Not Really Imp.
1	2	3	4

b) Provide analysis and interpretation of complex problems

Extremely Important	Quite Important	Somewhat Important	Not Really Imp.
1	2	3	4

c) Investigate claims and statements made by the government

Extremely Important	Quite Important	Somewhat Important	Not Really Imp.
1	2	3	4

d) Stay away from stories where factual content cannot be verified

Extremely Important	Quite Important	Somewhat Important	Not Really Imp.
1	2	3	4

e) Discuss national policy while it is still being developed

Extremely Important	Quite Important	Somewhat Important	Not Really Imp.
1	2	3	4

f) Be an adversary of public officials by being constantly skeptical of their actions

Extremely Important	Quite Important	Somewhat Important	Not Really Imp.
1	2	3	4

g) Be an adversary of businesses by being constantly skeptical of their actions

Extremely Important	Quite Important	Somewhat Important	Not Really Imp.
1	2	3	4

h) Set the political agenda

Extremely Important	Quite Important	Somewhat Important	Not Really Imp.
1	2	3	4

i) Concentrate on news which is of interest to the widest possible audience

Extremely Important	Quite Important	Somewhat Important	Not Really Imp.
1	2	3	4

j) Provide entertainment and relaxation

Extremely Important	Quite Important	Somewhat Important	Not Really Imp.
1	2	3	4

k) Develop intellectual and cultural interests of the public

Extremely Important	Quite Important	Somewhat Important	Not Really Imp.
1	2	3	4

l) Influence public opinion

Extremely Important	Quite Important	Somewhat Important	Not Really Imp.
1	2	3	4

m) Give ordinary people a chance to express their views on public affairs

Extremely Important	Quite Important	Somewhat Important	Not Really Imp.
1	2	3	4

14) Have you written any books or articles on your experience in the Middle East? If yes, can you name them?

15) On a scale of one to seven (where one means very frequent and seven means not at all frequent), rate how frequent you verify or conduct further investigation on the information released by the government on the Arab-Israeli conflict.

Very frequent   /—/—/—/— /—/—/   Not at all freq.
                    1   2   3   4   5   6   7

Access to Information:
16) On a scale of one to seven (where one means very accessible and seven means not at all accessible), rate the general accessibility level of government officials (ministers, government spokespersons and public information officers) for information on the Arab-Israeli conflict.

Very accessible   /—/—/—/— /—/—/   Not at all acc.
                    1   2   3   4   5   6   7

17) On a scale of one to seven (where one means very prevalent and seven means not at all prevalent), rate the prevalence of government leaks (secret distribution of official information to correspondents).

Very prevalent   /—/—/—/— /—/—/   Not at all prev.
                    1   2   3   4   5   6   7

Government Public Relations:
18) On a scale of one to seven (one being very frequent and seven being not at all frequent), rate the frequency of the government's use of the security issue as a justification for withholding information on the Arab-Israeli conflict.

Very frequent   /— /— /— /— /— /— /   Not at all freq.
                    1   2   3   4   5   6   7

19) On a scale of one to seven (where one means very often and seven means not at all often), how often, in your opinion, is government use of security justified for withholding information on the Arab-Israeli conflict?

Very often   /—/—/—/— /—/—/   Not at all often
                   1   2   3   4   5   6   7

20) On a scale of one to seven (one being very sufficient and seven being not at all sufficient), how sufficient are your informal sources (peers, colleagues, friends and acquaintances) for verifying government claims on controversial issues with regards to the Arab-Israeli conflict?

Very sufficient   /——/——/——/—— /——/—— /   Not at all suff.
                    1   2   3   4   5   6   7

21) On a scale of one to seven (where one means very credible and seven means not at all credible), rate the credibility of the government public relations machinery (e.g. public information officers, press conferences and press releases) in this country as sources of information on the Arab-Israeli conflict.

Very credible   /——/——/——/—— /—— /—— /   Not at all credib.
                 1   2   3   4   5   6   7

Culture:

22) On a scale of one to seven (where one means familiar and seven means unfamiliar) rate your familiarity level with Islam/Judaism.

Familiar   /——/——/——/—— /—— /—— /   Unfamiliar
           1   2   3   4   5   6   7

23) On a scale of one to seven (where one is native ability and seven is almost no ability) rate your ability of SPEAKING Arabic/Hebrew.

Native ability   /——/——/——/—— /—— /—— /   No ability
               1   2   3   4   5   6   7

24) On a scale of one to seven (where one is native ability and seven is almost no ability) rate your ability of READING Arabic/Hebrew.

Native   /——/——/——/—— /—— /—— /   No ability
         1   2   3   4   5   6   7

On the following open-ended questions, feel free to use the back of the pages if you need more space.

25) What are the cultural factors that you think might impede your access to information about the Arab-Israeli conflict in this country?

26) What do you think the government is trying to do in its dealings with the news media? Does it flood you with information or give you the minimum on the Arab-Israeli conflict? Explain.

27) How many Egyptian/Israeli friends and acquaintances do you have in this country?

28) Does religion play a role in your access to information about the Arab-Israeli conflict? Explain.

29) Does language play a role in your coverage of the Arab-Israeli conflict? Explain.

30) In your opinion, is the security issue misused by the government in not releasing information about the Arab-Israeli conflict?

APPENDIX C: TERMS, DEFINITIONS, AND QUESTIONS

Term	Definition	Question
Correspondent's age	age in years	• In what year were you born?
Correspondent's language	fluency in language of foreign government	• On a scale of 1 to seven (where one is native ability and seven is almost no ability), rate your ability to SPEAK Arabic/Hebrew. • On a scale of 1 to seven (where one is native ability and seven is almost no ability), rate your ability to READ Arabic/Hebrew. • Does language play in a role in your coverage of the Middle East conflict? Explain.
Correspondent's religion	The correspondent's past and present religion, if any	• In what religion were you raised? • What religion do you practice now?
Correspondent's familiarity	Familiarity with the official religion of foreign country	• On a scale of one to seven with religion (where one means familiar and seven means unfamiliar), rate your familiarity level with Islam/Judaism. • Does religion play a role in your access to information about the Middle East conflict? Explain.
Correspondent's education	The highest educational degree	• What is the highest educational degree that you hold?
Correspondent's years of operation	Years of operation in years/months	• How long have you been a foreign correspondent? • How long have you been stationed in the Middle East?

		• How long have you been stationed in this country?
Culture	Cultural context of the foreign country.	• What are the cultural factors that you think might impede your access to information about the Middle East conflict in this country?
Journalistic roles	Investigative (interpreting complex problems)/neutral (detached dissemination of information)	• How important do you think the following roles are that the news media do or try to do today? (Weaver&Wilhoit's scale).
Relationship between government and correspondents	Newsmaking model on the journalists' part/asymmetric model on the government's part	• What do you think the government is trying to do in its dealings with the news media? Does it flood you with information or give you the minimum on the Middle East conflict? Explain.
		• On a scale of one to seven (where one means very frequent and seven means not at all frequent), rate how frequently you verify or conduct further investigation on the information released by government on the Middle East conflict.
Access to official information	Correspondents' accessibility to government's ministers, spokespersons, and public information officers	• On a scale of one to seven (where one means very accessible and seven means not at all accessible), rate the general accessibility level of government officials (ministers, government spokespersons and public information officers).
Government leaks	Secret distribution of information from government officials to correspondents	• On a scale of one to seven (one being very prevalent and seven being not at all prevalent), rate the prevalence of government leaks (secret distribution of information).

Security issue	Correspondents' perception of the frequency of government's use of national security as a justification for withholding information. National security information includes military, foreign affairs, strategic and economic information that, if released, would threaten the national existence of the state.	• On a scale of one to seven (where one means very frequent and seven means not at all frequent), rate the frequency of the government's use of the security issue as a justification for withholding information on the Middle East conflict? • On a scale of one to seven (where one means very often and seven means not at all often), how often is government use of the security issue justified for withholding information on the Middle East conflict? • Is the security issue misused by the government in not releasing information about the Middle East conflict?
Sufficiency of correspondents' informal sources	Correspondents' use of peers and colleagues, friends and acquaintances as sufficient sources of information on the Middle East conflict	• On a scale of one to seven (where one means very sufficient and seven means not at all sufficient), how sufficient are your informal sources (peers, colleagues, friends and acquaintances) for verifying government claims on controversial issues with regards to the Middle East conflict. • How many Egyptian/Israeli friends and acquaintances do you have in this country?
Government public relations' credibility	Correspondents' perception of the credibility of public relations machinery as information sources on the Middle East conflict	• On a scale of one to seven (where one means very credible and seven means not at all credible), rate the credibility of the government PR as sources of information on the conflict.

REFERENCES

Abramowitz, J. (September, 1998). Personal interview.

Almaney, A. (1972). Government control of the press in the United Arab Republic, 1952–70. *Journalism Quarterly*, 49 (2): 340–347.

Altheide, D.L., & J.M. Johnson (1980). *Bureaucratic propaganda*. Boston: Allyn & Bacon.

Andersen, R., R. Seibert, & J. Wagner (1998). *Politics and change in the Middle East: Sources of conflict and accommodation*. Englewood Cliff, NJ: Prentice-Hall.

Angevin, P. (December, 1998). Personal interview.

Arnett, P. (1994). *Live from the battlefield: From Vietnam to Baghdad, 35 years in the world's war zones*. New York: Simon & Schuster.

Asante, M., E. Newmark, & C. Blake (1979). The field of intercultural communication. In *Handbook of intercultural communication*. (Eds. M. Asante, E. Newmark, & C. Blake). London: Sage Publications. Pp. 11–22.

Aspell, T. (October, 1998). Personal interview.

Ayad, C. (November, 1998). Personal interview.

Bailey, S. (1990). *Four Arab-Israeli wars and the peace process*. New York: St. Martin's Press.

Barakat, H. (1993). *The Arab world: Society, culture, and state*. Berkeley: University of California Press.

Bass, A.Z. (1969). Refining the "gatekeeper" concept: A UN radio case study. *Journalism Quarterly*, 46: 69–72.

Battah, A., & Y. Lukacs (1988). *The Arab-Israeli conflict: Two decades of change*. London: Westview Press.

Beattie, K. (1994). *Egypt during Nasser years: Ideology, politics, and civil society*. Boulder, CO: Westview Press.

Bell, S. (1980). American journalism: practices, constraints, and Middle East reportage. In *The American media and the Arabs* (Eds. M. Hudson & R. Wolfe). Washington, DC: Center for Contemporary Arab Studies. Pp. 51–58.

Ben-Rafael, E., & S. Sharot (1991). *Ethnicity, religion, and class in Israeli society*. New York: Cambridge University Press.

Beyer, L. (September 1998). Personal interview.

Bickerton, I., & C. Klausner (1998). *A concise history of the Arab-Israeli conflict* (3rd ed.). Englewood Cliffs, NJ: Prentice-Hall.

Blitzer, W. (1985). *Between Washington and Jerusalem: A reporter's notebook*. New York: Oxford University Press.

Block, I. (2000, November 10). Media distort crisis in Middle East. *The Gazette*, p. B13.

Boulding, K.E., & L. Senesh (1983). *The optimum utilization of knowledge: Making knowledge serve human betterment*. Boulder, CO: Westview Press.

Boullata, I. (1990). *Trends and issues in contemporary Arab thought*. Albany: State University of New York Press.

Boyd, D.A. (1993). *Broadcasting in the Arab world: A survey of the electronic media in the Middle East*. 2nd ed. Ames: Iowa State University Press.

Brandon, H. (1988). *Special relationships: A foreign correspondent's memoirs from Roosevelt to Reagan*. New York: Macmillan Publishing Company.

Brown, C. (1988). "The June 1967 war: A turning point." In *The Arab-Israeli conflict: Two decades of change*. (Eds. A Battah & Y. Lukacs). London: Westview Press. Pp. 133–146.

Buccianti, A. (November, 1998). Personal interview.

Burrell, J. (December, 1998). Personal interview.

Bushinsky, J. (October, 1998). Personal interview.

Cadoret-Manier, R. (September, 1998). Personal interview.

Cantor, G. (1998, April 15). "Too much remains uncertain, not enough secured as Israel turns 50." *Detroit News*, p. 1.

Chibnall, S. (1977). *Law-and-order news*. London: Tavistock Publishers.

Cohen, R. (1990). *Culture and conflict in Egyptian-Israeli relations: A dialogue of the deaf*. Indianapolis: Indiana University Press.

Contreras, J. (September, 1998). Personal interview.

Curtiss, R. (1986). *A changing image: American perceptions of the Arab-Israeli dispute*. Washington, DC: American Educational Trust.

Curtius, M. (2001, January 22). Peace talks begin amid pessimism. *Los Angeles Times*, p. 4.

Dabbous, S. (1994). Egypt. In *Mass media in the Middle East: A comprehensive handbook*. (Eds. Y. Kamalipour & H. Mowlana). Westport, CT: Greenwood Press. Pp. 60–73.

Dachs, G. (September, 1998). Personal interview.

Daniszewski, J. (October, 1998). Personal interview.

Diller, C. (1994). *The Middle East*. 8th ed. Washington, DC: Congressional Quarterly, Inc.

Donahue, R., & M. Prosser (1997). *Diplomatic discourse; international conflict at the UN: Addresses and analysis*. Greenwich, CT: Ablex Publishing Company.

Doucet, L. (September, 1998). Personal interview.

Drees, C. (2000, November 22). Israeli envoy: Egypt influenced by biased coverage. *The Jerusalem Post*, p. 3.

Drummond, J. (2001, February 8). "Middle East: The Israeli election." *The Financial Times*, p. 14.

Dunn, D. (1969). *Public officials and the press.* (Reading, MA: Addison-Wesley Publishing Company.

Edelstein, A., Y. Ito, & H. Kepplinger (1989). *Communication and culture: A comparative approach.* New York: Longman.

El-Hodaiby, M. (2000). Islamic fundamentalism does not foster violence. In *The Middle East: Opposing viewpoints.* (Ed. M. Williams). San Diego, CA: Greenhaven Press. Pp. 86–95.

Emery, M. (1995). *On the front lines: Following America's foreign correspondents across the twentieth century.* Washington, DC: American University Press.

Ericson, R.V., P. Baranek, & S. Chan (1987). *Visualizing deviance: A study of news organization.* Toronto: University of Toronto Press.

Ericson, R.V., P. Baranek, & S. Chan (1989). *Negotiating control: A study of news sources.* Toronto: University of Toronto Press.

Fawaz, G. (1995). Egyptian-Israeli relations turn sour. *Foreign Affairs*, 74 (June): 69–78.

Foighel, H. (October, 1998). Personal interview.

Foisie, J. (1985). "A new boom or an old hand? *Nieman Reports, 39* (Winter): 15.

Foxman, A. (2000, November 29). "Media bias: Real or perceived? *The Jerusalem Post*, p. 8.

Franceschini, E. (September, 1998). Personal interview.

Freedman, R. (1979). "The Soviet Union and the Arab-Israeli conflict." In *World politics and the Arab-Israeli conflict.* (Ed. R. Freedman). New York: Pergamon Press. Pp 53–86.

Freedman, R. (1998). Introduction. *The Middle East and the peace process: The impact of the Oslo accords.* (Ed. R. Freedman) Gainsville: University Press of Florida. p. 4.

Friedman, T. (1989). *From Beirut to Jerusalem.* New York: Farrar Straus Giroux.

Frohloff, A. (September, 1998). Personal interview.

Galnoor, I. (1977). *Government secrecy in democracies.* New York: New York University Press.

Galnoor, I. (1982). *Steering the polity: Communication and politics in Israel.* London: Sage Publications.

Galtung, J. (1988). "The peace process: Twenty years later: Failure without alternative?" In *The Arab-Israeli conflict: Two decades of change.* (Eds. Y. Lukacs & A. Battah) London: Westview Press. Pp. 231–331.

Galtung, J., & M.H. Ruge (1965). The structure of foreign news. *Journal of Peace Research*, 2: 64–90.

Gandy, O.H. (1982). *Beyond agenda setting: Information subsidies and public opinion policy.* Newark, NJ: Ablex Publishing Company.

Gans, H.J. (1979). *Deciding what's news: A study of* CBS Evening News, NBC Nightly News, Newsweek, and Time. New York: Pantheon Books.

Gauch, S. (September, 1998). Personal interview.

Gelie, P. (September, 1998). Personal interview.

Geyer, G. A. (1980). The American correspondent in the Arab World. In *The American media and the Arabs*. (Eds. M. Hudson & G. Wolfe). Washington, DC: Center for Contemporary Arab Studies. Pp. 65–72.

Gieber, W., & W. Johnson (1961). The city hall "Beat." A study of reporter and source roles. *Journalism Quarterly*, 38: 289–297.

Goldberg, N. (September, 1998). Personal interview.

Goren, D., & R. Rothman (1982). Government–news media relations in Israel. In *Government and news media: Comparative dimensions*. (Eds. D. Nimmo & M.W. Mansfield). Texas: Baylor University Press. Pp. 243–270.

Graber, D.A. (1997). *Mass media and American politics*. 5th ed. Washington, DC: Congressional Quarterly, Inc.

Granham, D., & M. Tessler (1995). *Democracy, war, and peace in the Middle East*. Indianapolis: Indiana University Press.

Grossman, R. (September, 1998). Personal interview.

Gruen, G. (2000). Israel and the American Jewish community: Changing realities test traditional ties. In *Israel's first fifty years*. (Ed. R. Freedman). Gainsville: University Press of Florida. Pp. 29–66.

Grunig, J. (1992). *Excellence in public relations and communications management*. Hillsdale, NJ: Lawrence Erlbaum Associates, Publishers.

Grunig, J., & L. Grunig (1989). *Public relations research annual*. Hillsdale, NJ: Lawrence Erlbaum Associates

Grunig, J., & T. Hunt (1984). *Managing public relations*. New York: Holt, Rinehart & Winston.

Guibal, C. (December, 1998). Personal interview.

Gunther, I. (November, 1998). Personal interview.

Gutter, R. (November, 1998). Personal interview.

Halevi, Y. (2000). A separate peace. *The New Republic, 223* (4): Pp. 14–15.

Haque, M. (1997). Elements of cross-cultural communication and the Middle East. In *The U.S. media and the Middle East: Image and perception*. (Ed. Y. Kamalipour). London: Praeger. Pp. 16–24.

Hauser, C. (October, 1998). Personal interview.

Henningham, J. (1996). Australian journalists' professional and ethical values. *Journalism Quarterly*, 73: 206–218.

Hess, S. (1984). *The government/press connection: Press officers and their offices*. Washington, DC: The Brookings Institute.

Hess, S. (1996). *International news and foreign correspondents*. Washington, DC: The Brookings Institute.

Hinnebusch, R. (1985). *Egyptian politics under Nasser and Sadat: The post-populist development of an authoritarian-modernizing state*. London: Cambridge University Press.

Hockstader, L. (October, 1998). Personal interview.

Hogrefe, J. (September, 1998). Personal interview.

Hohenberg, J. (1964). *Foreign correspondence: The great reporters and their times*. New York: Columbia University Press.

Hohenberg, J. (1998). *Israel at 50: A journalist's perspective*. New York: Syracuse University Press.

Hollander, J. (September, 1998) Personal interview.

Holmes, P. (September, 1998). Personal interview.

Hosein, H. (September, 1998). Personal interview.

Hutcheson, R. (2001, April 2). Bush and Mubarak agree to work quietly for peace. *Pittsburg Post-Gazette*, p. A-5.

Huth, P.K. (1988). *Extended deterrence and the prevention of war*. London: Yale University Press.

Jenkins, S. (November, 1998). Personal interview.

Jensen, S. (October, 1998). Personal interview.

Johnstone, J.W., E. Slawski, & W. Bowman (1972). The professional values of American newsmen. *Public Opinion Quarterly*, 36 (2): 522–540.

Johnstone, J.W., E. Slawski, & W. Bowman (1976). *The news people: A sociological portrait of American journalists and their work*. Urbana: University of Illinois Press.

Kamalipour, Y. (1997). *Introduction The U.S. media and the Middle East: Image and perception*. (Ed. Y. Kamalipour). London: Praeger. Pp. 1–5.

Karl, P. (1983). In the middle of the Middle East: The media and U.S. foreign policy. In *Split vision: The portrayal of Arabs in the American media*. (Ed. E. Ghareeb). Washington, DC: The American-Arab Affairs Council. Pp. 283–298.

Katz, E. (1971). Television comes to the people of the book. In *The use and abuse of social science*. (Ed. I.L. Harowitz). New Jersey: Transactions Book. Pp. 249–271.

Kerr, M.H. (1973). The Arabs and Israelis: Perceptual dimensions to their dilemma. In *The Middle East: Quest for an American policy*. (Ed. W.A. Beling). Albany: State University of New York Press. Pp. 3–31.

Kirat, M. (1987). *The Algerian news people: A study of their backgrounds, professional orientations, and working conditions*. Unpublished doctoral dissertation, Indiana University at Bloomington.

Kruglak, T.E. (1955). *The foreign correspondents*. Geneva: Droz Library Press.

La Belle, G. (November, 1998). Personal interview.

Lambert, D. (1956). Foreign correspondents covering the United States. *Journalism Quarterly*, 33: Pp. 349–356.

Lancaster, J., & K. Richburg (2001, January 4). Arafat accepts Clinton proposal to renew talks. *The Washington Post*, p. A1.

Lederman, J. (October, 1998). Personal interview.

Lehman, S., & A. Schejter (1994). Israel. In *Mass media in the Middle East: A comprehensive handbook*." (Eds. Y. Kamalipour & H. Mowlana). Westport CT: Greenwood Press. Pp. 109–125.

Lesch, A., & D. Tschirgi (1998). *Origins and development of the Arab-Israeli conflict*. Westport, CT: Greenwood Press.

Lesch, M., & M. Tessler (1989). *Israel, Egypt, and the Palestinians: From Camp David to Intifada*. Bloomington: Indiana University Press.

Lewin, K. (1947). Channels of group life. *Human Relations*, 1: 143–153.

Lewis, B. (1999). *The multiple identities of the Middle East*. New York: Schocken Books.

Liebes, T. (1997). *Reporting the Arab-Israeli conflict: How hegemony works*. London: Routledge.

Liebman, C., & E. Don-Yehiya (1983). *Civil religion in Israel: Traditional Judaism and political culture in the Jewish state.* Berkeley: University of California Press.

Lippmann, W. (1922). *Public opinion.* New York: Macmillan Company.

Luijendijk, J. (November, 1998). Personal interview.

MacLeod, S. (November, 1998). Personal interview.

Manoff, K., & M. Schudson (1986). *Reading the news.* New York: Pantheon Books.

Maxwell, W. (1956). U.S. correspondents abroad: A study of backgrounds. *Journalism Quarterly.* 33: 346–348.

McDermott, A. (1988). *Egypt from Nasser to Mubarak: A flawed revolution.* New York: Croom Helm.

McLean, I. (1996). *The concise Oxford dictionary of politics.* New York: Oxford University Press.

McQuail, D., & S. Windahl (1993). *Communication models for the study of mass communication.* 2d ed. London: Longman Publishing.

Meehan, M. (September, 1998). Personal interview.

Menaker, D. (November, 1998). Personal interview.

Metz, H. (1991). *Egypt: A country study.* Washington, DC: Federal Research Division.

Mogulof, D. (September, 1998). Personal interview.

Molotch, H., & M. Lester (1974). News as purposive behavior: On the strategic use of routine events, accidents, and scandals. *American Sociological Review*, 39: 101–112.

Morris, N., & B. Demick (2001, February 7). Sharon's win brings uncertainty to Mideast. *San Jose Mercury News*, p. 1.

Mowlana, H. (1997). Images and the crisis of political legitimacy. In *The U.S. media and the Middle East: Image and perception.* (ed. Y. Kamalipour). London: Praeger. Pp. 3–15.

Mufti, M. (2000). Israel and the Arab states: The long road to normalization. In *Israel's first fifty years.* (Ed. R. Freedman). Gainsville: University Press of Florida. Pp. 67–94.

Murphy, C. (1994). Egypt: An uneasy portent of change. *Current History*, (February): 78–82.

Murphy, D. (1976). *The silent watchdog: The press in local politics.* London: Constable & Company.

Nassar, J. (1997). The culture of resistance: The 1967 war in the context of the Palestinian struggle. *Arab Studies Quarterly*, 19 (22): 77.

Nasser, M. (1982). The Middle East press: Tools of politics. In *Press control around the world.* (Eds. J. Cury & J. Dassin). New York: Praeger. Pp. 149–186.

Nasser, M. (1990). Egyptian mass media Under Nasser and Sadat: Two models of press management and control. *Journalism Monograph*, (124): 1–26.

Netanyahu, B. (2000). *A durable peace: Israel and its place among the nations.* New York: Warner Books.

Nimmo, D. (1964). *Newsgathering in Washington: A study in political communication.* New York: Atherton Press.

Nuechterlein, J. (2000). Peace when? *First Things*, 108 (December): 7–8.

O'Hefferman, P. (1994). Mass media roles in foreign policy. In *Media power in politics.* 3rd ed. (Ed. D.A. Graber). Washington, DC: Congressional Quarterly, Inc. Pp. 325–336.

Omestad, T., et al. (2000). The spiral of war. *U.S. News and World Report*, (October 23): 25.

Othmerding, H. (September, 1998). Personal interview.

Palmer, A. (1997). The Arab image in newspaper political cartoons. In *The U.S. media and the Middle East: Image and perception*. (Ed. Y. Kamalipour). London: Praeger. Pp. 139–150.

Pedelty, M. (1995). *War stories: The culture of foreign correspondents*. London: Routledge.

Peretz, D. (1998). U.S. Middle East policy in the 1990s. In *The Middle East and the peace process: The impact of the Oslo accords*. (Ed. R. Freedman). Gainsville: University Press of Florida. Pp. 347–364.

Peri, Y. (1993). The Arab-Israeli conflict and Israeli democracy. In *Israeli democracy under stress*. (Eds. E. Spinzak & L. Diamond). Boulder, CO: Lynn Rienner Publishers. Pp. 343–357.

Perlmutter, A. (1978). *Politics and the military in Israel: 1967–1977*. Postland, OR: Frank Cass Inc.

Plett, B. (November, 1998). Personal interview.

Powell, E. (November, 1998). Personal interview.

Prosser, M. (1978). *The cultural dialogue: An introduction to intercultural communication*. Boston: Houghton Mifflin Company.

Radin, C. (2000, October 16). Pessimism grows despite summit. *The Boston Globe*, p. A1.

Rauch, M. (December, 1998). Personal interview.

Rees, M. (2000). Hard times, hard man. *Time*, 156 (22): 67–68.

Reeves, P. (2001, February 9). Arab bombers send messages to "criminal" Sharon. *The Independent*, p. 13.

Rodenbeck, M. (November, 1998). Personal interview.

Rodgers, W. (September, 1998). Personal interview.

Roscho, B. (1975). *Newsmaking*. Chicago: The University of Chicago Press.

Rosenblum, M. (1981). *Coups and earthquakes: Reporting the world for America*. New York: Harper Colophon Books.

Rosenblum, M. (1998). Netanyahu and peace? From sound bites to sound policies. In *The Middle East and the peace process: The impact of the Oslo accords*. (Ed. R. Freedman). Gainsville: University Press of Florida. Pp. 35–80.

Rosten, L. (1937). *The Washington correspondents*. New York: Harourt, Brace & Company.

Rothschild, M. (1998). Interview with Robert Fisk (British correspondent). *The Progressive*, 62 (7): 36–41.

Rugh, W. (1987). *The Arab press: News media and political process in the Arab world*. 2d ed. Syracuse, NY: Syracuse University Press.

Safire, W. (1993). *Safire's new political dictionary: The definition guide to the new language of politics*. New York: Random House.

Said, E. (1978). *Orientalism*. New York: Vintage Books.

Said, E. (1981). *Covering Islam*. New York: Pantheon Books.

Said, E. (2000). *The end of the peace process: Oslo and after*. New York: Pantheon Books.

Salhani, C. (1998). *Black September to Desert Storm: A journalist in the Middle East*. Columbia: University of Missouri Press.

Saunders, H. (1985). *The other walls: The politics of the Arab-Israeli peace process.* Washington, DC: American Enterprise Institute for Public Policy Research.

Savir, U. (1985, March 7). An Israeli view of the American media. *USA Today*, p. 32.

Schleifer, A. (1987). Conflict and coverage in the Middle East. Paper presented at the Advista Arabia Conference, Cairo, Egypt.

Scott, W. (1965). "Psychological and social correlates of international images. In *International behavior: A Socio-psychological analysis.* (Ed. W. Scott). New York: Holt, Rinehart & Winston. Pp. 1–12.

Seib, P. (1997). *Headline diplomacy: How news coverage affects foreign policy.* London: Praeger.

Sela, Avraham (1998). *The decline of the Arab-Israeli conflict: Middle East politics and the quest for regional order.* New York: State University of New York.

Shadid, A. (November, 1998). Personal interview.

Shaheen, J. (1984). *The tv Arab.* Bowling Green, OH: Bowling Green State University Popular Press.

Shoemaker, P.J. (1991). *Gatekeeping.* London: Sage Publications.

Sigal, L. (1973). *Reporters and officials: The organization and politics of newsmaking.* Lexington, MA: D.C. Heath & Company.

Snyder, G.H., & P. Diesing (1977). *Conflict among nations: Bargaining, decision-making, and system structure in international crisis.* Princeton, NJ: Princeton University Press.

Starck, K., & E. Villaneuva (1992). Cultural framing: Foreign correspondents and their work. Paper presented at the International Communication Division of the Association for Education and Journalism and Mass Communication, Montreal, Quebec, Canada.

Strentz, H. (1989). *News reporters and news sources: Accomplices in shaping and mis-shaping the news.* 2nd ed. Ames: Iowa State University Press.

Tatro, N. (September, 1998). Personal interview.

Tofall, B. (November, 1998). Personal interview.

Trigoboff, D. (2000). War of words. *Broadcasting & Cable*, 130 (44): 12.

Tunstall, J. (1971). *Journalists at work.* London: Constable & Company.

Turk, J.V. (1986). Information subsidies and media content: A study of public relations influence on the news. *Journalism Monographs*, 100: 1–20.

Ulf, H. (1998). Reporting from Jerusalem. *Cultural Anthropology*, 13, (4): 548–574.

Weaver, D., & C. Wilhoit (1986). *The American journalist: A portrait of U.S. news people and their work.* Bloomington: Indiana University Press.

Weaver, D., & C. Wilhoit (1996). *The American journalist in the 1990s: U.S. news people at the end of an era.* Mawah, NJ: Erlbaum Associates.

Webster, N. (2001, January 6). Too much baggage, not enough time: So-called right of return, Jewish settlements complicate peace efforts. *The Gazette*, p. B7.

Weick, K.E. (1979) *The social psychology of organizing.* 2nd ed. Reading, MA: Addison-Wesley.

Wells, A. (October, 1998). Personal interview.

Werkman, W. (September, 1998). Personal interview.

Werr, P. (November, 1998). Personal interview.

White, D.M. (1950). The gatekeepers: A case study in the selection of news. *Journalism Quarterly*, 27: 383–390.

Whitelaw, K. (2001). Ariel Sharon fires his opening salvo. *U.S. News & World Report*, (April): 38.

Wiegand, K.E. & A. Malek (1997). Islam and the west: Cultural encounter. In *The U.S. media and the Middle East: Image and perception*. (Ed. Y. Kamalipour). London: Praeger. Pp. 201–211.

Wilber, D. (1969). *United Arab Republic of Egypt: Its people, its society, its culture*. New Haven CT: Hraf Press.

Windfur, V. (December, 1998). Personal interview.

Wise, D. (1973). *The politics of lying: Government deception, secrecy, and power*. New York: Random House.

Wolfsfeld, G. (1997). *Media and political conflict: News from the Middle East*. New York: Cambridge University Press.

Yaacobi, G. (1982). *The government of Israel*. New York: Praeger Publishers.

Yaacobi, P. (September, 1998). Personal interview.

Yael, L. (1998). Israel at 50: Zionism's cultural revolution. *Race and Class*, 40 (1): 71.

Zaharna, R. (1997). The Palestinian leadership and the American media: Changing images, conflicting results. In *The U.S. media and the Middle East: Image and perception*. (Ed. Y. Kamalipour). London: Praeger. Pp. 37–49.

INDEX

Islam: Constitution of, 45; and the establishment of Israel, 2; holy book of, 44; misrepresentation of, 45–48; and the Moslem Brotherhood, 63; principles of, 43–45; and role in Egypt's cultural values, 62; and Western journalists, 176–177

Israel: and the 1967 War, xiv, 7–10; and the 1973 War, 11–13; and accessibility of officials, 149, 157–159, 172; Ashkenazic Jews in, 66; and bilateral relations with Egypt, 17–18; culture of, 64–70; ethnic diversity in, 65; foundation of, 2–4; and government leaks, 137, 163–164, 170–171; Government Press Office (GPO) of, 80–81, 109–110, 157–158; governmental public relations of, 148–149; and government-press relationship, 110, 136–139, 170–173; image in U.S. media, 42; and informal sources for Western journalists, 163, 166, 168; and news media scene, 159, 178–179; and Oslo, 23–34; and peace treaty with Egypt, 13–16; and press censorship, 116–117, 136–137, 166–167; and secret negotiations with Jordan, 11; secularization in, 64; and the use of security, 136–139, 164–165, 166–167; Sephardic Jews in, 66

Jerusalem, 79–80; and the 1948 War, 4; and the 1967 War, 10; and Camp David, 16; and checkpoints, 78; East Jerusalem versus West Jerusalem, 79–80; Israeli settlements in, 4, 8; and the Oslo accords, 25; and Palestine National Council, 7; Palestinian suicide attacks in, 26; Sadat's visit to, 14

Johnson, Lyndon, 8–9

Jordan: and crackdown on PLO, 11; and the Oslo Accords, 24; and secret negotiations with Israel, 11

Journalistic norms, 132–133

Judaism, 2, 7, 176–177

Kissinger, Henry, 32; and the 1973 War, 13; and Arab-Israeli agreements, 14

Meir, Golda, xiv, 11

Mossad (Israeli intelligence), xiv; and leaks, 163

Moussa, Amr, 26, 31

Mubarak, Hosni, 26, 35–36, 59, 115, 133, 135–136

Nasser, Gamal Abdel, 59, 114–115, 133–135; and the 1956 War, 4, 6; and the 1967 War, 7–8; and direct censorship of the press in Egypt, 114; *A Durable Peace: Israel and Its Place among the Nations,* 28; and nationalization of the press, 115; and the notion of group solidarity, 60; and relations with the Soviet Union, 5

Netanyahu, Benjamin, 26–29, 160

Newsmaking model, 118–122, 151–154, 169; and assimilation, 127–128; and beats, 122–123; and leaks, 126–127; and information subsidies, 129–130

Organization of Petroleum Exporting Countries (OPEC), 12

Oslo Accords, 23–26; correspondents' memoirs about, xv; Egypt's reactions to, 25–26;

Palestine: and Camp David, 29; and the establishment of Israel, 2–4; and the foundation of the PLO, 7; and *Intifada,* 20; and the new *Intifada,* 30–31; and the Oslo Accords, 24; and Palestinian nationalism, 10; and "The Question of," 3

Palestine Liberation Organization (PLO): and the 1967 War, 7–10; charter of, 7, 25; and Fatah, 7; foundation of, 7; and Occupied Territories, 24; and the Oslo Accords, 23; and secret talks with Israel, 24

Palestine National Council (PNC), 7

Palestinians' image after, 49–50; results
of, 25; signing of, 24
Peres, Shimon, 24, 26, 148–149
Press conference, 145–146, 186
Press release, 144, 146–147, 186
Public information officers, 147
Public relations: model of, 142–143;
two-way asymmetric model of,
143–145, 151–154, 171, 173, 186

Qaddafi, Moammar, 49

Rabin, Yitzhak: and the 1967 War, 8;
assassination of, 24; and the Nobel
Peace Prize, 24; and Oslo negotiations, 24
Rodgers, Walter, 182

Sadat, Anwar, 59, 115, 133–135; and
the 1973 War, 11–12; assassination
of, 16; and Camp David negotia-
tions, 15–16; and Nobel Peace
Prize, 16; visit to Jerusalem, 14
Said, Edward, 3, 28, 29; *The End of the
Peace Process: Oslo and After,* 25;
Orientalism, 46
Schleifer, Abdullah, 41
Sharon, Ariel, 30, 34–36
Sinai I agreement, 13
Sinai II agreement, 14
Sinai Peninsula: and agreements be-
tween Egypt and Israel following
the 1973 War, 13–14; and Israeli
occupation in the 1967 War, 8–9;
Israeli tourists' visits to, 19; Israeli
withdrawal from, 14–15, 17
Soviet Union: and the 1956 War, 6;
and the 1967 War, 8–9; and the
1973 War, 13; and arms deal with
Egypt, 5; and criticism to Sadat's
visit to Israel, 15, 33; and role in
Middle East conflict, 10, 13, 23,
32–34
Stereotypical image: of Arabs and Israelis, 41–42, 49, 52; definition of,
39–40

Suez Canal: 1956 invasion of, 5; and
the 1967 War, 9–10; and the 1973
War, 12; nationalization of, 5
Syria: and the 1948 War, 3–4, and the
1956 War, 6–7; and the 1967 War,
8–10; and unity with Egypt, 8

Tatro, Nicolas, 159, 165
Tel Aviv, 15, 26, 76–77, 80

United Nations: and the 1956 War,
6–7; and the PLO, 14; and resolution 181, 2; and resolution 242, 9;
and resolution, 338, 13
United States: and the 1956 War, 5–6;
and the 1967 War, 10; and the 1973
War, 12–13; and Camp David, 29;
and the Oslo Accords, xv; and role
in the Middle East conflict, 32–33,
36; and support for the establishment of Israel, 2; and the United
Nations Emergency Force, 6

War: the 1956 War, 4–6, 7; the 1967
(Six-Day) War, xiii-xiv, 7–10; 1982
Lebanon War, 138; Arab-Israeli,
1–3, 7–12, 15–16; Gulf War, xvi;
October 1973 War, xiv, 11–13, 117;
World War I, 143; World War II,
2–3
Weizmann, Chaim, 3
West Bank: and the 1967 War, 8; and
Camp David, 29; and checkpoints,
78–79; and *Intifada,* 20; and Jewish
settlements in, 16, 26; and the Oslo
Accords, 24; and withdrawal of Is-
raeli troops, 26; and the Wye River
Plantation Agreement, 27–28
Western correspondents: and cultural
familiarity, 41, 47, 52, 180–182. *See
also* Foreign correspondents
Windfur, Volkhard, 162, 164, 167
World Zionist Organization, 3
Wye River Plantation Agreement, 27–28

Yom Kippur, 12

Zionist movement, 2, 67–69, 116, 137

About the Author

MOHAMMED EL-NAWAWY is an Assistant Professor of Journalism at the University of West Florida. He has done extensive research in the fields of international communications and intercultural communications.